BETTER STRONGER FASTER

BETTER STRONGER FASTER

Build it, scale it, flog it:
the entrepreneur's step-by-step
guide to success in business

Brad Rosser

Copyright © Brad Rosser, 2009
The right of Brad Rosser to be identified as the author of this book has been asserted in accordance with the Copyright, Designs and Patents Act 1988.

First published in 2009 by
Infinite Ideas Limited
36 St Giles
Oxford
OX1 3LD
United Kingdom
www.infideas.com

A CIP catalogue record for this book is available from the British Library

ISBN 978–1–906821–15–9

Brand and product names are trademarks or registered trademarks of their respective owners.

Cover designed by Cylinder
Text designed and typeset by Nicki Averill
Printed and bound by TJ International Limited, Cornwall

CONTENTS

INTRODUCTION

I believe that start-ups and entrepreneurs are the future of any country. They drive innovation, employ millions of people and have the guts to stand out.

Did you know that three out of every four start-ups survive their first year? So far, so good. But, did you also know that only one in five of those survive through their next four years, and only a small percentage of those actually get sold? Come on, agree with me: that's just not right.

It is heartbreaking to think that so many entrepreneurs invest so much time and effort on promising start-ups that ultimately fail. In most instances, these people could not find help or received advice from individuals or consultants who did not know what they were talking about. All they needed was a guiding hand from someone who knew the rules and had worked through each stage of a business's development.

I decided to do something about it. I set out to write a book that would give entrepreneurs the help they deserve – a book that addresses the hard issues and helps entrepreneurs to avoid the inevitable pitfalls that await them on their journey, right from developing a commercial idea through to a profitable sale.

The book draws on experiences from both my own ventures and working directly with some of the world's most successful, controversial and colourful entrepreneurs, including Virgin's Sir Richard Branson and Australian billionaire Alan Bond.

They proved to me that it is no accident that some businesses succeed and others don't. Successful entrepreneurs don't just have the drive and will to succeed, they also have something else. They have the critical skills, the action plan to battle each stage of development, and the right team and partners around them. They make it look easy because they know the rules.

So, you will find that I have strong views on what works and what doesn't; what to do when, and how to do it. This book is your personal mentor. It is unique in that it not only reveals precisely what to do at every stage of your business's development, but it is also supported by fun, sometimes dramatic, yet always informative examples from real-life cases that I was personally and directly involved in. No guessing or theorising – just the real deal.

So the objectives for my book are straightforward:

- To demystify the 'secrets of the successful entrepreneur' smokescreen that the self-serving/uninformative 'gurus' like to hide behind.
- To provide insight and advice based on my first-hand experience.
- To demonstrate that building a successful business can be done with the right application.
- To develop the skills, confidence and motivation that will enable readers to get up and have a go for themselves, and make it a success.
- To tackle the non-trivial, hard-hitting, and (sometimes) controversial issues of entrepreneurial business building.
- To be very clear about what to do and what not to do at every stage of start-up development.

Enjoy reading through the whole book before you embark on your journey. As you progress, reread the chapters as you reach each stage of your business's development.

It is confidence-building and inspiring to know that all entrepreneurs have struggled at some stage. However you have a secret – you will now know in advance the problems and issues that lie ahead and how to deal with them. You will beat those damned statistics!

Good luck.

PART ONE
BUILD IT

CHAPTER 1 **THE BULLETPROOF IDEA: YOUR FOUNDATION FOR SUCCESS**

Proof that an astute business brain lies behind the bearded grin and jeans comes with Branson's hiring of Brad Rosser, in 1994, as Virgin's corporate development head. Effectively the group's new-business manager, it is Rosser who is charged with maintaining Virgin's relentless quest for pastures new. Hundreds of new business proposals cross his desk annually.

– 'At the court of King Richard', *Management Today*

Great quote. It's really flattering – that's why I used it. It reflects a time when I was the brains behind the brains behind the beard.

What the quote doesn't tell you is that while I was besieged by ideas from people wanting to associate with Virgin, one of the world's great brands, I was desperate – desperate to find commercial ideas good enough to help me do my job. Out of every hundred ideas presented to me, I rejected ninety-nine.

The problem was – and is – that so many people are passionate about ideas they simply haven't thought through. Often they waste years on no-hope projects.

The bedrock of any successful business – a bulletproof idea

So, why am I telling you this? Because the first, fundamental truth of business is that no matter how perfectly you execute an idea your business will eventually fall apart unless the idea is good – so good that it's what I call bulletproof.

Does this sound negative? Well, it's not. Read on. This chapter will strengthen your business idea and make it bulletproof.
Or again, it might help you work out that your idea isn't going to cut it. In that case, abandon it and look for a new one.

Believe me, there's no shortage of new ideas out there and this chapter can help you find one. But there is a shortage of people who think hard and really challenge their idea to ensure it's good enough. Let me show you how to be one of them.

It's a popular myth that entrepreneurs fly by the seat of their pants

It's a popular myth that entrepreneurs fly by the seat of their pants, that they act purely on impulse, that they don't spend time carefully thinking through issues. In truth, successful entrepreneurs tend to either rewrite history or gloss over the less exciting parts of growing a business. It's in their nature.

They are positive people who are always restlessly moving forward. They find it boring (and it makes them sound mortal) to recount the difficult dark times blow by blow. They also don't tell you about the ideas they abandoned (or which failed) before hitting on their successful formula. Therefore, you simply cannot always believe what they say they did – or why.

It's like a Hollywood version of reality. I have worked side-by-side with a number of the world's most successful entrepreneurs and can assure you they spend a significant amount of time simply devoted to hard thinking and careful planning.

I find it absolutely essential too. Successful businesses are based on the same solid foundation: a good idea that has been thoroughly and carefully thought through. This careful thinking is not just at the beginning of the business either; it is a process that needs to continue throughout the life of the business in order to constantly look for ways to improve and make more profit.

So let's start to get a flavour of what constitutes a good idea by returning to my days at Virgin. It was like being Caesar, in a way: thumbs up and you're funded; thumbs down and it's goodbye.

Thumbs up, thumbs down

Here's a tale of two ideas. One got the thumbs down, despite the fact that the two men behind it had devoted years of their life and thousands of pounds to its development. The other received the thumbs up as well as considerable financial backing and ultimately became an industry leader. See if you can work out why.

The first idea was presented by two extremely nervous gentlemen who came to me when I was at Virgin. They were looking for support for … well, something. They shuffled into my office, proceeded to rummage through a plastic bag they'd brought, pulled out two cartons of some substance or other, and threw them onto my desk. I kept my poker face, but quickly glanced around the room to see if there were any hidden cameras.

The idea simply wasn't commercial: two years wasted!

We sat there in silence as I tried to work out exactly what it was they had brought. One carton was branded 'Woofit' and the other 'Meowit'. Both appeared to contain a horrible brown liquid. I began to worry that if one of the cartons leaked it would burn a hole through my desk.

I waited patiently for them to enlighten me. Eventually they realised that if they wanted us to invest in their product they might have to actually explain what it was. Finally, one of them gave us the scoop: the cartons contained an energy drink for cats and dogs – quite the revolution! Not surprisingly, the drink for dogs was called Woofit and the one for cats was Meowit. He then sat back in his chair and they both looked at me like they'd just developed the cure for cancer.

At this point, two of my colleagues got up and excused themselves. I could see them fighting to stifle their laughter as they disappeared.

I soldiered on: I wasn't going to dismiss these guys out of hand, as they'd clearly worked hard on developing their idea. Perhaps there was something I'd missed.

So I began to ask questions. Why did they think there was a market for their product? Who were their customers, the pet owners or the pets? How many pet owners would actually pay a premium to buy their cats or dogs an energy drink when milk was so cheap and water cost next to nothing? Where did they think their product would be sold – pet stores or supermarkets? How many pet stores were there actually in the UK?

Unfortunately, their responses weren't heartening. The more I spoke to them, the more it seemed they hadn't done their homework. Convinced they had a good idea, they'd simply developed a product, at considerable expense, that matched their own idiosyncratic tastes. Unfortunately, they'd wasted a great deal of time, effort and money because they hadn't bothered to think things through. But they were entrepreneurs, and they had a can-do attitude. With a different idea, perhaps things would have gone differently.

Compare that with the team who pitched us the idea of Virgin entering the fitness market.

They knew their market – right down to the giant toothbrush!

They began by explaining the clear market gap they were targeting and how their gyms would be differentiated from existing competitors – better facilities, a greater lifestyle focus, improved customer service, at a great location, at the right price. They were very specific in the details on each of these, right down to the large toothbrush-shaped fountain that would be the centrepiece of the children's' pool. They knew their market – they had been senior managers in the fitness industry for years (doesn't mean that you have to have directly relevant experience, but it helps if one of your team does.). They'd also done a thorough evaluation of what did and didn't work in the existing health club model. They knew the market was growing. They knew which segments of the market were the most attractive. And they understood the drivers of the business – the profile of the health club customer, what these individuals were looking for in a health club, and what existing players simply weren't providing. They also knew what their price limits were, and what people would and wouldn't pay. They even had specific properties earmarked. Nothing seemed left to chance. Virgin Active is now the fifth-largest fitness chain in the world.

Perhaps you're beginning to see what distinguishes a solid commercial business idea from an inevitable failure; the difference between a Virgin Active and a 'Woofit'! Is there a rapidly growing market? An unmet customer need? Do you have a clear understanding of the target market? All of these elements are important but no single one provides the entire answer.

What you need is a structured framework that will enable you to test your idea to maximise its commercial potential. This is how to build up 'the bulletproof idea'.

The bulletproof idea

1. Can anyone make money in this market?

2. Can my product satisfy an unmet customer demand?

3. Can I sell it for more than it costs to make today and in the future?

4. Can I get my product to market smarter than my competitors?

5. Can my project make money?

6. Can I manage the inherent risks in the business?

Interrogate your idea in bite-sized chunks. That's more than half the battle

I have developed this framework over the past twenty years. It draws heavily on my experience at McKinsey, the world's leading management consulting company. McKinsey is renowned for its rigorous analytical thinking, with corporations paying millions of pounds for its recommendations on the strategic challenges that they face. I took the McKinsey approach to developing analytical frameworks and adapted it to provide a valuable tool for analysing new business proposals at Virgin. Finally, I adapted and refined the framework further each time I launched and grew my own start-ups.

This process of refinement has led to the framework that you see today. It is extremely powerful if used correctly. It is your gateway to a great commercial idea that will become the bedrock of your future success and be a great source of confidence as you face the inevitable ups and downs of a start-up. Believing in yourself and your idea will at times be the only thing that you have to hang onto. To ensure you begin your project with a bulletproof idea with maximum commercial potential, I need you to use it in the following manner:

> **Assessing your Ideas truthfully and without ego is the hallmark of all great entrepreneurs**

- Answer the questions truthfully and frankly. No gloss! The ability to do this is a hallmark of all successful entrepreneurs. Deceiving yourself will only end up wasting your own time and money.
- Use these guides to inspire and direct you. Ask people; look for solutions on the internet; leave no stone unturned till you're sure the idea's bulletproof.
- Review how your idea performed against each question and overall. This is not a school test. You don't need a perfect score for every question. There is no such thing as the perfect idea. Consider the questions as challenges to help you improve your idea, ensuring you have an edge over your competitors.
- If you apply the 'bulletproof idea' test and realise that your idea is not cutting it, then look for a new idea. There is no point in wasting your time and money on a loser. As I have already mentioned, successful entrepreneurs do this all the time.

■ Continue to apply the 'bulletproof idea' test throughout the life of your business. Just as no idea is perfect, so the competition never stands still. You must constantly challenge yourself for ways to improve and strengthen your idea.

So let's go through the bulletproof idea testing process. It allows you to interrogate your idea in bite-sized chunks and be creative to ensure your idea's a winner. You'll find the sub-questions in the test are simple; not at all daunting. If you work on them now and as you go along, then you'll beat the competition.

1. Can anyone make money in this market?

► How large is the market?
► How quickly is it growing?
► How competitive is this industry?

Unfortunately, not all markets are created equal – it's far easier to make money in some markets than others. Take the first two questions together. When a market is large and growing, it's easier to make money in than when it's small and stagnating or declining. It's always going to be easier to ride on the coat-tails of an industry on the up. If the market is stagnating or declining, you're going to have to work a hell of a lot harder to achieve the same results.

You need the market to be working for you so you can hang onto its coat-tails

Take the example of the early days of the personal computer (PC). If you were a PC manufacturer, a components maker, or even a technical support provider, you were able to ride the explosion of demand for PCs and related products and services. Sales volumes skyrocketed as schools, universities, businesses and individuals realised that they simply couldn't live without a PC. Life during this time was much easier for shops selling PCs than for shops selling electronic typewriters.

The third sub-question deals with competition. The harsh reality is that the more competitors there are in an industry, the harder it will be to succeed. Where there are lots of competitors there will be a dog-eat-dog environment with everyone fighting over scraps. So, how do I assess the level of competitive tension in a market? I use the following simple test:

- Count the number of competitors that exist in the market.
- Examine what happened to prices in the market over the past two years.

Take the DVD player, for example. When DVD players were first launched, fast-moving manufacturers of the machine and related accessories were able to exploit the inevitable shift of consumers from the ubiquitous video recorder to a new technology that offered vastly improved vision and sound. The potential was enormous and no manufacturer then dominated the industry. A great time to enter the sector! But today life is hard: the market is mature; there are hundreds of competitors; margins are thin. You can pick up a DVD player for almost the price of a DVD. Not such a good time to enter the industry, wouldn't you say?

In a low-growth, competitive industry your product must work that much harder

To understand the nature of the market you're operating in can be the difference between success and failure. To make the point, let's look at two businesses that were owned by the same company. The owner desperately wanted both companies to succeed and devoted the same time, effort and resources to both companies. However, one business operated in a crowded, mature market while the other operated in a fast-growing market with few competitors. Despite the concerted efforts of the parent, one business prospered while the other languished. No prizes for guessing which was which.

A tale of two markets

McKinsey was a long-term adviser to Kingfisher. Indeed, I had worked on a project with them when I was at McKinsey in the early 1990s. In 1982, Kingfisher purchased FW Woolworth. Woolworths was a discount retailer of products as diverse as home goods, music, clothes and stationery, and was an institution in the UK, having opened its first UK store in Liverpool in 1909. By the time of the Kingfisher acquisition, there were hundreds of Woolworths stores. These stores had been struggling for some time and the plan was to put in place a new strategy to turn them around. In addition to those stores, Woolworths had one lonely B&Q, which was an outlet selling a large range of home improvement products.

There is some conjecture about whether Kingfisher even knew that the B&Q outlet existed when it first bought Woolworths. At any rate, Kingfisher had soon developed ambitious growth strategies for both businesses and set about implementation, throwing considerable resources in equal measure behind them. But the two businesses operated in very different markets. Woolworths was in a mature, stagnant market. B&Q, on the other hand, was perched on the cusp of an explosion of interest in DIY home improvement in the UK. This was an almost perfect control experiment: two businesses, both with talented management teams, considerable resources, and ambitious growth plans, the only real difference being the markets in which they operated.

You must list your product's tangible advantages

The results could not have been more different. Despite the laudable efforts of its management team, Woolworths continued to struggle. It battled against a large number of nimble competitors – every time Woolworths implemented something new, its competitors would swiftly copy the move. It was under pressure from the emergence of speciality stores such as the music 'megastores' and also from the rise of the cut-price retailers like Asda, who were increasingly moving into new product ranges such as clothing, music and books. The competition was cut-throat and prices were being slashed. There was blood in the aisles. B&Q was a completely different story. DIY was booming yet there were very few established competitors in the market. It was a footrace to become the number one DIY retailer, but the field was small and everyone was starting from the same position. No one was particularly concerned about what their competitors were doing. They simply had their heads down and were desperately trying to meet the massive groundswell of demand. There was more than enough business to go around – you almost couldn't help but make money!

Kingfisher was able to rapidly expand the number of B&Q outlets and within five years had more B&Q outlets than Woolworths had stores. B&Q was a godsend for Kingfisher, which ultimately ended up selling off Woolworths to focus solely on the home improvement opportunities B&Q offered. As a footnote, Woolworths succumbed to the dire economic conditions of 2008/9 and went into administration.

It's not impossible to be successful if you enter a low-growth, competitive industry but the odds will be stacked against you. It will mean that you have to try just that much harder and you will need to have a real advantage somewhere.

2. Does my product satisfy an unmet customer demand?

▶ Why would anyone buy my product?
▶ How many people will buy it?

I'm often approached by people with 'a great idea'. My response is always the same: 'Why is it great?' My heart invariably sinks when they respond with '… because I've always wanted the product … and I've told my friends and my mother, and they think it's great too'. Believe me, you need a better reason than that. You must have tangible and concrete reasons why a customer would buy your product. This is the acid test for any business.

I have devised a two-step test for you to challenge your idea. The first part of the test is to look at the characteristics of your idea to see whether it's truly different and compelling enough for people to buy it. The second part of the test provides an insight into how many people might purchase the product or service.

This is a little chicken-and-egg: you may have identified an unmet need and developed a product to meet it, or you may have developed a product and are looking for a market. It really doesn't matter which comes first – normally both happen at the same time. However, to assess the commerciality of your idea, the best approach is to test the features of your product and then challenge yourself – what are the potential sales? This will force you to adapt your idea to ensure its commercial. Does it have the potential for large numbers of sales? Sales are the cornerstone of any large, profitable business.

Adapt to ensure the market's large enough. And, NO, your mum loving the idea doesn't cover it!

So let's start with the first test. Is there a compelling customer proposition? Technical jargon for: 'given what's already out there, will they want it?' When asking 'would anyone buy my product?' the following questions need to be answered:

- **Is it unique?**

  Is it a design? A brand? A technology? What is it that you have that nobody else does?

- **Is it better quality than existing products?**

  Be concrete: write down the features of your product that are superior to those of your competitors. The benefit(s) must be tangible.

- **Is it cheaper than existing products?**

  Perhaps you can offer your product at a significantly lower price than your competitors or offer more features for the same price. Get out and there and do some competitive shopping and compare prices.

■ **Does it save the consumer money?**

Some products succeed because they are designed to save the purchaser money (e.g. energy-efficient light bulbs).

■ **Does it make the consumer money?**

Perhaps you have an investment product that will make the consumer a whole heap of cash.

■ **Does it save the consumer time or effort?**

Your product might enable the consumer to do the activity faster, more economically, or do more of it (e.g. online price comparison sites).

It must be something that the consumers could not easily achieve themselves; otherwise they won't pay.

It isn't essential to tick every box, but the more positive responses, the better. The most important point is to identify at least one tangible, truly compelling reason why people will buy.

If there's an industry 'buzz', that's a sure sign of a growing market

OK, so now you are confident that people will buy your product – but how many? You won't be precise here, of course. The good news is you don't need to be. Use your common sense and follow your nose. You're just looking for hints. The concern here is that you may have identified a product that offers a compelling customer proposition, but only to a market so small that you'll never sell enough to make money. If you do find this, then go back and see if you can expand the potential market you can sell to – this makes your idea commercial.

I ask myself the following questions to help me understand the potential sales volume:

- Is it a new, exciting, growing industry (like DIY when B&Q prospered)?
- Are similar products already offered and how many do they sell?
- What do market research reports that provide industry overviews say?
- Are the newspapers full of 'buzz' about the product/industry?
- Can I contact some major potential customers to gauge how they would respond to the product?

To bring this to life, let's move onto one of my favourite examples: the birth of Virgin Atlantic. Virgin Atlantic encapsulates perfectly the holy grail of matching a compelling customer proposition with a large (and rapidly growing) demand. It's a much lower-risk strategy to adapt an existing product in a growing industry. When that's the case, you normally can't help but to sit back and watch your bank balance grow.

A killer customer proposition – with wings

Much has been written about the success of Virgin Atlantic and many writers have hypothesised about the reasons for its success – friendly and good-looking flight attendants, the handing out of ice-creams, in-flight massages, onboard amenities, luxurious departure lounges, Branson's attention-grabbing PR stunts – but these are all pure gloss. The real reason that Virgin Atlantic was so successful was that Richard designed a product that met a very specific and growing unmet customer need.

Let me explain. Almost all businesses have in place strict travel expense rules that prohibit employees from flying anything more expensive than business class. As you can imagine, these employees enviously eyed the first-class cabin, resenting senior management and employees of other businesses who were able to fly in the lap of luxury. So what did Richard do? He created 'Upper Class' and promised 'first-class travel at business-class prices'. Upper Class was officially designated a business-class fare even though it was the highest class offered on Virgin Atlantic flights.

This meant that businesses would pay for the flight but business travellers were also happy because not only did they feel they were getting a superior product than traditional business class but they were now also travelling in the highest class available on the flight – they would no longer suffer the indignity of being seated on the wrong side of the ropes cordoning off the first-class cabin. What an ingenious solution. Some mystery shopping with British Airways ensured that the prices Virgin charged were always below those of its fierce rival. And to top it all off, a generous air-miles programme also ensured strong customer loyalty.

Virgin had a killer idea in a growing market. It blew BA away!

So far, so good: a very clever product that solved a clear, unmet need. But were there enough potential customers for Virgin Upper Class? Virgin spent considerable time investigating the market. They talked to travel agents and also to the travel departments of large businesses. They talked to businessmen and women who were regular travellers.

They also did a lot of desk research. All their research pointed to the fact that air travel for business was rapidly growing. More specifically, their research suggested that there were two routes that were growing particularly strongly: London–New York and London–Hong Kong. Virgin also knew that transatlantic flights were the lifeblood of BA and that business and first-class tickets drove the profitability of these flights. So Virgin was now both confident that there would be enough customers for their service and they knew precisely which two routes they would target first (with other routes to follow later). Virgin now had a killer customer proposition and a very specific market (that was both large and rapidly growing) to target. There are no guarantees in business, but the odds appeared stacked in Virgin's favour. Richard launched Virgin Atlantic and the rest is history.

OK, the die is cast: you have your product refined and you are convinced that it will sell. Does it have a margin, though? No margin, no profit.

3.

Can I sell it for more than it costs to make today and in the future?

- ▶ Can I sell it for more than it costs to make today?
- ▶ How large is the profit margin?
- ▶ What flexibility do I have in my pricing/cost structure?

Sometimes, the obvious questions are the most difficult. When I ask people 'Can you sell your product for more that it costs to make?' they usually look at me like I'm an idiot.

The answer usually runs: 'Of course! If it costs me £10, then I'm simply going to sell for £10, plus my profit'.

Don't be an idiot! Will they pay more than it costs you?

But does it really work like that? Unfortunately, it doesn't. Consumers will only pay what they're prepared to, regardless of what it costs you to make.

After leaving Virgin, I advised Unilever on the launch of several start-up ventures, including Rocket. I want to use Rocket as a perfect example of the pitfalls of making wrong price assumptions – which if not addressed will have disastrous consequences.

Rocket: Cutting costs to lift off

Rocket was a UK company that produced and sold chilled kits of fresh ingredients that took only minutes to cook into high-quality meals. The ingredients were top-notch and the meals were marketed from great-looking mobile kiosks to commuters on their way home from work.

The retail outlets were expensive, but it was felt they were important to appeal to the target customer – the cash-rich, time-poor worker. It was a succinct, easily understood customer proposition taken to a large target market.

But there's a but. Rocket made the mistake of thinking that they could simply charge higher prices to cover their high costs.

Here's the dream: develop the idea, then sell to someone who can add profit immediately

They couldn't, of course. If the meals were priced too expensively, pre-packaged meals from the likes of Marks & Spencer and take-out restaurant meals became more attractive to Rocket's target customer. After taking all its costs into consideration, the company actually sold at a loss. It could not raise prices to compensate. If it couldn't find a solution – and fast – it was out of business. Eventually I found Rocket a supplier who could produce the meals more cheaply, so it now had a profit margin. It now had a foundation for a successful business and could go to work.

As an epilogue, Rocket eventually went on to be bought by a large manufacturer who could increase margins even further.

This was a case of developing a business and then selling to someone who can incrementally add profit almost immediately – not a bad strategy for some start-ups to work towards from day one.

Here's a simple checklist to ensure you have a margin.

- Don't assume that you can charge what you wish. Customers will only pay what they are prepared to pay.
- Figure out what your costs are and then compare this with the price of competing products. Can you actually make a sufficient margin?
- Challenge yourself to find ways to improve your margin. Can you lower your costs in some way? Can you distinguish your

product such that you will be able to charge a premium?

- Be prepared to face future price and cost pressure.

Distinguish your idea in the consumer's eyes. You can then charge a premium

So far so good – you have a great product and an attractive price – but smart entrepreneurs realise that any competitive advantage could disappear any time. They are constantly looking for a new angle that will give them an edge. They also understand that one of the most powerful ways to create a truly formidable competitive advantage is to develop an innovative way to inform and deliver to their customers.

4. Can I get my product to market smarter than my competitors?

- ▶ Do I have an innovative way of letting people know about my product?
- ▶ Do I have an innovative way to deliver my product to customers?

What we're doing here is defying convention. So think hard and really challenge yourself. A truly innovative way of informing people about your product and getting it to customers can even overcome the problems of operating in a crowded, stagnant market, or any other disadvantage your business has.

You can see it; competitors can't – the advantage no-one can take from you.

Let's return to Rocket for a moment. Rocket utilised mobile kiosks in the foyers of city offices where they knew people would be working late. They positioned their shop kiosks at railway stations where busy commuters would be passing by, and they even designed a very clever carry bag with a shoulder strap that would enable commuters to carry their product without adding to the already onerous burden of a briefcase, bag, ticket, etc. Each of these ideas helped to raise the profile of Rocket and also to provide a very clever way to reach the target customer.

Another clever way to develop an advantage is to look at other industries. What works there might be good for you, even if the sector's totally different. When starting a business the ability to get your message across can be the difference between rags and riches. So let's now look at an example of a businesses that did this very successfully, and in the process transformed its prospects.

The direct route to success

The management of Virgin Vie – Virgin's cosmetic business – wanted the business to operate from a network of traditional, high-street stores. The management argued that this was how the Body Shop and other successful cosmetic retailers operated and that it was therefore vital that they had the same to promote the brand and to attract customers. The management were convinced they were right. But when the business was launched, the stores remained resolutely empty. The expensive, glitzy, flagship store was simply not attracting customers.

A simple, deadly winning tactic is to take a delivery mechanism from one industry and use it in another

This was hardly surprising: the cosmetics industry is highly competitive and difficult to break into, and industry margins are low. Doesn't sound particularly appealing based on the criteria in Question 1, does it? Any new player looking to enter the industry needs to offer something truly new and innovative. Virgin Vie was able to chug along (although by no means being a success) because it benefited from the strong Virgin brand.

Fortunately, Virgin's management at the head office in Holland Park insisted that Vie also consider alternative distribution methods.

Brainstorming sessions were held, and everyone was tasked with thinking creatively about how Vie could bring a new twist to the cosmetic retail model.

Everyone knew that people enjoyed working for Virgin. The Virgin brand was synonymous with fun, anti-establishment leanings and bringing the consumer a better deal. Staff often viewed themselves as mini-Richard Bransons with their own entrepreneurial enterprises. This sparked the thought that perhaps there was a way to harness the pool of individuals out there who would leap on the opportunity to work for Virgin.

In further discussions, the name of Avon was raised several times. They had successfully refined the concept of door-to-door selling but Vie did not simply want to be another door-to-door sales company. Then someone mentioned Ann Summers and the home 'parties' that they organised for women to purchase lingerie and other products.

Over a period of six months, taking elements of each of these, a proposal was developed for an alternative distribution method for Vie: selling direct to consumers through Tupperware-style parties held by commissioned sales agents. This would combine the most attractive elements of each of the competitor businesses considered.

What saved the business was having an open mind and brainstorming over a glass of wine

---

It was a novel way to introduce the product to the customer and the follow-up mail-order distribution was a cheaper cost of client acquisition than the retail. What Virgin Vie had hit upon with its direct sales model were two benefits: first, a very low-cost route to customer acquisition by maintaining a large, commission-based roving sales team; and, second, a very low-cost method of actually distributing goods to the end customer, as the sales agents transported their own stock and paid cost plus the cost of delivery.

The Vie business was saved by this simple but innovative way of getting its product to its customers. It wasn't rocket science – just having an open mind and brainstorming over a glass of wine.

The point's simple: develop an edge and keep it. It's vital to success, particularly when you're cash-strapped and struggling for survival. Just follow these simple steps:

- Develop the mindset that any advantage you have can be taken away tomorrow, which means that you must constantly look for ways to develop new competitive advantages.

- Challenge yourself as to how you will let customers know about your product and how you will deliver your product to them. Do not accept the status quo and convention.

- Do this by brainstorming among your team and talking to as many people as you can. Remember Virgin Vie? No one person came up with the ideas that saved the business. But you must assume responsibility for getting the right people together and driving them to come up with truly innovative solutions.

- Copy selectively from other industries or competitors. You don't have to copy the whole business; you are simply looking for good ideas that you can apply. If it is successful in another market, then there is every chance that it will work for you too. The cleverest entrepreneurs are able to take something that has worked in another industry and apply it to an entirely new context.

There are rules to follow if your project is to make money ...

5.

Can my project make money?

- ▶ How much profit will I be making when I am up and running at full capacity?
- ▶ What is my break-even point, and how realistic is this when compared with the overall size of the market? And how long will it take me to break even?
- ▶ Will entering this market provide a springboard to further opportunities?

This section wraps up all the previous questions together to see whether you will actually be able to achieve your ultimate business objective (i.e. to make enough money to become financially independent). You must understand how big the potential pie is, and how long it will take you to get to turn a profit. Pragmatic entrepreneurs understand that if the pie is not so large and it takes too long to get stuck into, then it may not be worth chasing or might disappear before they get to it.

You must bring that break-even point forward

If the numbers don't stack up or some things cost too much, don't simply give up. Go back and revisit each of the elements of the bulletproof idea and look for ways to improve it. That is the real beauty of this approach: things don't need to be perfect from day one. You can build, innovate and refine your way to your bulletproof idea.

So let's drill down on those sub-questions.

The rules for profit making

Question	Implication	Action
• How much profit will I be making when I am up and running at full capacity?	• If the potential pot is not large enough, why are you bothering to chase it? • The size of the prize is almost never as big as you think it will be – because of competitors, unexpected costs, etc. • If you're only looking at a small profit, it probably won't even turn up; if it's large, at least some of it is bound to be there.	• Look for ways to increase the breadth of your product's appeal (e.g. is your product too expensive?). • Are there other channels to market (e.g. direct sales as well as through retailers, like Virgin Vie)?

Continued ...

Question	Implication	Action
• What is my break-even point, and how realistic is this when compared with the overall size of the market? And how long will it take me to break even?	• Don't just assume that because there's a large market out there for your product that you're naturally bound to grab a slice of the pie. • You must build the financial case for your business from the bottom up – how many units do I need to sell to break even? When do I think I will be able to hit those targets? What will I be making month by month before I get there? • Only after doing this, do a top-down reality check: if my calculations say I need to sell so many units in the first six months to break even, let's just double check to see if the market is big enough for that. • Furthermore, the longer you have to wait, the more potential risks are involved, and the higher the likelihood you won't be around when that much-awaited day arrives.	• If you are predicting that you are going to be able to quickly capture 2–3% of an established market, then that is probably reasonable as long as you have a compelling product. If you are predicting that you are going to rapidly achieve a 10–15% market share, then you may need to rethink. • Look for ways to lower your break-even (e.g. are there any further costs you can strip out, like Rocket did?). • Is there any way you can break even faster (e.g. pre-selling your product to get the money in faster, like Virgin Active)?
• Will entering this market provide a springboard to further opportunities?	• There will always be opportunities that open up for potential exploitation – you simply have to keep your eyes open and be receptive to them.	• Your job is to explore potential new opportunities and decide which to pursue and when. At the same time, you must keep your management team focused on the day-to-day management of the business.

Let's take another look at an example of a business that had developed clear strategies for each of these questions well before they launched and which reaped the benefits as a result – Virgin Active, the health club chain.

Fit for riches

Two guys approached me when I was at Virgin with the health club concept that eventually became Virgin Active. They were proposing to take the template of a health club one step further by including more of the life-style amenities consumers were increasingly demanding, such as libraries, social spaces, food courts, etc. They wanted to combine that with good management, good customer service, fair prices and desirable sites.

Not only was the idea a good one – an improved product in a growing market – they also understood their economics perfectly. All their forecasts were built from the bottom up: they didn't simply assume that they could take '10% of the market', they built up their forecasts on a club-by-club basis. They also did not simply accept that break-even might take a while.

Heaven: the idea was going to break even before the first brick was laid!

They challenged themselves to lower the break-even point and actively looked for ways to reduce the time it would take. They carefully selected their initial locations in order to be able to rapidly capture large pools of members to generate immediate cash-flow. They knew exactly how many members were required to break even for every club and how many it would take to make the target level of profit.

But they pushed even further and developed an aggressive marketing campaign of 'pre-sales' whereby they would offer individuals significant discounts if they signed up for membership before the gym even opened. This meant the team could be confident of breaking even before they had even finished fitting out the gyms.

At full-run rate, each gym was highly profitable with annual membership fees more than covering the costs for the upkeep and maintenance of existing facilities and equipment. Furthermore, the opportunity was not simply to open a lone gym, but they could realistically expect to operate twenty gyms in the UK, with significant international expansion opportunities available as well.

You can mitigate risk – but not by sticking your head in the sand!

The absolute beauty of this area is that it brings it all together. Your objective is to make sure the pot's big enough and it doesn't take too long to capture. It imposes a financial health check – or should that be sanity check? – on your idea. So, revisit the detail in the table on pages 23 and 24 with an open mind. And look again at the earlier questions (1 to 4) until you're satisfied you've married your idea to a profit. Even if that's the case, you still have to manage risk.

6. Can I manage the inherent risks in the business?

▶ What risks does the business face?
▶ What can I do to manage these risks?

So, after using the elements of the previous five questions to analyse, develop and adapt your idea, it is now bulletproof. Or so you might think.

But hold on a minute, there are risks in every business: things that you have no control over; things that may dash your hopes. So, you need to keep your eyes open and your wits about you. Successful business-builders identify the risks they think they might face and come up with a plan to address them.

From the outset, I want to make it clear that the best way to ward off risks is to focus on doing what you do, and doing it better than the rest. Challenge yourself to deliver a truly exceptional product. If you do this, the risks should take care of themselves. Too many people agonise over every little action their competitors take, but completely ignoring potential risks is not wise either. So, what I have done below is to outline the generic risks that a start-up can face and some strategies to mitigate them.

You're an entrepreneur, not an inventor. You want a successful idea – anybody's idea!

The major risks that you need to consider are:

Potential risks	Questions to ask
Competitor	• What steps might they stake to retaliate?
	• Will they reduce their prices?
	• Will they strong-arm distributors to stop them stocking my product?
	• Will they launch a large marketing campaign?
	• Will they copy my product?
Legal/regulatory	• What legal/regulatory requirements currently exist?
	• Are these likely to change or become more onerous in the foreseeable future?
Supplier risk	• Am I highly dependent on one or two key suppliers?
	• Will I be able to find substitutes if one of my suppliers fails or attempts to raise prices?
Customer risk	• Are my customers' tastes/income/purchasing behaviour likely to change?

The good news is that there are strategies available to help you manage these risks:

■ **Protect your idea:** Securing legal protection (e.g. a patent) of your idea is the most effective way to protect against competitors copying your product. Unfortunately, this is not always going to be available. You should however, whenever possible, sign exclusive contracts with customers and suppliers. This could prove decisive.

■ **Copy what works elsewhere:** If it has worked somewhere else, then it should work for you too. You don't have to copy an entire business model. You might. But you might also simply copy parts of a business model that are particularly impressive and which could be applied successfully in your own business. You may draw on businesses that are both within and outside your own industry. Remember, you're an entrepreneur, not an inventor; just because you didn't think up the idea in the first place doesn't in any way mean it's less worthy or less likely to be a success.

- **Partner with established players:** If you feel that you have a weakness in some area – contacts, expertise, etc. – then you might want to look for a partner with complementary skills. You might also want to look to partner with a powerful brand. At Virgin we frequently partnered with expert management teams or businesses with the operational expertise to complement our marketing and customer-acquisition skills.

- **Have options:** Smart operators always ensure that they have back-up options. You don't want to be dependent on any one thing. You should have a potential alternative in mind for every single relationship that is critical to the ongoing success of your business (e.g. suppliers, distributors, even customers).

The last word

This chapter has blown away the myth that successful entrepreneurs fly by the seat of their pants without thinking or strategising. Nowhere is this more important than when developing your idea. It's no accident that the bedrock of successful businesses is an excellent idea. Poor, non-commercial ideas will fail, however well delivered. You now have the questions to interrogate your idea and the means to answer them. In short, you have the firepower to ensure that your idea's not mundane – in fact, that it's bulletproof – and so much so that you can and will beat off the competition, something to give you supreme confidence in the heat of battle when it's lonely and all those around are doubting you. OK, let's move on: it's time for battle.

Dos and don'ts

1. **DO** choose a market that's fat and growing, and not overcrowded. If you don't, you're making it hard before you start. Often this means your choice will be a new market or one experiencing a resurgence.

2. **DO** ensure your idea solves your customers' problems in a tangible way. It must. Go back and drill down. List out how it does this. You must have at least one concrete reason – a price advantage, better quality, etc. – to start with.

3. **DON'T** assume you can sell your product for more than it costs to make. The market determines the price. Either screw down the cost or add benefits to it so you can charge more. At any rate, ensure you have a margin.

4. **DO** challenge yourself to get your product known and delivered to your customers in a unique way, or in a way competitors find hard to copy or, better still, are unaware of. Do be creative and look outside the box. Draw from other industries.

5. **DO** look for ways to lower break-even and increase the size of the pie you're chasing. If your time to break-even is long, and your reward low, it's probable that you'll never get there in one piece.

6. **DON'T** stick your head in the sand. Understand and consider solutions to possible risks. The best solution is always to run your business better than your competitors. But you must be ready to act.

7. **DO** be disciplined. Every now and then, challenge your business against the bulletproof idea. Markets and competition rarely stay still. Nor can you.

CHAPTER TWO **LAUNCH SMART: WHAT TO DO (AND, ESPECIALLY, *NOT* DO!)**

Three businesses in four succeed in the first year. So far so good, but only 20% of the remaining three quarters make it to the sixth year. I find that figure truly shocking. So, what causes this terrible waste of time, effort and money?

In the majority of cases it's simply insufficient income that causes failure. I'm not talking about generating first sales. In fact, preoccupation with the first sale is extremely dangerous. Don't be distracted from the real objective, which is to achieve a sustained, high volume of sales that drives a consistent profit. A second, related issue is spending money on the wrong things. Spending money sucks in time, drives down margins and does not buy you the time to achieve sustained sales. The objective of every start-up is survival. Survival depends on having more cash coming in than going out. Cash coming in depends on sales. Anything else is window dressing.

Survival depends on more cash coming in than going out. Anything else is window dressing

Let me set the scene.

How not to do it!

Virgin Vie was Virgin's attempt to take the cosmetics and toiletries world by storm. The highly energised management team were gearing up for success and were intent on making everything perfect. With a war chest of some £20 million behind them, they felt invincible. The management team's strategy was to rapidly roll out a network of high-street stores. Vast sums were spent on design consultants and branding experts. Millions were devoted to engineering the products. Elaborate designs for stores were rejected in favour of ever more sophisticated ones; each made the Taj Mahal look like a utilitarian block of council flats. The 'perfect' design was finally settled upon, and a hugely expensive flagship store on Oxford Street was fitted out to its precise specifications. And this was all before Vie had made one single sale! Preconceived notions tested on 'focus groups' were relied on at every turn.

As the company developed, I would frequently visit the head office in Chichester. Every time I visited, the number of staff appeared to have grown exponentially. When I asked why they were recruiting so many staff I was told that all the staff would be working flat out as soon as the business hit the forecasts in the business plan. My visits would also involve a close inspection of the operational and financial set-up. I looked in awe (well, actually, horror!) at the elaborate (and hugely expensive) stock-ordering and warehouse systems they had put in place, not to mention the finance and accounting systems.

The cocktail of ego, knowing best and perfectionism is always lethal

When I had the temerity to ask whether these complex systems were really necessary for a business that was yet to achieve any major sales, they simply scoffed and told me again that once the business hit its targets they would be invaluable.

So, what happened when Virgin Vie launched? Initially, the Oxford Street store had a lot of visitors – but few turned out to be customers. People were attracted to the store because of the brand but very few spent money once they were inside. Something was simply not right. Feedback from real customers (not those focus groups) quickly suggested that the products did not have a Virgin 'feel'. The problem was that the management had wasted so much money in the set-up phase on things they did not really need that they were beginning to run out of money now that sales had fallen vastly below forecasts. The grumbling among the management team began. They wanted to spend money on new marketing campaigns and to revamp the products but they had already emptied their war chest.

Fortunately, Richard Branson and I had been adamant from the start that Virgin Vie should also be sold directly through Tupperware party-style cosmetics evenings. And while visitors were not spending in the high street store, the feedback from Virgin's direct sales force was positive. Customers felt the evenings were unique events at which they could purchase premium products at discounted prices. The sales staff also liked these events, as they saw themselves as Richard Branson-like entrepreneurs.

Non-essential spend will consign you to the junkyard of start-ups

---

Over the next few months, commissions and incentives were reviewed and refined, home-delivery packaging was designed, and a host of other changes were made ahead of launch. Time pressure meant they had to learn on the job. Perfecting the offering had to wait. Yet today Virgin Vie is one of the leading direct sales cosmetic companies in the UK, and is the country's second-largest direct selling company with annual sales in excess of £60 million.

What about that elaborately fitted-out Oxford Street store? Well, it required a further injection of funds before eventually being closed down!

Virgin Vie was extremely lucky. It had both a household brand and financial backers with deep pockets to support it during the radical revision of its strategy. Can you imagine what would have happened if Vie hadn't had the Virgin brand? I suspect the retail stores might not have had a single customer without it. If you'd ploughed all your capital into an extravagant retail launch only to realise that you weren't generating any sales and that there was no impetus for visitors to your stores to actually buy anything then you'd join the statistics as another failed start-up. And you'd rue the money spent on accounting systems and the like that were never needed.

This chapter will ensure that you don't make the same mistakes.

You're going to use your time effectively, only spending money on what is absolutely necessary to build your business (the front end versus the back end). And, crucially, you're going to achieve a sustained, high volume of sales.

What to spend your money on

I want to begin by telling you in no uncertain terms what you can and can't spend your precious cash on during the survival stage.

Spend money on the 'front end' of your business. The front end involves every aspect that gets people in through the front door and achieves sales. It includes, for example, your product and all sales and marketing initiatives, such as advertising, brochures and press. At this stage, sales and customers come before everything else. It's all you should worry about. A mindset that focuses on sales generation is one of the most important determinants of success in the survival months.

The back-end spending was absurd; Rocket needed Unilever to bail it out

Do not spend any money on the 'back end' of your business. This involves any part of the business that's invisible to the customer, such as administration and support systems. The back end is obviously important but it doesn't generate all-important cash. At this stage, you should only worry about IT systems if you're selling them. Otherwise they will not make you a penny. Inevitably, there will come a time in the future when if you don't invest in the back end it will start to adversely affect your customers. This is the correct time to make further investments. Not before.

Sounds obvious, doesn't it? But you'd be amazed how often people get this wrong.

A cash till too far

Rocket, the ready meals business I was involved with, is a great example of a business that made the mistake of focusing on the back end rather than the front end of its business at launch. I remember attending one particular management presentation which drove this fact home to me. One of the management team was demonstrating the new till system that he had just spent a small fortune implementing. 'So if you press this button, you can record the customer's purchase, automatically re-order stock for the next day, generate real-time financial reports and closely track every employee's productivity for the day at every Rocket kiosk,' he told me earnestly. I listened to this in amazed silence.

Unfortunately, I wasn't amazed at the fact that here was a cash register that seemed able to do everything short of achieving peace in the Middle East. What amazed me was that someone could actually think that we should be investing our limited funds in such an overly complicated system when we had just one kiosk at Waterloo train station, two staff and a largely untested customer proposition. The real questions they should have been addressing were: How are we going to get customers to the kiosk in the first place? What is it that the customer actually wants? How do we persuade customers to buy?

Rocket, like Virgin Vie, fell for the lure of investing heavily in back-end developments. Its investment plans read like a checklist of no-go areas for start-up businesses.

- Elaborate till systems? Avoid!
- State-of-the-art stock ordering systems? Avoid!
- Top-of-the-range finance systems? Avoid!
- A large finance team? Avoid! Avoid! Avoid!

So, to make sure you don't make the same mistake, put together the graphic below, which illustrates the elements of the front end and back end of a business.

FRONT END

➤ Product
➤ Packaging
➤ Pricing
➤ Marketing
➤ Sales pitch
➤ Sales close
➤ Sales staff

BACK END

➤ Manufacturing
➤ Information technology (IT)
➤ Human resources
➤ Finance
➤ Logistics
➤ Administration

➤ Product development
➤ Market research

This classification is straightforward and commonsense but there are two elements, market research and product development, which are special cases. They're front-end expenses but you need to treat them, as I'll demonstrate later, as back-end expenditure.

I've made it a rule that I will only invest in the back end of any business if, in not doing so, the customer is adversely affected. As the front end of your business expands, there will be a point where the back end starts to groan under the weight. When there's a risk that you'll not deliver on your customer promise, it's time to invest. Indeed, as I highlight in chapter 8, there'll come a time when you'll do serious damage to your brand and reputation if you fail to invest in your back end.

Don't let back-end systems spending make positive cash-flow an impossible dream

I now want to look at four common back-end expenditure mistakes that entrepreneurs make in the survival stage of their business. Indeed, they are some of the most expensive mistakes that you can make.

How to avoid back-end error number one

Any expenditure should reflect current volumes of business and not some predicted future volume levels that may never arrive. For example, your IT manager may tell you that although you have just twenty-five clients and have only been operational for one month, it's vital to invest in a system that will allow the business to comfortably service a potential client base of 1000. Indeed, your IT manager may absolutely believe this and put together a highly seductive argument. But it's like a dieter buying an outfit in a smaller size in the anticipation that one day he or she will fit into it. How can they be sure? And will it still be fashionable? How can you be sure that, if the IT manager is right and the customer base reaches 1000, you will still need that system? It may be obsolete by then.

How to avoid back-end error number two

Don't let senior staff build empires through unnecessary expenditure. Challenge every proposal for expenditure on the back end. The first question should always be: 'Will this provide a benefit to the customer?' You should consider whether there's a cheaper alternative, whether the expenditure can be delayed, whether you really need that many people to deliver whatever it is and whether it would be cheaper to outsource the function.

You need to have a fast-moving front-end machine that's constantly putting pressure on the back end

How to avoid back-end error number three

Keep under control any staff who try to 'keep up with the Joneses'. Every single IT manager I have ever met has told me: 'We absolutely have to have this because it is smaller/faster/more efficient.' But do you really need them? What's wrong with using simple Excel spreadsheets?

Is the business really going to grow so rapidly that you need accounting software designed for a company the size of GE Capital or Nestlé? Only agree to these requests if they save costs or deliver better solutions to your customers.

How to avoid back-end error number four

Failing to maintain enough flexibility in your cost base during the early stages – particularly in the back end – can be fatal. Try to keep your costs variable. Unless an impressive office is critical to your sales generation (for example, if you're a financial adviser and it's important to convey a sense of permanence) then you should consider options around short leases or a location that might not be A1 but will offer you a lot better value for money. These may prove more expensive in the short term, but will provide you with valuable flexibility to scale up as your business grows and when you can actually afford to tie yourself into a longer term lease.

The front end of your business should be constantly pushing and straining on the back end. That is the way that good businesses operate. You should always find yourself in a position where your sales are growing at such a rate that your back end is struggling to catch up. Ideally you will never be in a position where your back end actually does so. Forget sophisticated telephony. Faxes still work and so do telephones.

When you know the product gels and the marketing works, pull the trigger and spend, spend, spend!

You might even just find that by forcing your staff to pick up the phone, they stay a little closer to their customers than they would if every last piece of customer interaction was managed by the world's most advanced customer relationship management system.

Achieving sustained sales

Now you have sufficient money for the front end of the business, let's make it a success. The objective here is to preserve cash while you test and understand your product and marketing. When you're convinced you've got it right, you'll pull the trigger and go flat out spending money on marketing campaigns that will work, with a product that customers want. When the latter begins to lose steam, you repeat the process: refresh, re-test, and re-launch.

What will become obvious to you – and is absolutely key – is that any preoccupation with first sales and launch will actually stop you from being successful in the longer term.

So I want to introduce three interrelated techniques that I have seen applied in every successful start-up I have worked with, and which, with the benefit of hindsight, would have worked wonders for Virgin Vie. They are: 'the pitch', the '80:20 rule' and 'leap and learn'. Together, these will help determine when it's time to pile in and spend your cash on a marketing campaign you just know will work, promoting a product that gels with customers. In other words, you pull the trigger.

Front-end technique number one: The pitch

You need as many compelling customer 'pitches' as possible. A pitch is your clarion call to customers; it's a compelling call to action that resonates with the customer. Everything you do at the front end is an opportunity for a pitch. Consequently, every single aspect of the front end needs careful thought and a disciplined approach to determine what that pitch should be.

Every single print advertisement, every radio commercial, every presentation, every conversation is a sales opportunity

In retailing, for example, the unique individual pitches include the store design, the floor layout, point-of-sale materials, packaging, the counter and the sales person behind it. Even the brochure displayed on the counter. Each opportunity needs to be carefully considered and a specific call to action developed. It might be to encourage a customer to enter the store, to approach a specific counter or to actually hand over their hard-earned cash for your product.

Front-end technique number two: Applying the '80:20 rule'

This rule states that once something is 80% 'perfect' then you should get on with it. This applies to almost everything you do during the early stages of your business. For example, once you have your product to a stage that is 80% perfected then it's ready to take to market and to begin the process of gaining valuable feedback. The same would apply to your marketing. Why waste your time, money and effort waiting for the perfect solution when you don't know even what the perfect solution is? You can't know whether that advertisement will work until you test it with real customers in a real-life situation. Some people fall into the trap of being perfectionists, or are so afraid of taking the plunge that they procrastinate in the hope that one day everything will be perfect and the launch of their product will be 100% risk-free. That day will simply never come. You need to get out there and begin testing.

The 80:20 rule could be the 70:30 rule or 60:40 rule. You get the point: once you've reached a stage where any further investment should really be based on actual customer feedback, take your product to market and test it.

Front-end technique number three: 'Leap and learn'

The third technique is that, right from the start, every business needs to 'leap and learn' with real customers. Successful entrepreneurs realise that they don't know (and can't know) everything about their customers before they engage with them. They need to launch, learn from genuine feedback from real customers and then make the necessary changes to their pitch, product, marketing and distribution. And re-launch. This iterative process will eventually lead to a model that works.

Use real customers and real customer feedback to perfect your pitches

Here is your chance to take the product that you have long talked about to real customers. It can be a little daunting at first, but now is one of the most exciting times in your business life.

During this phase of your business, there is a very clear need for hard thinking and quality idea generation. You must consider how to solve problems that you will inevitably face. And you will need to spend time thinking about how to develop and refine your call to action for each and every pitch opportunity. Use real customers and real customer feedback to perfect your pitches. Don't rush into doing things until you have thought them through carefully and tested their cost-effectiveness. This will take real discipline, but it also distinguishes the wheat from the chaff – entrepreneurs who do the hard yards and those that don't, the winners from the losers.

The techniques in action

If you apply these techniques you'll have a robust business from an early stage – and you may find when we get to the chapter on funding that you may not even need external funding, which is the ideal case.

I want to bring these techniques alive by applying them to some real-life case examples. These will help you understand how they work and interact, and realise how powerful they are when applied in unison.

So, let's return to our favourite whipping boy – Virgin Vie. You know the facts of the case already, but before we draw morals from the story, I want to clarify one point. You might think that the mistakes at Virgin Vie were the result of a weak management team. This assumption is incorrect. The management team was absolutely blue-chip and experienced. They genuinely believed that they were achieving something as they raced along spending money.

£500,000 just to secure the Oxford Street store? You have to shift a hell of a lot of lipstick to cover that!

So, now I hear you ask: 'How did it go so wrong with all that firepower? How did Virgin Vie fail so miserably to apply each of these three techniques?' Well, let's study each in turn and assess exactly where Virgin Vie went wrong.

Shop – or night club?

Virgin Vie is an example of a business that did not have a compelling pitch. It's very clear that its initial retail pitches did not connect with customers at any level. It relied heavily on the Virgin brand to draw people into the store. Now, they did come, but the conversion to sales was low. OK, the product wasn't perfect, but was still saleable, as demonstrated by the success of the direct sales force. Unfortunately, there was no compelling call to action within the store. Virgin Vie simply assumed that, once in the store, customers would inevitably buy. The store should have been overflowing with a range of different pitches such as promotions, special offers, club memberships, or flyers to ensure people didn't leave the store until they'd bought. However, there was no incentive to buy today.

Further, the staff were not quite right. People associate Virgin businesses with young, friendly approachable, perhaps even cheeky – but highly professional – staff. Virgin Vie recruited competent sales people, but they weren't classic Virgin employees. Careful recruitment, the development of compelling sales scripts and regular training would have made a world of difference to the effectiveness of the employees.

I recall talking to the management of Virgin Vie and being told that they had so much to do and were absolutely flat out. They had to get the final designs for the store, buy that couch, etc., etc. ... The management was focused on all the tangible (and completely wrong) outputs.

Perhaps they could have used Virgin Atlantic air hostesses

Management remained entirely focused on the brand at the expense of sales. They ran around like lunatics, but never had the discipline to concentrate on the important and difficult items, like the various sales pitches.

If they'd been single-minded about driving sales, they might have been really creative. Imagine how more more compelling the pitch would have been if customers buying more than, say, £200 of cosmetics would go into a draw to win flights on Virgin Atlantic. Perhaps they could have used Virgin Atlantic air hostesses as a channel to recruit engaging sales staff. Virgin Vie paid scant attention to every opportunity to pitch and had provided no call to action.

Virgin Vie also forgot to apply the 80:20 rule. The management were determined to have a perfect product and delivery, and spend a fortune before even knowing what their customers wanted. Virgin Vie spent almost £500,000 on a one-off payment to secure access to its Oxford Street store before its lease even started. It needed to shift a hell of a lot of lipsticks to cover that. The store looked more like an exclusive night club than a place where people could shop. Everything looked perfect, but ultimately customers didn't want to shop there.

You must know what your customers want if your business is to survive

Finally, Virgin Vie also failed spectacularly to 'leap and learn'. Rather than going into the market and testing their proposition, with the minimum amount of fuss, the management simply decided they knew best. They thought – wrongly – that they knew exactly what customers wanted, relying on their own views and questionable market feedback, of which there was surprisingly little. All their theories and preconceptions were simply wrong. Yet Virgin Vie spent vast sums of money rolling out a business before they even tested these theories. Virgin Vie should have been out in the market testing product with real customers in an actual sales environment and then making the required changes.

Unfortunately, once Virgin Vie began to receive negative feedback, there was little that could be changed in a short period of time. They couldn't simply close the doors of the Oxford Street store or demand that the factory making the cosmetics re-engineer the products. No entrepreneur wants to find themselves in that situation.

Virgin Vie is a clear illustration of the danger of ignoring the three techniques. If you do so, then you'll ensure that the front end of your business is ineffective. You'll fail to generate sales – and by launching too early you'll be spending precious cash prematurely.

I don't even want to mention at this point the disastrous situation you'd be in if you had made Virgin Vie's mistakes and also spent all your cash on the back end!

So, what happens when it goes right? I now want to take you through three case examples to demonstrate how powerful these techniques can be when applied in unison and in a disciplined manner.

The gain in Spain

The first example is perfect proof that success in business rarely happens by accident. The business in question is a Spanish restaurant in London where I assisted the owner (who later became a close friend of mine). Restaurants do not succeed simply because of the quality of the food. Of course, the food is very good but success requires more than that. It took the owner years to perfect his winning formula. The business has been incredibly successful, but only because the owner has worked tirelessly to refine his pitch, product and marketing. Every single day the owner is looking for ways to improve.

When used in unison these techniques deliver turbo-charged sales

He launched with a menu and wine list that he believed London diners would respond well to but he wasn't certain. He then listened to the feedback from his initial customers and began to tweak the menu and make additions to the wine list. He placed some simple advertisements in local papers but found that the clientele that he was attracting was less than ideal. So he racked his brains for new marketing ideas.

He began to network with groups that were likely to bring customers to his restaurant. He talked with local hotels that might refer business. He constantly looked for opportunities to have his restaurant written up in local and national newspapers.

He watched the local competition to see what he could pick up from them. He even managed to build relationships with several prominent Spanish tennis players who then brought along other well-known sporting personalities, creating a buzz about the restaurant. He truly leaves no stone unturned in looking for new and effective ways to market his restaurant and ensure that he delivers a product that customers want to return to again and again. His discipline in this approach has been rewarded with a thriving business that has been awarded 'Best Spanish Restaurant in London' and, more importantly, delivers significant profits. He now has three locations in London and is looking to launch additional restaurants.

Disciplined management was rewarded with a thriving business – one that makes very significant profits!

The second case I want to consider is a property business that I helped to build and in which I was a significant partner.

Tinkering to £750 million!

The property-sourcing business used our techniques to turbo-charge a small start-up. Take the example of advertising. What we did was take some advertisements used by overseas competitors, customise them, and place them in the paper. It was plain-vanilla stuff – no fancy consultants' artwork; a flat-out test.

The first ad pulled some customers. We asked for feedback, tweaked the adverts, and went again. Improved results. We kept at this low-cost tinkering, until we were confident we had wording that really resonated with our target customers.

Then, when we were confident that the absolute ball-breaking formula had been found, we piled in and backed that formula with cash. That's what you've got to do. When you've got it right, pile in and pull the trigger. However, while this was going on, the product was also being evaluated, tweaked and refined.

Real-life customers were asked for feedback at the roadshow events we had seen advertising at. The first event was best described as shambolic, but it went ahead. Customers asked for greater comfort on such things as snagging, furniture packs and rental guarantees.

We changed the adverts based on customer feedback. The conversion rate went up 20%

These additions were tested, refined and embedded. The end result? Conversions moved up 20 percentage points. The harmony of a product customers wanted with a marketing execution we knew would work was powerful. The result of this? A £20,000 initial investment from savings spread over time turned into £750m of property sold per annum within five years.

You will recall I said earlier that although product development and market research were front-end costs, they were to be treated with suspicion and thought of as back-end costs. Hopefully, the story about the property business demonstrates why.

I see little point in spending money until you have real customers. It's a crime to waste precious cash on back-end items prior to launch.

Our final example is the wonderful and infamous Wal-Mart Corporation and the story behind the development of one of the truly revolutionary pitches of the last century. The reason I like this example is that it once again demonstrates the massive pay-off that accompanies devoting time to careful thinking, idea generation and hard work.

The Wal-Mart revolution

When I was at business school in the USA, I had the good fortune to meet a member of the Walton family for a drink and a chat about the success of Wal-Mart. As the glasses emptied and the hours passed I was given a unique insight into the evolution of the Wal-Mart business. It is a fantastic example of 'leaping and learning' to develop a truly revolutionary pitch.

In 1945, after leaving the army, Sam Walton purchased his first store, a Ben Franklin franchise variety store in Newport, Arkansas, using a $20,000 loan from his father-in-law and $5000 in savings. Sam had worked for retailers previously and so was aware of the general principles of the trade. But he was not content to simply follow established thinking.

Sam constantly looked for opportunities to differentiate his store from others and to service his customers better. Sam spent countless hours pacing the aisles of his store, talking to his customers and racking his brains for ways to improve his offering. He focused on stocking the shelves with a wide range of goods with very low prices, having his store centrally located so it was easily accessible to many customers and staying open later than most stores, especially during Christmas seasons. But he continued to look for ways to truly differentiate.

As a result of 'leaping and learning' and listening to customer feedback, Sam began to experiment with discount merchandising. He began to purchase direct from the manufacturer, enabling him to lower his price per item. He was then able to sell a greater quantity of goods, thereby increasing his sales volume and profits.

'Stack 'em high, sell 'em cheap' was a revolution in retail experimentation

Sam's store was soon exceeding the sales and profits of the other Ben Franklin franchisees. In fact, his store became so successful that the landlord refused to extend his lease when it expired as he wanted to give his son the profitable store Sam had built!

With the $50,000 proceeds from the sale of his first store, Sam purchased another Ben Franklin franchise store in Bentonville, Arkansas, which ended up being called 'Walton's Five and Dime'. As part of the launch of the store, Sam staged his first sales promotion – what he called the 're-modelling sale'. Not long afterwards, Sam decided to start a second store in Fayetteville. Looking for a manager who would be able to continue the success of his other store, Sam developed a principle that he would apply so successfully later at Wal-Mart: he offered the prospective manager a percentage of the store's profits. It seems so commonplace today, but then it was revolutionary. Incidentally, he found the manager after searching around his competitors' stores for good staff. Remember what I said about copying best practice?

Despite his success, Sam refused to be complacent and continued listening to customer and staff feedback to find new ways to improve his business. He was one of the first to develop the concept of 'self-service', which allowed customers to pay for everything in one go rather than paying at various counters throughout the store.

Sam also continued to focus on developing an ever-wider range of products and special promotions. Sam sought to price his products more keenly and enjoyed some success. He never stopped refining his proposition. It was then that he hit 'pay dirt' and developed a truly unique pitch. Customers could expect to purchase three items and only pay for two if they shopped at his store. This was a truly revolutionary concept in retail at the time, one that came to be encapsulated in the famous phrase, 'stack 'em high, sell 'em cheap'. Sam also introduced the concept of offering a range of specials that were limited to that particular hour or day or week. Customers now had a clear reason to visit his stores as they knew they would be able to buy goods at the lowest price with high levels of customer service. Furthermore, they had a reason to visit the store regularly and buy immediately if they wanted to take advantage of the specials.

Tinkering led to £256 billion in revenue

This might not sound particularly revolutionary today – indeed, walk into any retail space in any city in the world and you are likely to see such promotions – but at the time it was ground-breaking. Sam Walton did not develop this pitch with the launch of his first store, but rather 'leaped and learned' and constantly refined it. He had an idea, implemented it, reflected on feedback, made the necessary changes and then tested the idea again. This is such a simple approach but it is so incredibly powerful. Can you see how central these ideas were to Wal-Mart's success?

I have only taken one example of how Sam refined his pitch – that of his pricing strategy – but I can guarantee that there was not a single square foot of those Wal-Mart stores that wasn't subjected to constant scrutiny and refinement based on customer feedback, with the objective of generating incremental sales through effective pitches every time. The rest is history. Today, Wal-Mart is a global phenomenon with almost 5000 stores across ten countries generating more than US$256 billion in revenue.

There are also some subtle lessons from these tales. It takes bravery to experiment and guts to defy convention. It also reinforces the understanding that no business has a perfect plan or straightforward journey. For those launching a business with a bulletproof idea, this mindset inspires confidence.

The last word

Smart entrepreneurs know that the objective of launching is to build sustainable sales. Rookies fixate on the first sale. You know this. You know precisely how to ensure your product gels with customers, and to make your marketing drive sales. You know what to spend, and what not to spend cash on – and, critically, when to spend. Now all you need is to hold your nerve and relentlessly, methodically, march forward. Your reward will be sustainable sales at a profit. That is, you'll have a real business. However, I do need to smooth your path for you. Next stop, building instant credibility. The battle continues ...

Dos and don'ts

1. **DO** preserve cash at all times, allowing you space to ensure you get the product right and that the marketing's effective.

2. **DON'T** spend funds on back-end operations – things that don't directly affect the customer, such as accounting systems, ordering systems, etc.

3. **DON'T** spend funds on systems, people or assets that you feel you may need, could need or might need, whatever management pleads. Essentials only!

4. **DON'T** spend lavishly on product development or marketing first launches. The only possible way to generate sales is to experiment through different sales, marketing and product pitches with real customers.

5. **DO** search for the right product and marketing formula in a live sales environment by:

    – using every point of customer contact to pitch and entice your customers to purchase now

    – not perfecting anything, product or pitches – use the 80:20 rule

    – learning from feedback – adjust, re-test.

6. **DO** drop all ego, preconceptions and perfectionist tendencies during the testing phase.

7. **DO** pull the trigger and spend flat-out when your testing delivers the right formula. That is, when you know your product is attractive to customers and that marketing does drive sales.

8. **DO** spend on back-end operations when it is obvious it's affecting your ability to service your customers.

CHAPTER THREE **PUNCHING ABOVE YOUR WEIGHT: WINNING THE CREDIBILITY GAME**

There I was, sitting on an uncomfortable old chair, with a plastic cup of cold, weak tea in my hand. I was waiting outside an office in a business park on the outskirts of Leicester. The meeting had been tough to set up, and it was proving even harder to make it past the rather frightening-looking secretary sitting in front of me.

But I had to persist. On the other side of Madam Medusa was an individual whose help I needed to secure a contract. An hour passed. Then another. Finally, I was told the meeting had been cancelled because of an overrunning commitment.

As I sat on the train for the long trip back to London, I thought fondly of the old days, the glory days – the endless queues of people trying to pitch their next big idea to me when I was at Virgin. Even Paul Keating (the former Australian prime minister) had tried to sell me on the idea of a new internet business.

Yesterday – dinner with an ex-prime minister; today – being treated like dirt by a secretary!

I thought about the dinners with musicians such as Peter Gabriel and a whole host of sports stars. I thought about the 'who's who' of prominent politicians, business people and celebrities that were desperate to be associated with us at Bond Corporation in the months after Alan's involvement helped Australia win the America's Cup.

I had taken it all for granted. Now here I was on a very late train, returning from a meeting that a middle-manager couldn't be bothered to take!

As unpleasant as I found this experience, you'd better prepare yourself for even greater frustrations. It's the business-builder's lot to be treated as the lowest of the low, unimportant, just another time-waster. Only when you succeed will you have them eating out of your hand.

But there's a catch. This is not just an ego problem, although of course it's unlikely to help your self-esteem. There's a very real threat to the survival of your business. You need to secure the help of suppliers, finance providers, employees, possibly partners – and, of course, customers – to have a business.

I finally understood Branson's obsession with PR and its critical role in start-up survival

All this got me thinking on the trip home from Leicester that day. When you're starting with just an idea, how do you get the right doors to open and have those key meetings scheduled? It all boiled down to credibility. People had to believe you could do what you were promising. Otherwise you were just wasting their time and money.

So I had to think seriously – very seriously – about credibility. My background was useful here. The fact that I had worked with Bond Corporation, McKinsey and Virgin could open certain doors. But others, as I now knew, remained resolutely closed.

Access – or lack of it – is a common complaint among business-builders. But I wasn't going to fall at the first hurdle; I had to develop strategies to get my fingers through the slightest cracks in the doors and prise my way in. Persistence, a thick skin and relentlessness will all help. But they will not be enough on their own. You need strategies and tactics.

One tactic became obvious: positive public relations (PR). Just watch people salivate when you can hold up a newspaper or magazine cutting that sings the praises of your product … or, at the very least, mentions it.

This is a tactic that I should have been aware of from day one. I had, after all, worked at Virgin and no-one uses PR to better effect than Richard Branson. During my time at Virgin, I did realise the value of PR, but took it for granted – it was available on tap! Doors would open, conversations light up and actions would be taken quickly with the benefit of reams of positive press coverage. Out in the harsh real world on my own, I quickly saw quite the opposite when I didn't have any press at all for my new venture. Absence certainly does make the heart grow fonder!

I finally understood Richard Branson's maniacal obsession with PR. Richard had never forgotten the value of PR in starting out and growing the Virgin brand.

I developed a forceful approach to securing positive PR. Want to peek?

One of the very few real dressing downs I ever received from Richard was when we received some negative PR about the float of Victory (on which more later), when the share price languished after listing. Richard felt that this affected his credibility in the financial services industry. This was the first time that I realised just how tall Richard really was.

Richard later sought me out and found me cowering under my desk. Richard had a strong belief that staff should be praised not criticised and wanted to apologise for how he had spoken to me. It was not a pleasant experience but it gave me a very clear view of his business priorities.

So, after I eventually realised that every start-up needed to have as much positive press coverage as possible, I went to work. I took what I learned at Virgin and modified it to get PR of some sort for each start-up I worked on. Once I had something, I could build from there.

Some modifications were required for my start-up press campaigns, as Virgin had obviously been in operation for 30 years and was an incredibly strong brand. When I was at Virgin, I would pepper Richard with questions about how things had been for him when he first launched his businesses and which tactics had worked the most effectively for him in the early days right across the business, including PR. So, the combination of my experience at Virgin and the many start-ups that I have since worked on has enabled me to develop a powerful approach to securing positive PR for new businesses. This is what I will share with you here.

Ensure people believe you'll deliver – then you will have credibility

To begin with, let's be realistic. PR is a war of attrition: it takes time and isn't available on tap – certainly not for start-ups.

It all starts with credibility. You have to be credible, above all else. And to be credible – to get other people, especially journalists, to believe in you – you have to employ the right tactics. Some of these tactics involve working the PR system. Some don't. There are other ways of establishing your credibility. We're going to walk through the lot together.

What exactly is credibility? It's quite simple. It's other people's belief you'll deliver on your promise. If you deliver, they'll profit, and so they'll listen.

So, how do people decide whether or not they believe you'll deliver on your promise? In my experience, people invariably ask themselves four questions. These particularly apply during the early stages of the business when your own credibility and that of your business are so closely intertwined. Keep this acid test of credibility in mind and ask the questions of yourself.

1. Do they think that your business idea is a good one that will work in practice?

2.   Do they believe that you can make it happen?
3.   Do they believe that you are absolutely committed?
4.   What evidence of success or commitment do you have?

Feel that you can confidently answer each of these questions? Got some gaps? Not so confident? So, let's look at some tactics that will help you to fill those perceived gaps. We'll start with some methods that will smooth your path to good PR.

Building credibility without PR

For the young and ambitious Alan Bond and Richard Branson, credibility helped get them where they are today. But who would be the pound-for-pound king if they squared up in the business boxing ring?

Blue corner – Alan Bond; red corner – Richard Branson

Alan Bond began life as a sign-writer, and went on to make, lose and re-make hundreds of millions. Richard Branson left school at fourteen and has also made a fortune. For both of them, credibility and reputation were very important and a major factor in their success. I had a bird's eye view of both of them and their strategies.

Round one – effort, planning and strategy. Both planned meticulously, leaving nothing to chance. There was a very deliberate set of rules to follow. Nothing to separate them here – even on points.

Round two – clothes and appearance. Richard's famous for his non-business attire and image. His audience is the man in the street. Alan was no less particular. His audience was big city banks so he wore perfect suits and flew in private planes. Again, too close to call.

Round three – presentation skills. Alan's ability to present opportunities was quite brilliant; always with a brief business summary, supporting facts and infectious personality. No bank could resist. Richard was also very appealing to the public, and clearly passionate, but Alan shades this round on points.

Bond v Branson? Too hard to call!

Round four — building credibility by association. Alan was seen and photographed with the world's who's who. He had impressive management teams and offices. Richard similarly. Who can forget the image of a young Richard arm in arm with Glenda Jackson at an anti-war demonstration? Round even.

Round five — PR as a weapon. Alan was Australian of the Year, won the America's Cup and was never out of the world press for long. But Richard with his Virgin business was clearly the absolute master balloon trips, boat trips, even dressed in a bridal gown! He had the press at his beck and call. Branson wins this round hands down.

So, the verdict? For me, it's a draw. From humble beginnings, they required credibility — and fast. They wanted to influence the most powerful boardrooms in the world and the man in the street. I learned that credibility is a strategic game — you consider your tactics, deploy them and keep following through.

So, let's outline the lessons from Alan and Richard, and what's worked for me.

Sell the vision, but don't forget the facts!

You have your bulletproof idea but unfortunately that isn't enough. You need to be able to sell it. You need energy. You must be able to sell your idea with such force that people are left in no doubt it's going to be a success. Your vision must be shared in such a compelling way that people can't help but be enthused.

Many people have energy and enthusiasm. To succeed, though, you must be a thinker as well as a doer. You must leave nothing to chance. So I want you to take the bulletproof idea questionnaire from chapter 1 and add the relevant data points you need to sell your vision to others. Use this as part of your presentation and learn it off by heart. Now you're differentiating yourself from the pack. Not only are you a visionary, but your vision has substance.

Tool kit

Here's a very brief take on the business trappings – the ever-present 'tool kit' that's a concise, compelling expression of the business and yourself. (For real detail on this, see chapter 8.)

- **PowerPoint presentation:** This should provide a concise and compelling summary of your business and vision. You will need to tailor the presentation for specific audiences but it would typically consist of four to five slides covering the following:

  Alan Bond was never without his four-page explanation of how he'd change the world

  – Vision: how you'll change the world

  – Your bulletproof idea with data points

  – Describe the team that will deliver

  – Description of operations/key suppliers

  – Summary financial projections.

- **Business cards and stationery:** Image is everything, and well-designed and professionally printed business cards and stationery will ensure a professional image.

- **Website:** You don't need to have the world's most advanced website, but it should clearly set out what your business does and look like the site of a serious, well-established business. It cannot look and feel like you bought it off the shelf.

Team

To get your business going you obviously must have a team of
people so that when you go to meet external parties, you and your
team will be able to present a compelling argument as to why
those prospects should become involved with
your business. Sorry? What did you say? You
have no team? It's just you?

**Find 'grandfather'
non-executive
directors – they lend
instant credibility**

Relax. To have early-stage credibility, anyone
you're dealing with merely has to believe you'll
get the job done. They don't expect large teams,
but you absolutely need the following:

- **You:** You must be able to sell yourself and your vision for the
  business convincingly. In the early days of your business, there
  is no real distinction between your identity and that of the
  business.

- **A finance director:** External parties will certainly want to
  see that a credible individual is controlling the business's
  finances and back-end operations. A fully qualified chartered
  accountant must be available – full-time or part-time, just
  make sure you have one. The beauty is that they can, as and
  when required, play the role of managing, operations or
  finance director.

- **A technical head:** Some industries (e.g. biotechnology or oil
  exploration) require specific technical skills. If you don't possess
  those skills then you must have someone in your team who does.

- **A beefy board:** Simply be cheeky and go and ask a well-
  respected industry figure to be your mentor – or, better still,
  to be on your board. Scour the press or *Who's Who* looking for
  someone in their 'grandfather' business stage of life. Seriously,
  they will help. Just keep asking. But here's the absolute key:
  they must agree to be publicly associated with your business.

Home is where the heart (of credibility) is

It's probably true to say that fellow business-builders would empathise with you about the cost and hassle of acquiring and kitting out a business space. They lament the expense and question its worth. Others might even argue that you don't need such a headache; that a home office will suffice. This is wrong, wrong, wrong!

In the real world you absolutely must have an office. Even if people say that it does not matter to them whether you have an office or not, I guarantee that either consciously or subconsciously they will be dismissing you as lacking substance and real commitment if you don't have one. You don't need to lease a whole floor of the 'Gherkin' in central London, but you do need to find a space that is suitable for your purpose and audience.

> **Beg, steal or borrow – but in the real world, you absolutely must have an office**

External validation

The power of external validation cannot be overstated. People will always be looking for this. The most powerful way to make them feel more comfortable about your inevitable success is to provide written testimonials. Ideally, these testimonials would be from paying customers, but in the early stages get them from wherever you can, including suppliers, industry experts – whatever and whomever you can think of. Another testimonial, of course, can be your product. Nowhere is this more important than when your product is a technical solution to a customer's need, as the following story reveals.

No discounting the value of testimonials

When I became partner in a group that was seeking to establish itself in the customer-loyalty market through a series of cash-back sites, I undertook review of the project – as I always do. There were a number of initiatives I wanted to get on with. The business was stagnating after a solid run. It was being hampered by a lack of credibility and no real awareness of us in the wider world.

> So, we immediately set about a number of tasks. First, external validation. We revamped sites to include customer and supplier testimonials. We repositioned the founder to be a champion of the industry as chairman of the Loyalty Association.
>
> The external validation built credibility. The press took an interest in us, whereas before they were only interested in the competitors. This, in turn, led to new, exciting joint venture opportunities – ways to grow the business. With this armoury, we were able to launch a second site, which became number two in the market in record time.
>
> Even now, we never underestimate the power of testimonials, and are always trying to build our credibility to another level.

Wear the uniform

The clothes you wear, the car you drive, even the watch on your wrist will all send messages. You need to think about these things carefully.

We've already seen Richard Branson's strategy. That's why every time you see Richard he seems to be wearing jeans and a woolly jumper. His clothing was part of the 'uniform' of the music industry and helped cement his credibility with the youth audience buying his records and the bands his label was signing. But now Richard's a little older, you occasionally catch him hobnobbing with the great and the good. That's when he wears a suit – it's the uniform, after all.

Unless people see that you absolutely can't afford to fail, you won't get the time of day

Skin in the game

Let me tell you something: all the tactics above are worthless if you don't have any skin in the game. Let me repeat that: you must be perceived to have skin in the game. What do I mean by that? It means that you must be perceived to have invested a considerable amount of your own time, effort, money and reputation in making the business a success and that you stand to lose it all should the business fail. External parties will always want to see that you stand to lose significantly unless you make the business a success.

It's easy to see who's committed and who's not. Alan Bond and Richard Branson were always committed and had a sixth sense about who else was 100% in. The signs to look for are people working part-time on their project or giving up a secure job. Is cash at risk? What about reputation? You must be committed, and visibly so.

OK, so there you have seven powerful tactics for rapidly building credibility. Use them; they will also help you mount a successful PR campaign. Success, of course, involves avoiding disaster, as the following tale demonstrates.

The disaster story that never took off

Let me share a wonderful PR story from my days at Virgin. On 5 November 1997, a Virgin Atlantic Airbus A340 aircraft was forced to undertake an emergency landing at Heathrow Airport as a result of an issue with its landing gear. This was a serious incident and no journalist would normally have hesitated to splash the word 'crash' across the front pages of any newspaper. This was a potential PR disaster that could inflict unimaginable damage to Virgin Atlantic's business. So, what did Virgin do? Virgin's pressman grabbed his phone, headed straight for the airport and began arranging to meet as many journalists as he could. He knew most of the journalists already and his goal was to downplay the seriousness of the incident so that they would not consider it worthy of reporting at all.

After several hours' drinking, the disaster story of technical failure changed to a tale of the pilot's bravery and skill!

His primary concern was *The Sun*, because he knew that this was a story made for *The Sun's* front page. He managed to track down the journalist at *The Sun* who was going to be covering the story and invited him out for a drink at one of the airport bars. At great length, he sat with the journalist, slowly turning the story around. After several hours of drinking, the story was no longer the disastrous tale of failed landing gear and a resulting crash landing but rather the story of a brave and highly skilled pilot who became a hero by landing the plane safely in 'a textbook emergency landing'. Virgin's PR man did not leave the journalist's side until he had filed this moving story.

Pretty impressive, but no fluke. This was borne out of a very deliberate PR strategy that Virgin had perfected over many years. PR was an enormous priority for Richard. He would devote at least 30% of his time to ensuring that Virgin companies were being written about and that the coverage was positive. He was absolutely committed to this and worried constantly about how to maintain a flow of positive news stories that were furthering the objectives of Virgin. Richard would always go out of his way to respond to journalists' requests and constantly sought to build new relationships in the media.

Building credibility through PR tactics: A step-by-step guide

It's a three-principle guide: relationships, relationships, relationships. Understanding how journalists think and work requires you to build relationships with them, and to provide them with stories that they want and that benefit your company.

Richard was running an empire, but still devoted 30% of his time to PR

Understanding this intimate inside working of the press will provide you with the same insight that Virgin has with its surprisingly small but effective PR team. It's an incredibly powerful but simple three-step process. You'll be able to do it. However, like many things in life, it's the nuances, the small things, that ensure you win. That's what I learned from Richard. That's what I use in my own business life. Let's get down to it.

Step one: Build relationships with journalists

There's no short cut on this one. To get good press coverage, and plenty of it, you have to build empathetic relationships with the journalists you come into contact with. You've got to get them on your side.

Inevitably, some relationships will be closer than others. Some will just be acquaintances. Others may become life long friends and confidants. Richard Branson will drop everything to talk with a journalist and will go out of his way to make them feel like they are part of the inner sanctum of the Virgin family.

First up, you need to understand their mindset. Journalists share many common traits. They're idealists, in the main. They want to make the world a better place. They do this by reporting the truth, for better or for worse. They are hungry for knowledge and keen to learn. All idealists also want to be inspired. Journalists are no different. As they get older, many of them, at least those covering business, typically become jaded and somewhat cynical but those original ideals still lurk beneath the surface.

Journalists get schmoozed by the biggest con men in the game. You have to show them you're the real thing!

Most journalists are also highly inquisitive. They're often very bright and refuse to take things at face value. They will probe and question until they believe they have got to the essence of truth. Remember, they report the news, and live in abject fear of writing a false or misleading story. A start-up represents a risk, and that's why we spent half this chapter on building your credibility, so you can convince journalists you're the real deal, not a con man.

The good news is that many journalists are extremely ambitious: they crave acceptance and praise. They want promotions. They want to win awards. But to do all of these they need exclusives and scoops. Understanding that and helping them with titbits of information about your business and offering your insights into and gossip about the sector will help them get just that. They'll want to have a good relationship with you, and they'll naturally tell your story, and that of your business, in a reasonable and fair way – which is all you can ever really want.

So, let's look at how the master of this particular game likes to play it. Richard Branson has always worked tirelessly to build and maintain relationships with individuals in the media. Many of those individuals that he built relationships with in the early days are now editors. As his empire grew, he still maintained his focus on relationship building. When I was at Virgin, my efforts to secure time in his diary were always a distant second in line to meeting with the press. He was constantly looking for ways to make them feel special.

Good quote? Not 'a new, more comfortable seat', but 'the first and biggest fully flat bed in the world'!

Here are my tactics, based on my business experience and careful observation of PR sorcerers like Branson.

- Use your tactics to ensure your credibility.
- Let them see you're human too: break bread with them; talk about your family. Remember, Branson would invite them to his house. And wear your heart on your sleeve: be honest about your business objectives and fears.
- Inspire them. You're a visionary. You're going to change the world. And they can get in on the ground floor of a long ride to the top.
- Listen to them. They report on your industry. Ask for and show respect for their views. Allow a little time in your diary specifically for this.

Step two: Provide the ammunition – a good story

All journalists want is a good story. That means a story they can sell to their editor and that the paper will run. If you give the journalist the right information, then he or she can craft a great story. The key is to know what elements the journalist is looking for.

A story for a journalist is a pantomime. A pantomime has a beginning and an end. It has drama and a moral. In short you must provide:

- **Central characters:** Who is doing what to whom?
- **Good guy/bad guy:** Who is righteous and who is the villain?
- **Action:** What event, action, decision has happened or is about to happen?
- **Motivation:** Why is it happening/has it happened?
- **Location:** Where is it happening and who/what will be affected?
- **Timing:** When is it happening?

Richard Branson naturally provided journalists with the ammunition they needed to write a compelling pantomime. It was part of his PR genius. He would always bring the story to life by including superlatives, real people and specific examples, always looking at it from the perspective of the average reader. Of course, Richard never forgot to provide a villain. For example, when Richard announced that Virgin Atlantic was introducing a new type of seat in Upper Class on their planes, it wasn't just 'a new, more comfortable seat' but 'the biggest fully flat bed of any airline's business class in the world. In fact it is over a foot wider than BA's first-class beds! The seat cost millions of pounds to design and engineer, and maintains Virgin's position as simply the most luxurious business class in the skies.' In that one short quote, Richard has managed to include superlatives ('biggest', 'any ... in the world'), very specific examples ('fully flat bed', 'a foot wider'), and also managed to disparage his old enemy BA. One tends to forget that he is actually talking about a seat! But that is the point.

> **Providing research will earn you brownie points that may lead to articles focusing solely on you**

Creating a story is not nearly as hard as you might think. So, let's look at some examples of stories you might like to try:

- Bad guy/trouble. All pantomimes have a bad guy so make the journalist's job easy and give them one. At Cashback Kings we paint ourselves as consumer champions providing the customer the same product at a cheaper cost. The villain, who's forced by us to pass on some of his margin, is the retailer.

- Your business is going to revolutionise the world. You're offering customers something new that's in the public interest. You're a new business, for goodness' sake, so outline your customer benefits and back them up with testimonials. Don't forget, you're putting investment back into the economy in employing people.

- The appointment of well-respected individuals to your management team or your board is a story that most trade publications will carry.

- Statistics and data. Journalists crave unique data, particularly information relating to the public's behaviour. What are people buying? Why? How? How confident are they? So, first consider your customers. Conduct a survey of your own customers' attitudes. As long as you have sufficient customers, this can be a cheap way to generate some interesting insight that journalists could use in a wider industry article. If you don't have the customer base to do this, commission a third-party research body (e.g. YouGov) to conduct a survey of attitudes on your behalf. This might cover investors' attitudes to the property market, the major fears of investors over the age of fifty, the favourite holiday destination for those between twenty-four and thirty-five, etc. The great thing about a survey is that if the results are topical they are likely to be picked up by a broad range of media. Journalists often struggle to find reliable statistical data for many of their stories and they view surveys as a credible, independent source. The results of your survey will often be quoted in broader articles and will usually continue to be quoted until more up-to-date figures become available. Remember, you've got to start somewhere. Providing research will also earn you brownie points that may lead to future articles that focus solely on you.

Richard Branson in a wedding dress world front page news

- Target the local press with a story about your positive impact on the local community. For example, publicise how many staff you employ in your local area.
- Identify a case study within your customer base that has an interesting twist and build a story around it. For example, at my property business we had many clients who were building property portfolios for their children. We received significant coverage by building a story around this growing trend and illustrating the point with some interesting real-life case studies.
- Organise a 'stunt'. Richard Branson was brilliant at organising exciting stunts to showcase his new business ventures. Virgin Bride was a classic example, with Richard deciding to dress up as a bride himself on the day of the business' launch. It was such a simple idea but managed to secure Virgin Bride press coverage not only in every UK newspaper and TV news bulletin, but also in newspapers from San Francisco to Tokyo. So get creative and think about what stunts you might be able to organise to promote your business.

Let's now put these lessons into a process to get those column inches.

Step three: Run the process – identify the publication and the journalist, and follow through

Now you have the inside story, the scoop. Note how much work is required. Nothing happens by accident. Even in a contentious industry, a well-run process delivers.

An elephant among pygmies

At the early stages of the property company I was building, we needed some press. It was growing fast using a contentious seminar model. The press eyed it with suspicion. We had had some success targeting regional press through commissioned research, but nothing earth-shattering. So when the call came from a reporter from the *Financial Times Magazine*, it was time to act.

First, I had to get him to the office to meet the team. I had to prove we weren't working from a garage hiding behind a website. Presentations developed with audited data, customer testimonials and financial returns – all put together in a neat summary. While this was being prepared, I tried my best to build a relationship. There was to be no doubt in his mind that we viewed him as important. At the same time, I had to build empathy. I was bleating that we were misunderstood, and could he, as a stand-up guy, at least come into the office?

After much discussion, we taxied him to the office – twice. What he saw blew him away – a clearly committed team, with a finance director, and non-executive directors, all housed in a real office. The presentation was given by the chief operating officer. I risked not doing it myself as a sign of faith in my management team.

We built our story. We were misunderstood, and were championing the consumer, in contrast to traditional real-estate firms. All this was backed up by real-life customers with pictures and interesting quotes.

After he left, I continued to call him. When I picked up the magazine I was speechless. I will never forget the kicker – he called us an elephant among pygmies!

While it would be nice to be able to pick and choose where your story will appear, at this stage you are going to have to face the fact that you are going to be grateful for any coverage at all. So, as beggars can't be choosers, you are going to have to target trade, local and regional press before trying for national interest.

Pick your battles: regionals are the better starting place

I have listed the publications in that order deliberately. The order reflects the difficulty of securing coverage, from easiest to hardest. You will find it easiest to get coverage in trade journals because these tend to be specialist publications providing detailed coverage of your industry. The second easiest is the local and regional press. These papers typically struggle for regular interesting content, so if you are able to approach them with a topical local story there is every chance that it will be carried.

The national newspapers are by the far the most difficult to crack. But they do sometimes pick up stories from trade and regional press. You will need to build the trust of the national journalists over time and will need to generate stories that are deemed to have a national interest. The national papers have different editors and journalists within each section of the paper, so you will ultimately need to focus on building relationships with those journalists who cover the sections that might be interested in your business.

Once you have the names of the journalists then Google them. Look at their previous articles. What are their likes and dislikes? Do they have a specific outlook or perspective? What angle are they likely to approach the story from? When you eventually meet the journalist, make reference to some of the articles that you have read and why you found them interesting. They love it, and it's a great first step in building a relationship.

Tell them you enjoy their articles, then stand back and listen to the sound of purring

Your next step is to invite them to breakfast, lunch or for a drink. Explain that you have a story they might be interested in and that you are keen to give them an exclusive.

When you meet with them for the first time, your goal is to build empathy and to lay the foundations for a long-term relationship.

Also produce a press release. I would recommend preparing no more than two additional pages. The first page details your story and the second provides a brief summary of your business, including key statistics such as number of customers, sales volumes, turnover, etc. Use whichever statistics present your business in the best light.

It's a good idea to write a nice (short) thank-you letter saying you are grateful to them for taking the time to meet you. Be polite. Make reference to the fact that the two of you discussed a particular subject and that you had wanted to provide some further information that you thought the journalist might find interesting and that would answer some of the questions that had been asked.

Finally, follow up. Not following up is such a rookie mistake. It is also sheer laziness. You have worked so hard on putting in place the foundation of a relationship and now you can't be bothered to follow up? You need to be like a dog with a bone. If you aren't, you will undo all the good work you have done so far. So make sure that you follow up prior to the article going to print to check that all is still okay and that you haven't suddenly been cast as the villain!

OK. We're almost there. But there's one further question I'm often asked: 'Should I recruit a PR company to help me?' The answer is probably no. You have limited funding and every penny you have must be spent attracting customers through marketing. After reading this chapter, you already have the knowledge to get column inches. You should only consider using a PR company if they have very close relationships with journalists that you need to influence (see chapter 7 on relationships with suppliers, particularly the 'stepping stones' sections). Despite their claims, you need to be certain that they do actually have these relationships.

An eat what you can kill contact can work

Using a PR company to fast-track relationships with journalists is one of the few things you should ever pay a PR company for. Another is an 'eat-what-you-kill' contract, if you can negotiate it. By this, I mean paying the company for the mentions and column inches they achieve for you – the equivalent of a commission-loaded sales contract to incentivise sales staff.

Above all, ignore the inevitable PR sales patter that they 'must first conduct an audit and develop a holistic PR strategy'. If you don't go down the pure coverage route, pay only for introductions to journalists, the time it takes to manage these meetings and perhaps a one-off fee to set up the initial relationship with the PR company. We are only talking about a few thousand pounds here. Once you are rolling in cash, then you may want to actually recruit your own in-house PR manager. It is likely to be far more cost-effective than relying on outside support.

The last word

Start-ups are often, unfairly, treated as time-wasters and ignored. Many doors are shut in their faces – a depressing fact of life for business-builders. To ensure this doesn't happen to you, you need credibility. People must feel you'll deliver on your end of a bargain. You now know the essentially cost-free tactics to build credibility. I showed you how to work the system known as PR – clearly the most important and cost-effective building block for credibility. Your journey to sustained sales is now significantly smoother. But you need to be able to close the deal. Now's the time to become a master negotiator. The battle continues ...

Dos and don'ts

1. **DO** describe your concept with zeal and passion. Sprinkle your description with important facts about market size, margin, customer benefits, etc.

2. **DO** have a basic tool kit – cards, website, presentation – to explain you and your business.

3. **DO** ensure your team includes a qualified finance person who can also act as an operations or managing director. You also need a high-profile non-executive director or mentor.

4. **DO** have an office – rent, borrow or steal one if you have to!

5. **DO** get outside accreditation. Customer testimonials are the most powerful.

6. **DON'T** ignore the power of PR or you risk being completely sidelined.

7. **DO** prioritise building a relationship with the press. Show your human side, and show an interest in their work.

8. **DO** build a story for the press – good guys, bad guys, human interest, excitement, fact-based quotes.

9. **DO** improve your chances of coverage by systematically building exposure with the trade press and regional papers, and finally the nationals. Work your press contacts.

10. **DON'T** engage a PR company for anything other than 'real' PR contacts. Negotiate a 'success fee' arrangement if you can.

CHAPTER FOUR **NEGOTIATION: THE ART AND THE SCIENCE**

Every budding entrepreneur I meet wants to pull off the perfect deal. Nobody wants to feel that they could have done better. It rankles. And it doesn't matter how successful or wealthy you are, that feeling of irritation is universal.

The objective of this chapter is to ensure you can close the deal and get what you need – easy to say and difficult to do. At the heart of it all is an attitude of composure. You've got to have ice in your veins, hold your nerve and not rush to impulsive decisions you'll regret later. I've got tactics to share with you that work – and have worked in practice for me – in various situations.

Apply the techniques of billionaire master entrepreneurs to your own start-up

Let's start with some real-life examples of how the big boys do it. Billionaires are some of the toughest negotiators around – it's in their blood. I learned about negotiation at the feet of a master: Alan Bond, one of Australia's most colourful and popular entrepreneurs, who, as we have learned, started as a sign-writer and became a billionaire. Along with his right hand man, Peter Beckwith, he was formidable. Virgin were no slouches either. Richard Branson might have a soft cuddly exterior, but he is one of the hardiest and canniest negotiators around. I need to make you a formidable negotiator too.

'Why?' I hear you say. 'I'm just a start-up, not quite a billionaire yet, so how does this apply to me?' Well, let me tell you, you are going to have to get up to speed because a start-up is essentially just a series of negotiations. You will need to negotiate with employees, suppliers and customers. And it is critical that you get this right; otherwise you won't survive.

The great news is that everything I learned from my billionaire masters is applicable to a start-up although, admittedly, you have considerably fewer bargaining chips if you're a start-up. I have developed a powerful approach to negotiation that ensures that you get what you need at every stage of growth.

A start-up is essentially just a series of negotiations

Firstly, I will introduce you to the 'four legs of the negotiation table'. These are the four prerequisites essential to any successful negotiation, but I have designed them with your position as a start-up specifically in mind. The next two steps are the 'science' and the 'art'.

The science will ensure that you are well prepared and don't make basic errors. The art is a series of highly effective negotiating tactics that will ensure you get what you need. Put all these together and you will inevitably be successful. Be warned, though, that a lot of what you read in this chapter sounds Machiavellian and ruthless. However, remember that you're fighting for your very survival. I will show you that ultimately all parties to a negotiation must win – or no-one wins.

So, let me set the scene. Imagine a smoky saloon bar. There's a crowd of guys sitting around a green baize-covered card table. They are playing poker. The atmosphere is tense. Their expressions are frozen. Nobody wants to lose the game because the side of his mouth twitched. Body language speaks louder than words. It's a scene you see in hundreds of movies, but it's the one that always springs to my mind whenever I enter into negotiations. This is the part where you horse trade, your preparation already done.

I love the atmosphere, the game-playing and the late nights. There's an adrenaline rush from negotiations. It doesn't matter if the deals are big or small, there's a buzz. But let me tell you about one of the truly big ones …

Poker playing – but for real

Back in 1995, Australian Mutual Provident (better known as AMP) was the sixteenth largest insurance company in the world and was desperate to break into the UK market. It had already bought UK-based London Life (the second oldest mutual in the world) and Pearl Assurance (at the time, the biggest acquisition of a British financial institution by an overseas company). Yet, despite their pedigrees, both of these deals had failed to set the world alight. They did not prove to be the platforms AMP needed to grow its UK business. AMP remained desperate to diversify away from its home market. It had an American chief executive who was under intense shareholder pressure to do a deal – a big deal.

It really does become a question of who blinks first

At that time, Virgin was offering financial services in the UK through a joint venture, Virgin Direct, which it had set up with Norwich Union, a well-known insurance company. There was nothing particularly wrong with the venture – but there also was nothing particularly exciting. So, Virgin had appointed consulting firm Arthur Andersen to seek out another potential partner to replace Norwich Union. Luckily Virgin had introduced a break clause when it first signed up with Norwich Union, which allowed it to replace the insurance company without any penalty but retain the Virgin Direct name. (Successful negotiators always have a get-out clause!)

When Arthur Andersen approached AMP, it was like all the cherries lining up in a slot machine. The American boss immediately saw the potential. While AMP understood how the UK marketplace worked, it had no real brand recognition here – but Virgin definitely did. And just imagine the kudos of having a business partner with a reputation for being fun, irreverent and on the consumers' side. It was a match potentially made in heaven.

There was a deal to be done – but at what price?

It was also my chance to prove myself. I had just arrived as Virgin's head of business development, and this would be my first major deal for the company. The first meeting between the two sides took place at AMP's head office in Victoria. (They probably thought it gave them some sort of home turf advantage.) The case was laid out.

AMP had the financial know-how and the funds. Virgin had the name and significant marketing experience. And the relationship with Norwich Union clearly demonstrated the value that a partnership with Virgin could create. Both sides knew there was a deal to be done – but at what price?

The only thing I was certain of was that Virgin was going to have 50% with only a marginal investment!

Virgin is a series of companies. Some are joint ventures. Some are owned outright. For example, we always used to joke that Boy George paid for Virgin Atlantic! It was sales of his albums that provided the capital needed to launch the airlines business.

A Virgin first: I negotiated for 50%, essentially just for the use of the brand

When Virgin enters into a business with another partner, it likes to establish joint ventures. Virgin will allow the joint venture to use the Virgin brand, but it will impose limits on what the venture can do. For example, a company selling Virgin branded umbrellas probably won't be allowed to diversify into swimwear and sunglasses. Virgin 'sells' licences to each joint venture; the licences specify exactly which services or goods can be sold using its brand. Remember this point – it becomes crucial to this whole deal.

When I joined Virgin I created a bit of a stir by suggesting that Virgin should be negotiating for 50% of new ventures simply in return for investing the use of the Virgin brand. Richard was an enthusiastic supporter of this idea, but it hadn't been done before. AMP would be the first time we tried to negotiate it.

So negotiations began with AMP. The other side had a large team and even flew in their top negotiators to make sure that the deal came off. And from Virgin there was, er … me! I was responsible for making sure that Virgin got what it wanted. And believe me, the pressure was enormous, particularly as I had also suggested we push for 50% for the use of the brand alone.

If Branson didn't like the terms, the deal was off – that was his ultimate tactic

I knew that Richard could say 'no' at any time. It didn't matter if we were poised to sign on the dotted line – if Richard didn't like the terms then the deal was off. That was his ultimate negotiating tactic!

There were certain facts that I discovered about AMP after a few preliminary meetings.

- Its chief executive wanted to do a deal. His job probably depended on it.
- The head of its UK operations was Desperate, with a capital D, to do a deal. He wanted to look good in the process and was keen to build a business relationship with Richard Branson.
- For some bizarre reason, AMP wanted sole responsibility for dealing with the City watchdog, now known as the Financial Services Authority.

Like any new relationship, it started with a few preliminary 'getting to know you' meetings. I did my best to be affable and charming, giving no clues to just how hard-nosed I could be about business. But, all the time, I was picking up information. I watched how the team interacted with each other – who deferred to whom. I was also assessing who was likely to be my ally in this process – believe me, you'll always find one. I was aware that the AMP side would be paying similar attention to me, so I was constantly on my guard.

Although the UK boss was ostensibly running the show, I swiftly worked out that the real power belonged to an Australian woman, who had flown in to help with the negotiations. If she said 'jump', the other members would shoot into the sky. She was highly intelligent but rather suspicious and I was finding it hard to develop a rapport with her. Yet to have any real chance of success, I had to strike a chord. Then, when I was on the point of banging my head hard on a brick wall, I heard her talking about 'the doggies'. Now some people might have thought she meant Fido and Rover, but being a fellow Australian I wondered if she was referring to the Canterbury Bulldogs, a rugby league team from Sydney. The penny dropped. This was how I could build a relationship with her.

It was a game of cat and mouse involving one hundred meetings!

Fortuitously Virgin had an interest in London Broncos, a rugby league team, and though I didn't know my full back from a scrum half, I invited her to a match. (I spent the night before with Tony Rae, the chief executive of the London Broncos, finding out exactly what it was all about.) It was a huge breakthrough. Her icy exterior began to melt (I even got a smile out of her), and we were able to build a constructive working relationship. And, as we did, I learned that she couldn't lie – not effectively, anyway; she simply wasn't capable of it. She lied and suddenly the room glowed red like a nuclear alarm. It was like an alarm bell – which at various points proved extremely useful to me.

After this initial courtship, the negotiations started in earnest. But I already had a sense of what AMP considered deal-breakers and what I might be able to get away with. What did Virgin want from the deal? Well, we wanted the maximum return for the least possible outlay. I initially went in all guns blazing, demanding 55% of the joint venture for Virgin and confirmed I wasn't prepared to invest one penny. I obviously knew AMP wasn't going to agree to that – it would be like turkeys voting for Christmas – but if you're going to be cheeky, be very cheeky.

The complete negotiation process took seven months from start to finish. It wasn't the only project I was working on, but it was the most significant. And I would be lying if I said there weren't some sleepless nights when I lay awake thinking that if I didn't get the deal signed, I was doomed. But I held firm. I knew what Virgin's ultimate objective was, and I set about achieving it. It was a game of cat and mouse. When AMP said a definite 'no' to 55%, I returned with a demand for 54.5%. I didn't concede a penny, unless I got at least a penny back in return. If I were to guess how many meetings we had, I would say one hundred. Just think about that. **One hundred** meetings, each lasting hours, at which I could never relax. At least if one of the AMP team felt tired, they could call on one of their colleagues. Occasionally I might bring in someone else, particularly when I wanted to play 'good cop/bad cop' – more of which later – but this deal rested on my shoulders.

I played hardball, reducing my demands in 0.5% increments, until AMP finally agreed on a 50:50 operation (my goal from the outset). I played hardball on the structure of the joint venture. And I played hardball on what the licences would allow AMP to do with Virgin's name.

AMP agreed to pay £900 million into the new Virgin Direct for the use of the brand, so we were winning. But, in return, AMP wanted licences from Virgin to cover a whole range of financial services, from banking to credit cards to PEPs to insurance.

AMP blew it to the tune of £250 million – just moments before the final meeting

That was probably fair. After all, AMP was putting almost £1 billion into Virgin Direct. But I knew that the most valuable licences covered banking and credit cards, and often used them as bargaining chips. Yet, when the deal finally came to be signed, Richard and I were in agreement that through clenched teeth we would give one or both away.

And then AMP blew it! They blew it to the tune of more than £250 million. They blew it because they were arrogant and didn't truly understand the art of negotiation. And they did so just moments before the final meeting.

The chief executive had flown in from Australia for the big signing. We were meeting at Virgin's offices in Holland Park, next door to

Richard Branson's house. Now, you've seen the way he dresses – it's coloured pullovers and casual trousers – and, although nobody could quite manage the sweaters, the Virgin team also usually dressed in a relaxed fashion.

The AMP chief executive pulled up in his big stretch limo, dressed immaculately in a business suit, and immediately started discussing the strategy for the final negotiations with his similarly suited and booted team as they climbed the stairs to Richard's first floor office. Remember those old wartime propaganda posters? 'Walls have ears.' Well, the walls definitely did have ears – my ears. I was walking a few steps behind them and I heard it all.

So what was this fantastic strategy that the chief executive couldn't wait to convey? Was he going to threaten to walk away unless the most valuable licences were given? Was he going to threaten to slash the price if they weren't part of the deal? No! I couldn't believe my own ears when he told his team that they should just forget about the hugely valuable licences to sell Virgin branded credit cards and Virgin branded bank accounts.

Adrenalin pumping, I asked Richard to step outside

He didn't realise that we were prepared to concede them at the final moment, but he wasn't prepared to take the chance that they might be the deal-breakers. The chief executive told his team to concentrate on licences to sell PEPs, insurance and a whole range of other financial services, and forget about the big ones ... for now.

As we walked into Richard's office, I managed to get him outside on some pretence and shared my new intelligence. And the deal that we had been prepared to sign was amended – to the detriment of AMP – without them even knowing!

Virgin later sold a 50% stake in Virgin One, a bank offering it established with Royal Bank of Scotland, for £250 million. MBNA now markets Virgin branded credit cards in Europe. And Virgin's credit card, which launched in the UK in 2002, is regarded as one of the most successful ever – with over 200,000 customers in the first year.

Hopefully this story whetted your appetite, so let's try to make sense of it to ensure that you employ the right negotiating strategy and tactics. Your survival depends on it.

There are three stages: getting the prerequisites for any successful negotiation right (the four legs of the negotiating table); preparing for battle (the science of negotiation); and winning the battle by using various tactics to ensure the deal sticks and you get what you want (the art of negotiation).

Bluntly, selling your vision is the difference between success and failure

Start-ups: the four-legged foundation

I want you to imagine a four-legged table. If it lost one of its legs, the table would be useless. Negotiation is that four-legged table. It needs all four legs if it is to have any hope of succeeding – particularly so when you are in the weak position of being a start-up.

1. You must have a clear vision of the opportunity that this deal brings to both sides, and be able to communicate that it is unique, highly desirable and achievable

I cannot emphasise this point enough. It's your business – your start-up. If you can't enunciate your vision powerfully and inspire and motivate people, then who the hell can? Your enthusiasm needs to be evangelical. People need to share your vision. They need to believe the business will be successful and that you – and only you – are the person to make it happen. Your vision is the biggest asset that your start-up has. Bluntly, selling your vision is the difference between success and failure. If no one believes in your vision, you have no chance.

Nearly forty years after he established Virgin, Richard Branson still extols the virtue of the strength and value of the brand at every possible opportunity. He hasn't forgotten the difficult times.

I also do it regardless of whether it's a start-up or an established business. It's just so ingrained in me. Think about that potential employee you're trying to convince to join you for next to nothing. They will need to be inspired and bursting at the seams to work for you, believing that you are the pied piper who will lead them to untold riches.

Build a personal relationship. Be honest about your hopes. People will appreciate it and trust you

But let's not forget the achievable part: if no one believes you can get the job done then what's the point of having a vision? You must articulate a strong 'can-do' and 'take no prisoners' approach. Point to any prior successes you or members of your team have had. In my early negotiations at my property company I would often refer to the other experts in my team who had many years' experience in the residential property industry (whereas I didn't). This was critical in getting deals done with major property developers.

2. You need to build relationships and trust

Think of all those hostage movies when the negotiator, usually Bruce Willis or Samuel L. Jackson, is called in to save the day. Before he even talks about strategy or listens to the kidnappers' demands, he builds a relationship with them. He makes them human. This is the 'nuts and bolts' of negotiation. If you have a good relationship with the other side then you're more likely to be able to complete the deal without needing a helicopter and a bag of unmarked money!

You can't build trust overnight. It takes time. Just recall my experience with the female negotiator on the AMP team. It took weeks before we developed a working relationship based on mutual trust and her love of rugby – and my willingness to freeze my butt off watching a game.

That's also the point: a successful negotiator will make any sacrifice necessary. And when you have a good working relationship, people let down their guard. You learn things that might become useful later on as bargaining tools. That might sound Machiavellian, but then try to show me anybody successful in business who doesn't use everything they learn – wherever they learn it. You won't find them.

Right from the word go in their business careers, Richard Branson and Alan Bond would always go to great lengths to start any business relationship on personable grounds. It might be a five-minute meet-and-greet or an hour-long discussion, but they made the other person feel important, interesting and more worthy than just another business contact. If they can do it, so can you.

It never ceases to amaze me how many people and companies are willing to assist start-ups at their own risk, sacrificing potential revenue, time and effort. But they will only do this if you can inspire them and if they actually like you. So if you are the type of person who is usually quite blunt and does not invest time in building relationships, then you better start doing it now. You simply must make the effort to build a personal relationship with the people you want something from. Be honest about your hopes and aspirations – they will appreciate it and will trust you more. Ignore the logical side of your brain and the doubters that will tell you that 'no one will ever do that'; they most definitely will do it if you use the four legs.

There is no room for ego in negotiations

3. Check your ego at the door to the negotiating room

The object of negotiation is to get the deal done on your terms. It doesn't matter if the other side cannot spell 'negotiation' and you have a PhD in physics, in the negotiating room you are both equal. If the other side wants to walk into the room first and hog the best seats or flash a platinum card around at lunchtime, let them! When I am in negotiations with another party, I don't care if they pull the chair out for me, stir my coffee or call me 'mummy'. I am there to get a deal done.

There's a great temptation when starting your own business to play the boss and put your ego first. But this is one of the biggest reasons deals fall over.

The only way I got the deal was by proving myself

Richard Branson has always been acutely aware of this, and you would never guess by his dress or behaviour that he was a billionaire. I remember when he and I met Paul Keating (the former Labor prime minister of Australia) to discuss a potential internet venture. Richard thought that, given his political persuasion, Paul might not take too kindly to Richard leaving in a Bentley or Rolls-Royce (at any rate, he never did). When it was time to go home, Richard decided that he would catch the tube. When Richard told Paul at the end of the evening that he would catching the tube home, Paul was visibly impressed. (He would probably have been less impressed had he known that it took Richard several hours to actually find his way home!)

4. You need to prove yourself and deliver on your promises

A start-up does not have a track record so you will often find that the only way to develop strong relationships is by proving yourself. This might take the form of a test. When combined with the other three legs this can be incredibly powerful. What it means is to ask that you be given a chance to prove yourself.

It can take many forms but still involves the person or company that you are dealing with taking a risk. For example, I remember at my property business we were keen build a strong relationship with a leading Orlando developer. But they had never heard of us, so they set us a test. We were asked to market and sell a small number of properties quickly. The targets kept growing until we proved to the developer that we could handle large volumes of properties, leading to an exclusive deal to market a resort complex with more than 1500 apartments. So combining the four legs got me started when we had no track record and ultimately led to a strong, very profitable, long-term relationship.

So, are you starting your negotiation on firm ground? If you were
to put something on the negotiation table, would it collapse?
If you are utterly convinced that all four legs are present – and,
believe me, no negotiation can ever be successful if they aren't
– then it's time to move on to the science bit.

Getting what you need: The science of negotiation

Now, 'science' is really just a fancy word for
'preparation'. But there is a real science to how
you prepare. You should know by now that one of

The science is simple. It ensures you won't make basic errors

my pet peeves is the myth of entrepreneurs who act like they never
prepare, pretend they had the perfect plan all along, and never put a
foot wrong. It's complete and utter rubbish (to put it politely!). They
all prepare meticulously – and do it in the way I am about to show
you. The best thing is that this will stop you from doing something
dumb (which, unfortunately, often looks quite clever at the time).

When winning isn't winning

When I worked at McKinsey, I was put on a team to assist a
company that specialised in energy consumption measurement and
the servicing of the relevant equipment. (Yes, I know: a management
consultant's life is such an exciting one!) Its UK operations were
highly successful at winning new contracts but, perversely, the
business was losing money. It was only a small office, and, as such,
vulnerable. It didn't take me long to discover that there was a lack of
communication between the sales and pricing teams.

The sales team were pricing contracts at below the cost to the firm.
They were successfully winning business that was unprofitable. You
may laugh, but you would not believe how many companies do this.
For instance, it wasn't until the mid-1990s that the Co-operative Bank
had a system in place that worked out how much money it made
from each customer. And that was pioneering stuff.

> ### Every contract negotiated was losing money, crippling the fledgling business
>
> When I suggested they might be under-pricing contracts, the sales team was outraged. They were deal-makers at the coal face, and I could politely 'eff off'! I had to physically work through the actual results of contracts that had been won, drawing attention to cost slippages and overruns and highlighting the implications for profitability, before realisation dawned. Once they accepted there was a problem, it could be solved – and the solution was pretty easy. I provided a framework and clear guidelines that the sales team should use when pitching for new contracts. This meant every win was a profitable one. Shortly after implementing that framework, margins within the business improved dramatically.
>
> That sales team had failed to appreciate the science of negotiation. They thought they were highly successful, while the reality was very different.

I believe there are three elements to the science of negotiation, which, used together reveal a strategy for the whole process. The elements are: identifying the points to create value from the negotiation; identifying what you want from the deal; and identifying what the other side wants from the deal.

1. Win–win: Identifying the points to create value from the negotiation

When you enter into negotiation, you are not doing so because you love the thrill of the chase. It's because you firmly believe that by working together the profit opportunity for both sides is greater than by working apart. The deal will create a larger 'pie' for both sides to share.

But a larger 'pie' needs to come from somewhere. This is your first job in preparation. It involves a comprehensive review of the deal and serious thinking. Are there synergies that exist between both sides that create additional value? Are there opportunities for other deals on which you could work together? Are there future opportunities?

Focusing on future opportunities can be a
useful tactic, which I use whenever possible. For
example, with suppliers I try to ensure they work
exclusively with me and offer them the carrot of
introducing other work opportunities. As a start-
up, that's maybe all I can offer on day one.

Providing future work opportunities can get a start-up the deal

2. The stop-loss: Identifying what you want from the deal

The second step is to identify all the outcomes that you hope to
achieve from a negotiation before it commences. Define what you
need to gain. What's absolutely essential? What's nice to have?
What can you live without?

If the deal doesn't achieve your absolute minimum objectives,
then walk away. It might be frustrating but don't fall into the trap
of doing a deal for its own sake.

This is exactly the process that Virgin goes through with every
potential deal:

'Must-haves'   Virgin retains control of the brand
                        Virgin has at least equal control of joint venture
                        Other party provides 100% funding, or
                        close to
                        Representation in day-to-day management

'Good to have'   More than 50% shareholding
                        Appoint or control management team

'Can live without' Concession on range of products' licences
                        granted in specific industry

Every time I did a deal for Virgin, I ran through this checklist.
And once I completed it from Virgin's point of view, I performed
the whole exercise again from the other side's perspective. That
is your third step. I thought about what the other side wanted to
achieve from the negotiation.

This is a critical part of the start-up negotiation process. The pressure to do deals, and be seen to make progress, can result in loss-making deals. Do the preparation properly (the science of negotiation, remember) and you won't sign those deals.

3. Identifying what the other side needs from the deal

You need to prepare the same list of must-haves and would-likes, etc. for the other side. It will take some detective work, and will become more accurate over time. Also, there's a subtlety here: you must also separate out what the key individuals in their team might personally require (and I'm not talking backhanders!). They might not have the same agendas as the companies they work for. They might be looking for a bonus for pulling off the deal. They might want prestige. Or they might hope for promotion.

Now I would never know any of those things if I didn't put the hours in getting to know the other side. I might go for a drink with them or a meal, and all the time I would be listening for titbits of information that I could mentally file away for another day. I was constantly watching them, studying the dynamics of their relationships and their temperaments. A good negotiator always remembers that he is dealing with people. (And never forgets that a deal can fall down because they got out of bed on the wrong side that morning.)

The guy opposite you isn't the same as his company. He might want a job!

Remember I mentioned earlier that the head of AMP's UK operation was very keen to get a deal done. It gave me confidence that, in order to present his board with a completed deal, he would concede some points: when he was making concessions, I had to present them as 'wins' for him and AMP.

My checklist of desired outcomes from the Virgin Direct negotiation for AMP and the UK head went like this ...

	AMP	**Head of UK Operations**
'Must haves'	• Business that promises strong future growth • Foothold in UK financial services market • Reduce dependency on Australian business revenues • Reputable partner • Control over regulation and compliance	• Any deal viewed as successful by the board • Must be 'seen' to be the key individual in the deal, particularly by the AMP Board and Richard Branson
'Good to have'	• More than 50% stake • Virgin contributing significant funding	• Possibility of future employment
'Can live without'	• Licences in areas of banking	• Anything that might derail a 'successful' deal

OK, this is a checklist for a multi-million pound transaction involving two huge companies. However, I swear it is just as valid for any sole trader, partnership or small company embarking on a negotiation. The only difference when you deal with a sole trader or a small company headed by the owner is that their desired personal outcome will match that of the business. But it is extremely important when dealing with large companies that you recognise that the motivations or desired outcomes of the representative of the company and the company itself may differ. Sense any future tactics here?

To find out companies' or people's motivations, think creatively. For example, when I worked at Bond Corporation, we had a rather unusual technique to research the motivation of companies we planned to do business with. We would interview their staff. On one occasion, we were considering investing in the UK

construction industry and had pinpointed housebuilder Taylor
Woodrow as a potential acquisition.

We placed an advertisement for a senior position in the
construction industry. As luck would have it, one of the
candidates for this entirely fictional position performed a senior
role within Taylor Woodrow. By the end of the interview,
with some carefully framed questions, Bond
Corporation realised that it would be able to
build a business from scratch for less than it cost
to buy Taylor Woodrow.

**Constantly assess
your position. Never
lose sight of what
you really need**

Negotiation can be a protracted process, and
you will find yourself making concessions as
you go along. It is vital that you regularly review
your 'desired outcome' position as you proceed. It will keep you
focused on your critical objectives at all times. And never concede
a point as soon as you become aware of an item that the other
side 'can live without' – it can become a vital bargaining chip.

The science bit has been pretty painless so far. These three bits of
research help in formulating strategy. Let me illustrate that with
my strategy for Virgin when I walked into the room for the final
meeting with AMP.

Virgin had already spent time and money developing compelling
forecasts revealing the largest potential opportunity possible for
both sides. In other words, I could show AMP that the deal was a
clear winner. Virgin was determined to get a 50% stake in the joint
venture without spending a penny. I had no intention of giving
away additional licences unless it became absolutely unavoidable.
But I had also developed some illusory bargaining chips. For
example, I knew that AMP was keen to handle the relationship
with the City watchdog and Virgin had no desire for that role – it
would be time consuming and, ultimately, unsatisfactory. AMP
didn't know that. I pretended that Virgin considered having a major
role in the regulation of the business as vital, and that it could
prove a stumbling block to a deal getting done. And, as I've already

highlighted, I had thoroughly analysed the motivation of AMP's UK boss. He wanted a deal to get done, he wanted to look good in the process and he was keen to build a relationship with Richard Branson. Virgin now had a clear strategy for its negotiations, and entered the room armed with that and a battery of tactics. So, now let's see what the tactics for a start-up might be.

Getting your fair share: The art of negotiation

Now this is the point where negotiation starts to become fun. It's time for tactics. This can be one of the most exhilarating and rewarding parts of business.

The best negotiators use tactics to their advantage throughout the whole process. They notice everything in the negotiating room. A cough that could signal discomfort. A quick glance between two people that might indicate a change in atmosphere. A twitch. They study body language. They quickly realise who is able to lie and who cannot. Here's a quick tip: reputable lawyers are unable to lie. The best they can do is to say nothing when asked a direct question.

Sooner or later, the more I get, the less he gets. Tactics decide who wins

An employee once told me that he hadn't invited me to his wedding because it was for friends and family. I retorted that it was fine, and now that I knew where our relationship stood it would be much easier for me to get rid of him. His face fell. He didn't know whether I was joking or being straight with him. He wasn't sure if he had overstepped the mark. He was at a disadvantage to me. That's the sort of atmosphere you want to create in a negotiating room – where the other side is discomfited because it really hasn't a clue what you are thinking.

Gung-ho entrepreneurs go straight into tactics. They don't put the groundwork in. They don't make certain that their negotiating stool has four legs, and they sure as hell don't conduct a scientific analysis of the deal that enables them to develop a winning strategy. They will tell you that they rely on their instincts and business nous. Fine! But if the other side has followed my advice, these people are merely lambs being led to the slaughter. The gung-ho approach has no fall-back strategy, no sense of the other side's strengths and weaknesses, and no sense of the doom that is inevitable!

One alternative is always to walk. The best and the bravest know this

I'm going to share a range of negotiation tactics that have served me well. I can't tell you when or where to use them; I'm not by your side to prompt you. It comes down to instinct. But remember this: say you have a solid strategy for the negotiation but you have reached the stage where the more one side gets, the less there is available for the other. You obviously want to gain the greater share, so you may need to adapt your negotiating style and approach to achieve this. Be flexible.

Below I set out a list of negotiating tactics and when you might use them, but I don't want you to feel that you must slavishly stick to these. They are just a guide. I want you to use whichever you feel is appropriate at whatever time you think will achieve the maximum impact. Let's continue with the AMP deal example. Where there is a nuance particular to a start-up, I'll highlight it.

Pre/early-stage negotiation
- Identify your alternative(s) to doing the deal.
- Determine most effective composition of your team.
- Choose most effective style, presentation and appearance.
- Identify a 'champion' within the other organisation.
- Build rapport as quickly as possible.

Normal course of negotiations
- Let the other side offer first.
- Bid high if you are selling and low if you are buying – be cheeky, not cheap.

- Be 'ruthless' at times and 'punch with velvet gloves' at others.
- Seek ways to disarm the other side.

Making concessions
- Use the good cop/bad cop routine.
- Check your ego – say you have to refer to a senior authority for approval.
- Use a senior individual as an external sounding board to keep you on track.
- If making concessions, make them count.

Getting back on track
- 'Park' difficult issues.
- Re-state the vision.

Identify your alternative(s) to doing the deal

This is always a good philosophy to adopt in all aspects of life, although perhaps not when it comes to my wife! In negotiations, having an alternative achieves two things. It keeps the other side on their toes, because they will always worry that you could walk away, and it gives you greater confidence and strength. AMP was always aware that the fall-back position for Virgin was to stay with Norwich Union, its existing partner.

The science of negotiation taught you that you always have an alternative, not to do the deal. However, your negotiating position will obviously be strengthened if you have a genuine alternative to doing the deal. However, simply making the other side believe you have an alternative can also be very powerful.

A bidding war from thin air!

Towards the end of my time there, Bond Corporation got itself into serious financial trouble. It was an open secret in the marketplace.

Bond owed FAI, an Australian insurance company, about A$180 million secured on its coal assets. Now, there is a whole lot more to this story than you need to know about, but the bottom line was that Bond hoped to sell these assets to FAI to repay the loan and generate additional capital. But FAI, smelling blood, wasn't playing ball. It wanted to pay significantly less than A$180 million, while other parties were putting in bids of around A$100 million.

This was a really important deal for Bond, and the challenge I faced was to convince FAI that there were some serious buyers around who were perfectly willing to pay the asking price. Or more. The only problem was ... there weren't. We spent weeks debating price and getting nowhere, and then it came to me. I had to conjure up a bidding war out of thin air. So if the mountain wasn't coming to Mohammed ...

I didn't think the MBO had a chance – but the other bidder did!

I convinced the management team of Bond's coal company to put together a management buyout (MBO). We went through all the numbers, drew up documentation and even persuaded Westpac (one of Australia's premier banks) to back it. Now, I didn't think for one second that the MBO had any real prospect of success, but I needed FAI to think it had. Suddenly, presented with a credible management team and Westpac's backing, FAI felt that there was a real risk that it could lose out. The company increased its offer to more than A$200 million – or double the nearest alternative bid. (Incidentally, when FAI collapsed years later, they still owned those coal assets.)

Determine the most effective composition of your team
Putting together a negotiation team requires careful thought. Negotiation is highly interpersonal, and it will always be much easier if the other side actually likes you and feels that they can trust you. Remember what I said before about leaving ego at the door? If you haven't developed the necessary rapport with the other side, withdraw from the team. Think carefully about the skill sets and qualities each member of your team has in

negotiation, and match these with the qualities of those on the opposing side. Understanding the other side is part of the preparation vital to a successful deal.

As I have already mentioned, it became apparent that the UK head of AMP operations wanted to develop a relationship with Richard Branson. In reality, I held a far more senior position in Virgin than he did at AMP but he was older than me and viewed age as an important factor in seniority. So, whenever it was possible, Richard would talk directly to him creating the sense that they were driving the deal together.

> **If my face doesn't fit, I get someone else to deal with it. I just want to get the job done**

As I also mentioned, I was pretty much a one-man negotiating team but every so often I needed somebody to back me up. If I felt the UK head was being obstructive, I might bring in Richard. If I wanted to appear that I was fighting to get approval for the concessions I was granting, I might wheel in a member of the finance team or another executive who would put on his 'hard man' act. Whatever it took to make those negotiations go smoothly, I did. In a start-up, relations are critical. So be disciplined: leave your ego behind, and put the right face forward.

Choose the most effective style, presentation and appearance

Appearance, style and presentation can play a vital role in negotiations. At Virgin, we usually wore casual dress and maintained a fairly informal attitude. On many occasions, I am convinced that the other side saw us as disorganised, poorly prepared or simply young upstarts. It disarmed them and gave them the false impression that they were in the driving seat of the negotiations. But when we needed to dress up – to meet a venture capitalist, say – we donned our Savile Row suits, crisp white shirts and polished shoes.

When the deal with AMP was hotting up, the company hired one of the top American investment banks to advise them. But on the Virgin side, it was still just me. Those masters of the universe, as they liked to view themselves, were used to dealing with the bosses of Britain's blue chip companies who couldn't make up their mind without conferring with their boards. They didn't realise the power I wielded. Yes, Richard held the ultimate veto, but I still had more chips up my sleeve than a croupier. And they never understood that. They thought because I was young, casually dressed and Australian (!), I would be a walkover. As a start-up, the opposite may be true. You may need to overdress, and hire a smart car to show your worth. At any rate, give it careful thought.

Identify a 'champion' within the other organisation

Large companies have huge layers of bureaucracy that can cripple deals. As a start-up, one of the biggest frustrations is getting the attention of the big boys. I have found that the best way through this is to find a 'champion' on the other side who will cut through the bureaucracy and make things happen. He or she will know the right people to talk to and how to keep the deal's momentum. The ideal champion will be senior and well respected in the organisation, and will passionately believe in the opportunity that the proposed deal brings.

> **A supporter from the other side's inner sanctum could be the difference between success and failure**

Now, I'm a realist. The 'champion' isn't usually a vocal supporter of the deal because he thinks Brad Rosser is a good guy who's kind to animals and walks on water. He's doing it because there's something in it for him. It might be promotion, positive media coverage or a bonus payment. He might even want a job in your organisation. But if you can find a suitable insider then it will speed up the process and improve the likelihood of success.

Ultimately, when it came to Virgin's deal with AMP, the internal champion was the Australian lady I initially found difficult to work with. There was a whole lot of office politicking going on that I couldn't hope to ever understand, but I realised that the bosses in Australia wanted the deal done. She was there to make sure that the UK team didn't blow it. And, as we got to discuss the venture more, she realised that it really was a great deal for AMP.

Build rapport as quickly as possible

The first time you meet the other side, you need an icebreaker (and I'm not talking a pick axe). If we are meeting in the office of one of the negotiating team, I will scan it for clues. Is there a photo of a family? Is there any hint of a favourite hobby? Engage in small talk. It will help you gauge the other side better. Do they appear uncomfortable when you mention certain topics? Open? Honest? Slick? If the rapport isn't there, then slow negotiations down. Suggest a few 'nights out'. Build the relationship. This isn't a one-night stand! If you know the other side well, then it becomes far harder for them to mislead you. This is in effect a restatement of the third leg, but, from a start-up's perspective, it's so important that it's worth repeating.

Before we even started getting down to the nitty-gritty of the AMP deal, I learned one of their team was a big fan of Richard. So I got the great man himself to sign a copy of his autobiography, and presented it as a gift. It proved a great icebreaker.

The only time I deliberately play games is when I sense the other side is going to make outrageous demands

Let the other side offer first

I always let the other side offer first. It reveals their 'dream outcome'. But don't let this influence your desired outcome. If their offer doesn't represent a sensible starting point, then don't be downhearted. Remind yourself of your ultimate objectives.

Put your proposal on the table with clear and careful reasoning as to why it's realistic. In the Virgin Direct negotiation, the other side wanted control of the business. This was eventually watered down to control over the relationship with the FSA (Financial Services Authority).

The only time I break this rule is when I sense the other side is going to be outrageous with their opening gambit – the price they want to sell at is going to be way too high, or their offer to buy is just too low to be serious. I will then make the first offer, thus setting the starting point of the discussions.

The level of concessions you make at the outset affects all future negotiations

Bring up your 'must-haves' close to the start of the negotiations. It is no good continuing if you require something that the other side has clearly no intention of ever providing. Setting out your markers at the outset will prevent time being wasted, and will also act as a clear demonstration of your strength. Like a wild animal, you are marking your territory. But if you believe the other side has the ability to fulfil your demands but simply doesn't like them, then you need to start thinking about raising the stakes. At the very beginning of the Virgin Direct negotiation, I made it clear that Virgin must have more than 50% of the business. Because I brought it up so early, over time it became a given, something that had anchored itself in the very fabric of the negotiation from then on.

Bid high if you are selling and low if you are buying – be cheeky, not cheap

Your first offer should be as high or as low as you can make it, and be detailed in positive terms. Don't start worrying about what is 'reasonable'. Demand the maximum possible. Just remember that the other side is never going to tell you that you have undercharged, or suggest you raise the price because they want to pay more.

You have one chance at an opening offer. Use it wisely. Don't offer something ludicrous that immediately irritates the other side. Aiming high and being cheeky is far better than being cheap. Be confident, you really can anchor them at a high or low point – so try it!

Once both sides have put their offers on the table, then a series of offers and counter offers will follow until a price is reached that both sides agree on. Consider carefully how to manage the other side's offer up or down. The level of concessions you make will affect their perception of the scope for further concessions. Widen or narrow the debate depending on your objective.

If you are selling a product or service and want to maximise the price, then talk in as large increments as possible. Thousands of pounds, not hundreds. If you are the purchaser and want to pay as little as possible, then obviously you should talk in small increments.

When Virgin entered discussions with AMP, I immediately demanded a 55% stake in the joint venture. My strategy was to scale back my demands in increments of 0.5%, but to make each concession as painful and drawn out as possible. AMP, however, should have been talking about cutting back my outrageous demand by offering a stake at least 10%, but preferably 20%, lower. They didn't.

> **Creating an element of confusion and tension can be used to your advantage**

Seek ways to disarm the other side

Use any opportunity you can during the negotiation process to disarm the other side. Change the location. Change the strategy. Change the lead negotiator. Richard Branson commonly disarmed the other side by holding negotiations at his home. It took them out of their comfort zone into a more relaxed environment where they might let their guard down. If you disarm them, they are more likely to reveal their thoughts to you either directly or indirectly. (Remember that walk up the stairs at Virgin's offices in Holland Park with me walking two steps behind the AMP team – otherwise known as the £250 million walk!)

As a start-up, you have to be on your guard to ensure you're not on the receiving end. It's all too easy to be intimidated by impressive offices and tough secretaries. Stick to your guns.

At some point during the negotiation, however, you are likely to be asked to make concessions. How should you manage this? How can you minimise the concessions you have to make? And if you do have to make them, how can you ensure you extract every last bit of value?

Use the good cop/bad cop routine

I don't care if you've seen it in the movies and found it laughable, the good cop/bad cop routine definitely works. People always fall for it. If one person on your negotiating team takes a hard line and appears reluctant to alter his or her stance, then any concessions eventually given by you appear to be real wins for the other side. And the harder the bad cop is, the more authentic it seems. It introduces a small element of doubt into the other side's mind that you can play with. It may also cause a rift between members of the other side that you can definitely exploit.

Never reveal that you're the one with the decision-making authority

At Virgin, we regularly positioned the finance department as the bad guys who were reluctant to relax the purse strings to allow us to do what we could to accommodate the other side's requests. I would huff and puff and say I really wanted to do the deal at the price they wanted, but then I would bang my forehead in frustration because the finance department just wouldn't let me. (Needless to say, the finance department were blissfully unaware of their tough-guy reputation.) It may sound obvious, but it creates an element of confusion and tension.

With a start-up, you'll have a tiny team, but you still need an accountant, of sorts, so use the 'financially prudent' team member to your advantage. Your good cop/bad cop routine can disarm the other side – particularly if, after weeks of aggressive negotiations, you turn into Mr Nice Guy!

Check your ego – say you have to refer to a senior authority for approval

Don't be afraid to say that you need to take the proposal back to the 'board' or to the 'shareholders' for approval, adding a few caveats as to why they might not accept it. I use this tactic every time I negotiate. I never allow myself the final say. I need a sounding board. In the heat of the moment, one proposal might sound like a silk purse when it is just a sow's ear. This tactic provides an opportunity to think through the appropriate response without being rushed into making a decision. It also maintains the relationship with the other side, because it is not you that is making the ultimate decision. Their frustrations at a proposal being rejected will not be directed at you. Indeed, they may even believe that you share their frustration.

In the early days of a start-up, they may challenge you on this. Make up a 'higher authority' if you have to.

> **Branson was my external voice of reason. He made sure I didn't lose my way**

On the flip side, if you are letting other people negotiate for you, then you should force them to apply this tactic as well. Richard Branson used to do this to me all the time. Knowing that any compromise I made would have to be run past Richard for his final approval kept me on my toes and allowed Richard to ensure he got what he needed. At the same time, as you grow and have untried employees, it's a great control.

Use a senior individual as an external sounding board to keep you on track

Have somebody waiting outside the negotiating room who can be used as a sounding board and provide a reality check on specific points and proposed concessions. Believe me, when you are immersed in a long negotiation you can get caught up in the moment and may find yourself relentlessly pushing for the finish line. Somebody outside the melee can give a cool-headed perspective on progress. You may not like what they are saying, but it is an effective control mechanism. There will be times when the other side is bombarding you with demands and the external voice of reason will make sure you don't lose sight of the ultimate outcome. This is why I often counsel very early-stage ventures to find an experienced partner or, at the very least, a mentor to take up this role.

If making concessions, make them count

You should maximise the value of any concessions you make to the other side. For example, you may have identified a feature as a 'nice-to-have' or 'must-have' for the other side, whereas you view it as 'can live without', then make them work for it – make them believe that that specific feature was something you hoped to achieve from the deal. As previously highlighted on page 90, at Virgin, we led AMP to believe that we 'must have' responsibility for handling the relationship with the financial regulators. In reality, we had no interest in performing this function, but we knew AMP did. So, from the start of negotiations, we were adamant that handling the financial regulators would be a sticking point for Virgin. If we didn't get it, then the deal was off. We used this as a highly successful bargaining chip to get the concessions we wanted, such as a 50% stake in the venture.

A canny negotiator never forgets he's dealing with people – flesh and blood

Remember what I said about building a rapport? I told you that we learned quite quickly that the UK boss was keen to do a deal. I knew he couldn't be seen to be losing. When I conceded the financial regulator point, I presented it as a major victory for him. Little did he realise that his triumph was anything but.

'Park' difficult issues

Closely related to the issue of managing concessions, you will often find during a negotiation that a time comes when you feel you have lost momentum, or that tensions are high, or even that you feel like the balance of power is beginning to turn against you. Or you may simply feel overwhelmed and need time to think through a number of issues that have been raised in more detail. What should you do to get back on track? How can you change the tide and recover your leading position?

'Parking' is one of the tactics I use to keep the negotiation on track. If too many contentious issues are being raised simultaneously and you feel you are starting to lose control, then park them. Promise that you will return to those issues shortly. Don't feel under pressure to make an immediate decision and resolve everything that's been raised – you may make a foolish decision. You should be in the driving seat of these negotiations; if you are not, take a break. At one point in the AMP negotiations, Virgin had parked more than twenty issues in just three days. Some were major. Some were minor. Some were never heard of again.

In a start-up, the pressure to make deals can really mount. Sometimes the other side can bombard you with demands. It's almost certainly a negotiation tactic. 'Parking' will give you time to consider the impact of each issue fully, to check back on your preparation (particularly your desired outcomes) and ensure that any trade-offs are valuable and you can live with them. It also enables you to manage the trading of concessions to ensure that you always receive one in return.

When the pressure is unrelenting, 'parking' issues always gives you the space you need

Re-state the vision

Again, this helps you to keep the negotiation on track. There will inevitably be times in a negotiation when the process starts to falter, people lose heart or, worse still, you feel that you are not getting your way. At this point you need to ensure that everyone steps back for a moment. Take time to restate your original vision and the opportunities available for both parties. Whenever I got stalled and things looked hard during the AMP negotiations, I reminded AMP (and myself for that matter) of the very attractive pot we were both chasing. So, describe your vision again, refresh, reload, and go again.

The last word

A start-up is in essence a series of deals. If you do not learn to negotiate you will ultimately fail. This chapter has shown you how to prepare scientifically for a negotiation, described the array of successful tactics at you disposal, and, critically, showed you when to use them. Gung-ho entrepreneurs slip straight into tactics. You know better than that. You've got to have ice in your veins, hold your nerve and not rush to impulsive decisions you'll regret later. So, another bend in the road's negotiated. But you may need funding to oil the wheels – the battle intensifies!

Dos and don'ts

1. **DO** respect the four start-up prerequisites in negotiating. Be clear on your vision of the opportunity and articulate it clearly. Build empathy with the other side. Build an open relationship and bury your ego. Focus on the end game. Build deals where there's room to prove yourself by delivering on your promises.

2. **DO** prepare properly. First ensure you maximise the opportunity. Then develop a scientific strategy by identifying what you need and would like. Compare this with the other side's must-haves and would-like-to-haves.

3. **DO** employ tactics when you've reached the point where the more you get the less the other side gets.

4. **DO** employ the following early-stage tactics to get off to a good start: develop alternatives to the deal, get a good team together, build a relationship with the other side and attempt to find a champion on their team who shares your vision.

5. **DO** ensure you position yourself well above your walk-away position in the middle stages of the negotiation. Let the other side offer first. Make strategic concessions and adjustments, and disarm the other side.

6. **DO** ensure concessions are minimised. Otherwise you could end up with less than you need. Employ tactics such as the good cop/bad cop routine, referring to a higher authority and external sounding boards.

7. **DO** use stalling tactics – such as restating the vision and parking issues – if you feel the negotiation is getting away from you.

8. **DON'T** accept less than your minimum outcome. Better to walk away.

9. **DON'T** chisel the opposition unduly. Leave them some upside so they won't renege on the deal.

PART TWO
SCALE IT

CHAPTER 5 **HOW TO GET THE CASH YOU NEED – WITHOUT GETTING EATEN ALIVE!**

This chapter's very simple. I'm going to give you a piece of equipment – a powerful tool in the form of a 'magical pitch'. The pitch will do two vital jobs: it will ensure you get the money you need (vital, obviously), and it will do so in a way that you acquire it while retaining the flexibility you need to operate effectively as a start-up.

But before I give you the pitch, I'm going to take you through the how and the why of its design. First, it provides you with the intimate motivations and concerns of the funder – a massive advantage in negotiation. Second, it ensures you don't make any rookie mistakes – that is, it stops you saying or doing something that might instantly destroy any hope of funding.

I'll take you on a journey that will examine different sources of funding and their pros and cons. Those sources can include traditional plain-vanilla banking, other modern-day funders, such as venture capitalists (not my favourite people, as you'll see!) and more exotic business angels (henceforth referred to simply as angels).

Pitch to the concerns of the other party: that's how to get funds and flexibility

Armed with your new-found knowledge it will become clear that the most profitable way for you to raise external funds will be using the magical pitch.

Getting funding is all about having the right pitch and props – which I'll provide for you. But there's one show-stopper not in my control. Fortunately, it's in yours.

Pitch of pure pain

During my time at Virgin, I had literally hundreds of people pitch to me for funding. Despite the fact that we were desperately keen to find quality business ideas to back, we struggled to find suitable ones. This was largely because most of the individuals didn't really understand how to pitch for funding. As a result they left empty-handed.

Even Branson cringed. You must have a winning attitude

I remember one pitch clearly that typified the poor-pitch experience. From the moment this guy walked into my office, I could tell he was incredibly nervous. This was understandable so I tried my hardest to put him at ease. I offered him a drink and tried a little chit-chat. I was also deliberately dressed down so that I wouldn't come across as intimidating.

After a few minutes of faltering small talk, the man began his funding pitch. He still appeared extremely nervous and was struggling to look me in the eye. I had actually already read the executive summary for the proposal and quite liked the idea so I tried to coax him along as he stumbled a little in the delivery of his pitch.

The pitch continued for about fifteen painful minutes. No matter how much I tried with the guy, he seemed so uncomfortable that he just wanted to race to the end of the presentation. Towards the end of the guy's pitch, Richard Branson himself walked into the room. Now Richard always deliberately adopts a very non-threatening approach (it is hard to be too threatened by a man in a thick-knit jumper!) and tried to put the man at ease.

But despite Richard's best efforts, the nerves now really kicked in. He rushed through the remainder of his presentation, and concluded by apologising for the fact that the business required funding and that he had not been able to find any capital elsewhere. Having finally reached the end of his pitch, the guy seemed relieved and wanted simply to throw his business plan onto my desk and then make a rapid escape from my office.

Remember: you're offering the funder a massive opportunity – one that's going to make you both rich!

Same old, same old. Once again, I was faced with a business idea that was actually quite good, but which would be very difficult to fund because neither Richard nor I could have any confidence that the guy could deliver what he promised.

Unfortunately, this tale is all too common. It happened to me repeatedly when I was at Virgin and it still happens now. But why is it that budding entrepreneurs have such difficulty asking for funding?

As an entrepreneur, you must have the right attitude, or you'll fail before you start. It's that simple. This is the right attitude: remember that you're doing as much for the funder as they're doing for you. They'll invest to allow you to scale – for which you're extremely grateful. You'll work incredibly hard and provide a great return. It's a win–win.

So look the funder in the eye as an equal. Park that weak, subservient attitude, which consigns you to the dustbin of failed funding pitches, and understand this reality: most businesses should be able to secure some form of funding if they ensure they have the right attitude and five prerequisites.

1. **A bulletproof idea:** This is essential and should be no problem after the hard work you did in chapter 1.
2. **Absolute commitment:** The funders must feel confident that your future's on the line, and that you'll keep driving forward until you've made the business successful and provided a handsome return on their investment.

3. **A winning business plan:** The best plans present a persuasive argument.
4. **Professional appearance:** First impressions are incredibly important, so make sure you look the part. You don't need to be wearing a Zegna suit, but make sure it's a suit and not shorts.
5. **Compelling presentation:** Dust off your credibility presentation and add some detail on the funds you need, and how you'd spend them.

With the right attitude and the five prerequisites, you will probably get funding of some sort. But, will it be the right kind of funding?

Our five pre-requisites notwithstanding, the practice can be tougher than the theory – as I found out when I struck out from Virgin on my own. I'll always remember Richard's comment: 'You only need one deal to take off to be on your way ...'

Blood, sweat and tears – cash, but no prize!

I thought I had found that first deal in the form of a canning technology company. I was a junior partner on the deal and set about finding funding. I was confident that we would be successful, given my experience over the years at Virgin and the fact that we had the five prerequisites in place.

It all sounded fair and reasonable – what followed was hell!

We had agreed a debt deal with the owner of the technology which would see us pay off the purchase price over time. Our plan was then to use an equity raising to obtain sufficient funds to both service the loan repayments and also to fund the growth of the business. I must admit I felt a little queasy about this proposal. But the owners of the technology promised us that if the business was ever short of cash that they would not hold us to ransom and would renegotiate the repayment terms accordingly. This all sounded very fair and reasonable. What followed was hell.

It all started rosy enough. Using the five prerequisites, we raised our initial funds and made the first quarterly repayment of the loan. We then set about growing the business. However, the business grew much more slowly than we had expected and cash inflows were lower than forecast. This led to delays in our planned capital raising. Suddenly we faced having to make repayments of our loan without the additional cash we expected from the capital raising. Things weren't so rosy any more. Every penny we had began to disappear into servicing the loan, leaving us with very little to invest in growing the business. We should have seen this coming. These were the inevitable growing pains of any start-up. The sleepless nights began!

We had to return to the previous owners and suggested that, in line with their original promise, we would need to renegotiate the debt repayments as things were a little tight. We quickly discovered that the previous owners weren't so reasonable and forgiving after all. We spent days, which stretched into weeks, attempting to reach some agreement, which almost always involved us being charged additional exorbitant fees we could not afford!

Why give up control? It's your deal!

Our quarterly debt repayments loomed over us like the shadow of the grim reaper. Every waking moment the management team had was spent worrying about how the loan was going to be serviced and trying to negotiate some flexibility with the previous owners rather than focusing on growing and improving the business. But our pleas fell on deaf ears. We had only ourselves to blame as we should have known better than to rely on their word.

Inevitably, suppliers started to go unpaid. Staff salaries were paid later and later. Our credibility was rapidly deteriorating. Staff began leaving and suppliers wouldn't deal with us any more. Our mail box was stuffed full of threatening legal letters. The management team started to turn on each other. It was horrific. The business was caught in a destructive downward spiral. The business managed to limp on for a year before collapsing spectacularly. All our blood, sweat, tears and sleepless nights had been for nothing.

So, that was my rather brutal introduction to the real world of funding start-ups. It was a truly life-changing; an absolutely horrible experience! We made some serious mistakes and paid the price. But, believe me, I learned lessons from this debacle that I have never forgotten, including:

- Having the five pre-requisites in place will enable you to secure funding but on their own they are not enough.
- All start-ups can (or, rather, will) grow more slowly that you expect, so you need flexibility in your funding.
- Legal debts are exactly that – you can be held to ransom!
- Funding needs to be there on time every time.
- Development milestones will always be delayed, but you will still require funds to deliver them.

My nightmare with the technology company taught me first hand how incredibly dangerous the inflexibility of debt repayments can be for a start-up with unpredictable cash flow. There is also simply no point in securing funding if it has so many strings attached that you can't grow the business or (in a worst case scenario) you lose the business altogether. At any rate, why should you be forced to risk personal assets? This led me to believe that equity is the most appropriate form of funding for early-stage businesses.

In the brutal world of start-ups, you simply have to get the right funding package

However, even equity has a disadvantage for start-ups. If you have little more than a business plan and an idea, it's likely that you'll have to give away control of your business. This struck me as particularly unfair. The odds seemed stacked in the funder's favour any way you looked at it. I stood to lose everything if things went bad –

and yet I've never met a funder who gave me anything additional if the business was a raging success! So what could I do?

Well, over the years I developed and refined a powerful financial pitch that can be given to any potential investor. It is a hybrid of debt and equity funding, and is a cunning way to take the attractive elements of both debt and equity and integrate them so that both your interests and those of the funder are protected.

The financial pitch has been developed to show the funders that you have their interests at heart and that you take your role as custodian of their funds very seriously. It also reduces the risk for funders. As a result, you should be able to secure the funds you need, at the best possible price, while retaining the necessary flexibility.

Now I've got you all revved up and ready to go get your funding, but hold on for one moment. I want you to ask yourself a fundamental question ...

Do you actually need external funding?

I am totally serious. Before you race out and hire your executive assistant and sign the lease on that plush new office, do you actually need external funding?

Try to avoid external funding: it comes with moral and legal responsibilities

External funding is expensive and will come with strings attached – it always does. The moment you take on external funding you have assumed a burden with both moral and legal responsibilities. But I would prefer you to retain control of your destiny, and it can be done ...

Keeping your powder dry

R-Points, a business I'm a partner in, is the largest online cash-back community in the UK. It launched and grew without the benefit of any external funding. How could that be?

Well, it matched cash inflows with outflows. The owners had to put in some hard graft, and went without for a while. They became jacks-of-all-trades: programmers, web designers and marketers. Nothing was perfect, but it worked well enough. Revenue was the priority. The business had to bring cash in at the earliest possible opportunity.

R-Points was seeded on graft and (brief) financial hardship

When money came in, some of it went to creditors and some went to growing the business. This was a period of tense phone calls (with creditors, mainly) and hard negotiation as the business struggled to survive. But survive it did.

The fruits of this labour? The owners retained the ability to control their own destiny. They can decide who to employ, how much to pay staff and themselves, and what dividend policy to set. There are no outside dictators.

Another crucial benefit was keeping the equity powder dry. The owners retain all the power and control. They can decide when and how to allocate equity to new partners, if needed for business development or growth.

So far, we've worked on how to launch smart – bringing revenue forward and delaying cost. The ideal is to launch without recourse to external funding. Backed with a small amount of (perhaps personal) cash, or maybe a government grant or two, let's see if we can get it done the smart way.

You'll need a lot of front, cheekiness and top negotiating skills

So how do you avoid the expense and hassle – from creditor or shareholder – that comes with external funding? Answer: match your cash inflows with your cash outflows. Sounds simple, doesn't it? Theoretically, it is, but this is going to take some real bottle. To put it into practice, take the following steps:

1. Review all budgeted costs and keep as lean as possible. Review chapter 2 to remind yourself what you should (and should not) be spending money on at this point.

2. Review your budget carefully and identify when cash will actually be received from your anticipated sales. Be conservative about quantum and expected date of receipt.

3. Look at what you are going to have to pay and map out a payment plan that matches with your cash inflows.

4. You'll need to negotiate with everyone that you're meant to pay money to over this period. This will include your employees, landlord, consultants … whomever. Convince them that it is in everyone's interest that you don't pay them for the first few months as this will enable you to grow your business faster, place more orders with them and reward them accordingly.

   This is going to take a lot of front, cheekiness and all those negotiating skills! Not everyone is going to be prepared to do a deal. For those who won't, you are simply going to have to get your excuses ready and be prepared to endure some rather tense phone calls and perhaps the odd legal letter as payment deadlines come and go. Don't worry: it can take months for a matter to move from a legal letter to a court action. By that time you will have the cash you need to pay off the creditor anyway.

   There are many sources of capital and you must understand what you're getting into

5. Look for ways to ensure that your debtors pay you as quickly as possible. You might offer a discount for a limited period of time if the individual pays you rapidly or you might be able to negotiate some portion of payment upfront. Failing these, then just make sure that you monitor your cash collection every day and hound your debtors for payment.

6. Once the money starts to come in, don't simply race out and pay off all your creditors – go back to point (2) and review your payment plan. Don't pay a single creditor until you absolutely have to. Even then, pay them a portion of the amount you owe

with a promise to get them the remainder soon. They will be so relieved to receive anything from you at this stage that they will gratefully accept it. This keeps some money for you for the next unhappy supplier and also for reinvestment in securing customers and generating new sales. The bottom line is spend wisely, be obsessive about cash-flow and build your credibility.

R-Points proves it can be done, but none of this is easy. The potential rewards, however, are enormous – the owners have complete control over their destiny and, of course, a successful business.

Securing external funding – without being fleeced!

Perhaps the nature of your business means that funds are required for launch, or you have plans on an ambitious scale. So, let's turn to getting those funds.

Before we dive into the magical pitch, I am going to take you, as promised, on a brief tour of the fund sources typically available to start-ups: family and friends, banks, institutional equity, and angels.

Family and friends don't have to give you cash; you need to sell to them

In an ideal world, you'll see that angel funding using the magical pitch is the perfect solution. But because other sources are legitimate and your particular circumstances may lead you there, you need to be familiar with all of them – that way, you won't get fleeced.

Let's consider each of these funding sources in turn.

Family and friends

Parents, uncles, aunts, grandparents or just a friendly neighbour might have funds they are willing to invest. This is a great option. It is clearly a lot easier and more comfortable dealing with family and friends than with a bank manager. Obtaining a loan from family and friends can also be cheaper than going to banks or to professional investors, although that is not always the case.

I don't want to dwell too much on this option – it is self-explanatory. However, if you are considering borrowing from family and friends, I would just make the following points:

- Don't take them for granted. This may be your best or even only option, so you need to pitch them in the same way you would any other investor. They may be your family and friends but they're under no obligation to give you any cash. You need to sell to them.

- Formalise your agreement in a written contract. A handshake is simply not good enough. You have to pay the loan back regardless. So, if nothing is documented and circumstances change and the family member wants the money back, you and your business could be deeply compromised.

> **Being at the whim of a lender is no way to live life**

Banks

All high street banks and building societies offer – certainly when credit is plentiful – a range of business loan products (see www.betterstrongerfastergroup.com for details). You agree to borrow a sum of money and repay it over time with interest and charges. Sounds simple, right? Well, let's pause to think about a past employer of mine, Bond Corporation, who thought the same thing ...

America's Cup ... but fails to stay afloat

Bond Corporation was a company formed by Alan Bond and was my first employer. I ended up as Alan's executive assistant. Alan was a former Australian of the Year and the first non-American winner of the America's Cup. He was Australia's highest profile entrepreneur during the heady days of the 1980s. He had set up a corporation with A$10 billion in assets. That's right, 10 billion! That's what it had.

Although the company had the cream of Australia's corporate finance talent advising on its debt structuring, it went bust in 1990 in the most spectacular corporate collapse in Australia's history. Why? Many reasons were offered but the reality was that it had gorged on debt to fund its projects, with most of its debt structured with variable interest rates.

Bond Corporation had the best advisers, yet debts still forced it into liquidation

When rates rose rapidly from about 9% to 18%, it began to struggle to meet its obligations. When it eventually defaulted on its repayments, the banks automatically began to move in on their assets and kept chasing them. The corporation ultimately went under.

So, you have been warned. Debt is appropriate for many businesses but it does entail some significant risks for start-ups:

- If you fail to repay the loan, then the bank can take any assets you own and sell them to recover the funds it has lent.
- Cash-flows in start-ups are notoriously difficult to predict and so regular debt repayments can rapidly become a major strain for the business.
- Interest rates can also rise rapidly and unpredictably.

Therefore, I want you to think long and hard before you load your start-up with debt.

Work the system. That will unlock the bank's vault

It's clearly beyond the scope of this book to go into great detail about the inner machinations of the large banks and the workings of their various credit committees. But I want to remind you of one guiding principle: banks all apply credit-scoring models when determining whether or not to loan funds.

These models rely on certain inputs such as the level of debt to equity, business assets, experience of the management team, etc. I have experienced this first hand when obtaining financing for major residential property developments in the United States. If you understand the criteria that are being applied, you can ensure that your application satisfies them. A good relationship with your local bank's business lending manager can help you find out what you need to do to make sure your application is successful, as my friend and I found out ...

Ticking the wine box

Several years ago, a great friend of mine was seeking funding to develop a winery in Australia. His family had operated a table grape vineyard for over 50 years and was already selling grapes to Woolworths (one of Australia's largest retailers). The market was changing and he believed that he could earn a higher return from a winery. What he needed was to invest in new machinery and equipment. He had spent several years in researching and developing the business plan, and it looked to be a sound bet. He had significant equity of his own that he intended to invest as well. Yet when he approached the bank for funding, something he thought was a mere formality, he was turned down. We were both stunned. Little did we know that our job was just starting and that we would have to embark upon a major detective investigation.

So we set about getting to know the bank manager to try to understand the reason why the application was rejected. Over a few dinners and a couple of drinks, we got to know him quite well. We continued to probe him about the loan application and why it had been unsuccessful. At first he was reluctant to tell us but he eventually conceded that he had actually really liked the business. However, the loan had not been approved by the credit committee because the committee had been unable to tick one of the boxes on their checklist regarding the assets of the business.

Within two weeks the money was in the bank – problem solved!

We naturally pushed the bank manager for more information so that we could understand exactly what the issue was. It turned out to be a very minor issue with the treatment of a specific asset that unfortunately altered one of the key ratios applied by the bank.

Fortunately, we could simply present the accounts with a slightly different treatment of some of our assets (totally above board, I might add!) and the box would magically be ticked We went away, prepared the revised accounts, and submitted the application again. Within two weeks my friend had the cash in his account and was on his way to establishing 'Oakover', now one of the most highly regarded wineries in Western Australia.

Institutional equity

Equity involves giving away a share of ownership in your company (a piece of the action) in return for funding.

You can no doubt tell from what I've already said that I believe equity is often the best form of funding for most start-ups, but I would just remind you of the following.

- You have a partner for life, which means you can no longer operate as though the company is your private fiefdom.
  Your new equity partner has a legal right to a say in how the company is run. They also have a right to a share of all future profits. We discuss the pros and cons of partners in chapter 7.
- If you don't retain 50% of the shares (i.e. control) you may be thrown out – if the other partner has more than 50% of the shares, they will have effective day-to-day control of the business, and could even fire you and/or sell the assets of the company.
- Having control doesn't mean you can ignore the minority – the law automatically provides protection for minority shareholders, so don't think you will be able to ride roughshod over the other shareholders.

Equity funding is appropriate for start-ups, indeed part of the magical pitch involves giving away some equity. Institutional equity, however – and essentially, we're talking about venture capitalists (VCs) here – is quite different.

I'd suggest it's probably a bad idea to give any equity to a VC. VCs don't understand start-ups. They're hard-faced guys in suits who don't like the uncertainty that's part of life in a start-up.

I have pitched to VCs as an employee of a major corporation (a relatively safe position) and as an individual looking for money for my own start-up (nowhere near as safe or as comfortable a position). The story is always the same. That's why, in the early days, Branson and Virgin never really got on with the City. Virgin didn't trust them, and they didn't trust him. In reality it was a case of square peg and a round hole. Why?

Address the funders' deepest concerns to get your deal – and control, too

The City financiers wanted a proven management team and a clear revenue model. But, hold on, isn't that why a start-up would need funding in the first place? Further, VCs like to control the deal. They turn it around so that you, the entrepreneur, work for them. If you do well, perhaps you can have some ownership back.

Now, this isn't good enough. You need money, but, critically, you also need to be in control. You need to be able to manage the twists and turns of the roller coaster ride that is a start-up. No wonder the fledgling Virgin stayed well clear – so should you.

My view of VCs is pretty damning: dealing with them is typically a nightmare. They negotiate extremely tough deals and are likely to take a very large chunk of your business and give you little, tortuously structured (watch out for hidden legal traps) funding in return. They do, however, have great relevance (as we'll see in chapter 9) in the sales process, so it's a good idea to keep them on side.

Angel investors

Sadly, angels are not enlightened beings put on the planet to tender to the spiritual needs of entrepreneurs. Rather, these are wealthy individuals or perhaps even a group who are happy to invest in early-stage, high-growth ventures. And this is where I believe most of you should ultimately be seeking your funding from.

Finally, we're ready. Time for me to deliver on my promise – I'm going to describe my unique and powerful funding pitch that will ensure that you capture the funds you need, at the best possible price, while retaining the necessary flexibility. I'll also detail the props that you need to deliver the pitch effectively, and I'll tell you where to find angels. Here, at long last, is the perfect pitch.

Getting your money on the best terms: The magical pitch

Well, it's close to magical – I hope! The magical pitch is an argument made to an angel to make him or her feel comfortable to provide you with some cash so you can grow your business. Now, let's have some fun. Let's detail your pitch, word for word, and pause after each sentence to expose the funder's inner thoughts. How do I know these inner thoughts? Because I've been on both sides of the desk in these negotiations. This was how I refined and perfected the deal structure. The order is critical, so pay close attention. The inner thoughts expose the funder's deepest concerns and reveal the arguments you must win to get your deal.

The pitch goes like this:

Me: So I will need £200,000 for a new venture that I'm launching.

Them: [Rueful smile] £200k? That's a fair bit of cash. For a venture that has yet to commence? Sounds a bit risky. Good idea though. Should I invest? At the very least I think I am going to push for more than 50% to make it worth my while.

Rationale: *You have now set an expectation for the total sum of funding that will be required. This is an important place marker as you will subsequently show the funder that this is not actually going to involve a single large, risky payment, as they now fear.*

Me: I want to take the £200,000 as a loan but with real
          flexibility in the repayments so as not to put the
          company under any pressure.

Them: [Frowning] What does he mean by flexibility? Am I
          ever going to get my money back? What's my upside?

Rationale: *By retaining flexibility, paying a nominal interest rate,
          and setting a far distant repayment date, you are taking
          a huge burden off the business in its early period. There
          will be no sleepless nights as a debt repayment looms
          that the business cannot afford. But from the perspective
          of the funder, things don't sound particularly attractive
          at this point. They are now a little offside. They do like
          the fact that they will get their money back but the loan
          terms do not sound particularly attractive. There's no
          upside. So, now is the time to tell them some good news!*

Me: In addition to repaying the loan, I want to give you
          a chunk of free equity.

Them: [First hint of a smile] Now this sounds a bit more
          promising. I get my money back and a share of all
          future profits. But it is still a bit risky handing over
          the £200,000 up front.

Rationale: *The funder has importantly now been positioned to
          understand that their profit comes from the equity and
          not the loan. It is all starting to make sense now, The
          flexibility of the loan and the low interest rate are the
          trade-off for getting their funds back and also enjoying
          a chunk of the upside.*

Me: I intend to draw the £200,000 down in four
          separate tranches of £50,000. I believe this is
          important because I want to prove to you at
          each stage that the business is growing in the
          manner that I predicted it would. I have complete
          confidence in the business, but doing this will
          obviously reduce your risk if something goes wrong.

	I propose to give you a chunk of equity with every draw-down as follows: 10%, 7%, 5% and 3% for a total of 25% of the equity.
Them:	[Looking thoughtful] I like the fact that the investment is broken down into tranches. I won't have to throw good money after bad. I will get my loan repaid and I will end up with 25% of the company. I think I'll push for a bit more than that, but 50% is probably a bit greedy.
Rationale:	*Now you have positioned yourself as sensible and a doer, and you're confidently backing yourself. At the same time, you are putting yourself in their shoes by not asking them to invest good money after bad. This significantly reduces the risk of the investment. In conjunction with the fact that you are going to repay the loan, you now have created a bargaining chip to insist on giving away a smaller chunk of equity.*

Setting the milestones also imposes a discipline on you and the business. You now have very clear targets to hit! |
Me:	I think it is important that you also know that until I have repaid the loan to you in full, I will only pay myself a subsistence wage. I will not increase this amount or pay any dividends until you have got every penny back that you invested.
Them:	[Leaning forward now with positive body language] Good to see that no money will be wasted and that I will receive my money back as the first priority. Now this all sounds good. He is respecting me and my money. That makes a nice change! I end up with a chunk of equity and I get my money back. All right, so let's see if I can tweak that percentage up a bit. Time to negotiate.
Rationale:	*This is the icing on the cake. You have now demonstrated that you are prepared to make a real*

sacrifice. Your intention is clear, you won't take any money (beyond a subsistence wage) until you have worked every waking hour to get them their money back. Then they will be in the deal for 'free' and you can both relax and enjoy the considerable upside!

So let's recap for a moment the key elements of this proposed deal structure. These are:

Loan

■ Long repayment date.

■ Nominal interest rate.

■ Repayments only to be made when the business can afford it.

■ The loan to be drawn down in individual tranches on the achievement of key milestones.

Equity

■ 'Free' equity (but less than 50%!).

■ Equity given away in chunks on the receipt of each tranche of funding.

■ Subsistence wage for you, which is not be increased until the loan is repaid.

Look at what you're offering: you won't take more money than you need; you won't waste their money; and you won't do anything but survive until they get their money back. And you'll both get rich at the same time. What's not to like? What are you waiting for? Let's get on and present.

Your step-by-step guide to get funded

As I said earlier, I have sat on both sides of the table – begging bowl out, and cheque book at the ready. Raising money is personal. It's a matter between you and the funder. And I know that, at any point, a loss of confidence means the game's over. But I've raised £1 billion, and I'm not about to let you fail, so forgive me if I'm very definite and prescriptive from here on in. It's personal for me, too.

Getting your funding is a five-step process:

1. Finding angels.
2. **Dress smartly:** Do the preparatory work prior to first meeting with funder.
3. **The ice-breaker:** First face-to-face meeting with funder.
4. **Sell the dream:** Your magical pitch.
5. **Show me the money:** Signing.

1. Finding angels

Angels come in all shapes and sizes and are not necessarily only professionals. They may, for instance, be tradespeople, mechanics or people who have inherited some wealth. Dame Anita Roddick's funder in the first Body Shop store was a garage owner who invested £4000 in return for 22% of the company! Your ideal angel is a 'grandfather' type who has built successful businesses and is now looking to back others and provide valuable mentoring. In addition to the cash they provide, angels will often contribute skills, experience and personal contacts.

It's personal: the funder needs to believe in you, your idea and your ability to deliver

Historically, angels tended to invest on their own and operated on word-of-mouth introductions from friends. Today, in addition to these individuals, there are numbers of more formal networks, many of which pool angels together as part of a syndicate. You will generally find it easier to deal with a single angel rather than a syndicate.

Single angels are typically willing to invest anywhere from £10,000 to £250,000. Larger sums will typically be invested via a syndicate, which is often organised through an angels' network. A syndicate investment will often require the appointment of a manager who will oversee the syndicate's investment. This entails fees, charges and some administration. The larger the syndicate and the more intrusive the role of the manager, the more formal it becomes, and the less attractive it is for an early-stage venture.

Build a list of wealthy individuals – people you really need to pitch

Finding the right angel is going to take some detective work. You will simply have to keep your eyes and ears open. Tell everyone in your own network that you are looking and let them help you spread the word. If you can arrange a personal introduction, you're a step ahead of the game. As you begin your sleuthing, you should try all of the following sources:

- **Ask your lawyers and accountants if they know any likely candidates:** Your advisers will have broad professional networks and a large client base that may contain appropriate individuals. A personal introduction from them will always help.

- **Ask your lawyers and accountants themselves!** Your advisers will often fit the profile, being wealthy individuals who are active investors and who can also bring specific skills.

- **Successful entrepreneurs in your own industry:** Scour the newspapers and look particularly for successful private companies. Set up a meeting with the owners, not the managers, as they will have empathy with your situation because they've probably been in a similar position.

- *Sunday Times* **Rich List:** This is a perfect pre vetted list of wealthy individuals who have all been successful in business in some capacity. There will be more than a few 'grandfathers' in there. Go direct to the actual people: they'll be the decision makers and the ones who will have empathy.

- **An angels' network:** These are useful resources to identify individuals who are actively looking to make investments. Such organisations change quite regularly but you can go to www. betterstrongerfastergroup.com for an update on the state of play.

2. Dress smartly: Do the preparatory work prior to first meeting with funder

Don't make the mistake of thinking that you can simply turn up at your funder's office and have a breezy chat, and that then they will

Differentiate yourself from the pack. Prepare an 'action plan'

hand over the cash. You only get one shot at this, so you need to be fully prepared. This is all about building credibility from a funding perspective. The funder has never met you before and will need to make a rapid assessment of whether you can truly deliver all you claim you can.

So, no argument, before you meet any funder you need to:

- **Set up a company and open company bank accounts:** These are such simple things to do but can greatly enhance your credibility as they show that you are already taking action and that you must at least have some degree of financial intelligence.
- **Appoint a lawyer and an accountant:** Simply having the name of a lawyer and an accountant on your pitch documents is impressive, and again shows that you are already moving forward with your idea – all without costing you a penny!
- **Build credibility in the funder's view:** Chapter 3 gave you the tactics to build credibility. The more of these tactics you deploy, the stronger your negotiating position will be. There are, however, four that are critical.

  I.   Your finance director (even if part-time) is going to play a crucial role because any funder is going to want to have confidence that the finances of the business are being appropriately managed.

  II. Your 'toolkit' (i.e. your presentation, website and business cards).

  III. Glowing testimonials. Ideally these would be from customers but if you don't have any, then use any reputable third party (e.g. suppliers).

  IV. Skin in the game. You must have something to lose. Chapter 3 covered it nicely.

PR has always played a key role in securing funding, whether for my own start-ups or for Virgin, so go out and get yourself some coverage.

- **Prepare props for 'pitch'.** There are three key props that you are going to require when you make your pitch:

   I.   **Business plan:** Every funder will want to see that you have prepared a business plan. They may never actually bother to read it in great detail, or even at all. But you must have one otherwise you will lose credibility. They will want to see a string argument, based on real, detailed data, not just a list of facts and figures. See examples of winning business plans at www.betterstrongerfastergroup.com.

   II. **Action plan:** This is where you differentiate yourself from the pack and build massive credibility. Everyone will have a business plan but far fewer people invest the time in developing an action plan. Your action plan sets out the concrete steps you will be taking over the first twelve months and the associated costs and revenues to get your business up and running. It shows very clearly where the money is going. You will leave your action plan behind with the funder after your pitch. You can see an example of an action plan at www.betterstrongerfastergroup.com.

   III. **Compelling presentation:** This is important – without question. It's the key to your pitch. It is a presentation enabling you to make the magical pitch. It should be no longer than fifteen slides. I've outlined it in great detail below so you can get it right.

The power funding presentation

Slide	Content of slide	No. of slides	Comments
Title page	• Business name • Company registration number • Your name • Your contact details • Name of lawyer • Name of accountant	1	This slide is all about building credibility and showing that you are already on your way with the basics covered. You are no financial novice Vision

Continued ...

Slide	Content of slide	No. of slides	Comments
• Your	vision for the business	1	This is your chance to capture the imagination of your funder with a clear and compelling vision of what your business will become. They are going to be a part of something that is unique and exciting
The opportunity	• Size of the market • The customer 'pain' that exists in the market – and how your product solves this • The unique aspects of your product • How you intend to distribute your product • Competitor profile	2 (max.)	Use your analysis from chapter 1 to drive home the compelling opportunity that exists and the unique features of your product that are going to ensure its success in the market. 'This is a well thought-through idea that is bound to succeed'
The team	• Outline the executives who will make the dream a reality	1	You need to have at least one FD along with yourself. Non-executives and mentors are also incredibly helpful. If it's technical have a technical head, don't outsource it. Be precise about roles and resposibilities
Financial forecasts	• Five-year, high-level financial forecasts • Supporting key metrics (demonstrate forecasts built from bottom up) • Total quantum of investment need • Key uses for funds sought	2 (max.)	You need to excite the funder about the future profitability of your business. This business has the potential to make a lot of money. The forecasts have been built bottom-up, from a deep understanding of the business. No assumptions have simply been plucked out of the air!

Slide	Content of slide	No. of slides	Comments
Action plan	• Major activities over the coming twelve months and related costs and revenues	1 (max.)	You know exactly what you need to do in the first twelve months to make the business a success
Proposed deal	• Your proposed deal	1 (max.)	You have already put the total quantum of funds you require into the mind of the funder. Now you need to hit them with your unique proposal. Watch that initial scowl turn into a smile as you work through your proposed deal
Summary	• Recap of vision, profit upsides/blue sky, amount of investment required, deal terms	1 (max.) or verbally	You are both going to earn a fortune!

IV. **Contact funder to set up meeting:** You know where to find them. Call them. If possible, orchestrate a personal introduction, which will always make life a little easier!

3. The ice-breaker: First face-to-face meeting with funder

Understand this: ultimately, the funder is doing a personal deal with you. He wants to be able to look you in the eye and feel confident that you are honest and a person of high integrity. You are a can-do person who will get the job done and ultimately return their money with a nice profit. Much of this assessment will be made on gut instinct, so it's critical that a funder gets to know you.

Leave absolutely nothing to chance. You have a role. Play it!

Follow a two-stage process when meeting with a new funder. The first meeting should be entirely devoted to relationship building, with only an overview-level discussion of the business. The second meeting will be the appropriate time to use your presentation, to make your financial pitch and leave behind your business plan and action plan.

It's time to put on your best suit, get the hair right, brush your teeth, and spray on your deodorant (because you're probably going to sweat!). Now is your chance to show what a stand-up person you are and go and get funding. You will:

- **Adopt the right attitude:** Remember – as I said right at the start of this chapter – that first impressions are *critical*. You must be armed with the right attitude or you will fail. This means being confident and self-assured at all times. I am truly amazed by the number of people who appear apologetic or embarrassed, or even act as if it is 'unnatural' to ask for funding. This is sending the wrong signal and will result in failure. You should have great confidence and optimism based on the following premise: you have a great business that is going to be hugely successful. This is a win–win scenario for both of you. You get the funds you need and the investor will receive a great return. You are doing each other a favour! This gives you every reason to be confident – but never cocky or arrogant; thankful – but never embarrassed or apologetic.

- **Humanise yourself:** First impressions count and you don't want to blow it at this early stage. Take this time to humanise yourself and to look for common ground between the two of you. Talk about kids, family, personal history and so on. You want the funder to see the passionate, committed person of great integrity that you are; that you're someone who can be trusted; but, most of all, that you're someone who is going to give them their money back!

> **Most funders would rather see you die than work half-heartedly on their investment!**

- **Demonstrate commitment:** You really should have grasped this point by now!

- **Sign a non-disclosure agreement (NDA):** An NDA is simply an agreement that a party will not steal your idea and put it into practice themselves. No one wants to sign an NDA but

forcing the issue raises the stakes. It makes people believe
that you must have something of value. So, play the game. In
reality, the protection it provides is minimal. Your lawyer can,
of course, prepare one for you but you can also obtain one for
free from websites, such as the Patent Office in the UK, which
provide free downloadable template NDAs. A quick search on
Google will highlight several other free providers of NDAs.

4. Sell the dream: Your magical pitch

Now the rubber hits the road. The funder thinks that you are
a can-do and honest person. You now need to convince them
that your idea will work, that you can make it a success and that
there's a big prize at the end of it all for both of you.

Dig out your presentation, take a deep breath
and go to work. You must be authoritative here
and demonstrate that you know everything there
is to know about the business and that you are
going to make it work. Keep the following in
mind to avoid the rookie mistakes:

**Forget the executive
jet and the ritzy
lifestyle – the funder
will run a mile**

- **Be specific:** Funders are going to want to know exactly what
  their money is going to be used for. You must be highly
  specific and all forecasts must be built from the bottom up
  (i.e. built up from metrics such as the number of units sold).
- **Show you have their interests at heart:** Funders are always
  frightened that you are simply looking for someone to fund
  your own lavish lifestyle. Hence, making provision for large
  expenditures on your own salary, cars, travel, plush offices,
  etc., will immediately arouse their anger. Nothing will
  undermine your credibility more quickly than providing for
  a large salary for yourself. So, budget a salary that only just
  covers your essentials (and, no, that does not include a yacht
  and an Aston Martin!). This will impress the funders, as they
  can see you are absolutely committed and believe that the
  business is going to pay you back in spades in the future.

■ **Demonstrate that you make money when they do:** It's critical that the funder understands that you will make money only when they do. Your pitch will achieve this by explaining that the funder will have their money repaid as a matter of priority and that you will both then benefit from your endeavours to increase the value of both your equity stakes.

Unfortunately, only 25% of businesses actually make it to their sixth year. Funders therefore want to understand how your business is going to evolve from a struggling start-up to a highly successful multimillion pound business. You need to provide them with a clear development plan that shows the evolution of the business. Don't forget that an equity investor is going to want to see that there is potential for a trade sale or possibly a stock market listing.

■ **Sell the dream:** During this presentation, don't forget to illustrate graphically the endgame, namely, the enormous profit potential and sale possibilities. Sweep the funders along with enthusiasm, can-do attitude and the idea that they will be part of a team that will make a difference to the world.

■ Leave them with the action plan and the business plan.

5. Show me the money: Signing

This is it. This is the deal – the whole point of this chapter (the whole point and pleasure of being in business for many entrepreneurs). You've got your funder to the table. Whatever you do, don't get funding that screws you and the business you've fought so hard to develop.

Be realistic, not greedy. Use your judgement

The funder has bought into you, your idea and your proposed deal structure. The niceties are over. It is detail time. He wants a higher rate of interest on his loan and a bigger chunk of equity. You are up to your neck in negotiations. Now's the time to go back to the section on negotiation (chapter 4) and refresh your tactics.

This is where your understanding of the implications of debt and equity pays off. You know the implications of what you can and can't live with. You know what is fair. So, you must not be bullied and should stick to your guns. However, like any good negotiator, you should also understand your position clearly. If this is your first deal, then you are going to have to give more away. If it is your third or fourth deal, then you get to keep a little more. So, be realistic, not greedy. Use your judgement.

You should always sacrifice a little more equity (but not control) in return for flexibility in repayment of debt. But you must also set a limit at which you won't do the deal. Remember, it's better to walk away than do the wrong deal. Also remember that you got the funder here – so there is a deal to be done. They won't want to miss out.

Keep your funders close – make them allies – because nothing ever goes exactly to plan!

During this negotiation you're going to need to keep your wits about you. If your funders (or their lawyers) are sophisticated, then they may just try to confuse you with reams and reams of documentation and corporate finance jargon. Don't be put off by this. They're just trying to tweak things in their favour. Come back to basics. Asking a few simple questions will make sure that the agreement reflects what you thought you had agreed. These questions are:

- Do I have to repay the funds or not? How much? When?
- What security do I have to provide? Are my personal assets at risk?
- How much control do I have to give up?
- What happens if I miss a payment?
- How much equity could the funder ultimately end up with?
- What minority protections are there?
- Does the funder have to provide future funding?

Finally, remember this: the only thing you can be certain of with a start-up is that nothing will go as planned. It's doubly important therefore to maintain a close relationship with your funders and provide them with regular updates on the business's performance. If you've taken my advice, the angel won't think you're greedy. You'll have a good, open relationship, and an ally if you ever need additional funds.

The last word

Driven entrepreneurs will avoid outside funding if they can. But, if this isn't possible, they understand that they must continue to be masters of their own destiny. Funding? Yes. At any cost? No. You now have the tools to ensure you can pitch to raise funding. You also understand that it isn't enough. Therefore, this chapter provides you with the intimate motivations and concerns of funders. You now know how to use that knowledge to craft a deal that works well for both you and the funder, who sees that it's a win–win deal. In short, you now have the firepower to get the funding you need on terms that will allow you the control and flexibility a start-up absolutely needs to grow and prosper. Next, we ensure you put the funds to optimal use. The battle is turning our way ...

Dos and don'ts

1. **DO** challenge yourself to reduce or even eliminate the need for any external funding. By matching inflows and outflows, negotiating hard with suppliers, and discounting receivables, you may avoid the legal and moral obligations of outside funding.

2. **DO** bring an attitude of being an equal to funding pitches. It's a win–win, where both bring substantive value to the proposition.

3. **DO** make the funder believe in you. The funding is a personal deal between you and the funder. Ensure you build empathy and trust.

4. **DO** examine all potential sources of funding: family and friends, bank debt, and institutional (venture capital) equity. However, business angels (angels) are typically the right source for start-ups.

5. **DO** pitch the optimal deal. It's a hybrid of debt and equity and satisfies all the funder's concerns. It will include milestones to trigger fund release, soft loans with long repayment dates, free equity granted for the provision of the loans, and no funds used for lavish personal lifestyle.

6. **DO** get the right props to ensure your delivery is powerful and compelling. You need a bulletproof idea, absolute single-minded commitment, a business plan, an action plan and a presentation that summarises your business and the amount, use and timing of funding.

7. **DON'T** forget about credibility. Credibility will dramatically improve your negotiating position. So, ensure you demonstrate commitment to your project (with no get-out clauses), recognised professional advisers, external testimonials, and a team that includes a finance director.

8. **DON'T** let greed scupper the deal.

CHAPTER SIX **FINANCES: LEAD FROM THE FRONT – DISCOVER THE VISIONARY AND REALIST IN YOU**

Here you are, absolutely gunning, smelling success. Your funding is in the bank; realisation of your dream is a heartbeat away. But here, I'm going to hose you down, slow you up, and give some method to the madness.

This is where the discipline comes in. Someone has to be disciplined in business – and this chapter has to be the disciplined part of this business book. No apologies.

The essence is this: if you're going to succeed you have to be something of a schizophrenic. I want you to be a visionary. I want you to dream of where you'll be one day, and plan for it. But when it comes to getting there – your method, your day-to-day decisions – I want you to be a visionary with your feet on the ground.

This will ensure you survive to realise your dreams. Bypass the gung-ho, ill-disciplined, non-professional entrepreneur – those are the types who fall by the wayside.

Bypass the gung-ho, ill-disciplined entrepreneur – you won't fall by the wayside

There's already plenty of tension between these two apparently opposing objectives, but it gets even more complex. Scaling your business and keeping it on track gets harder with every new employee. Let me offer you a real-life story to illustrate the point.

The wrong information

There I was standing outside the Virgin Vie Board Room absolutely fuming. I had just delivered a no-holds-barred tirade against the senior management of Vie. They had been left in no doubt as to what I was thinking but, in doing so, I had just broken Richard Branson's unwritten rule at Virgin that directors (or anyone for that matter) should only ever praise their colleagues and never criticise them.

Even now, as the memories of Vie come flooding back, I find myself shivering … the memories aren't pleasant. Virgin Vie was a high-stakes bet from day one. It was the first Virgin company to list on the stock exchange since Virgin had been taken private in the 1980s. If this one screwed up, it would be an unmitigated disaster for Richard, myself and everyone involved. It was also a project that I'd pushed aggressively, as I was under a huge amount of pressure to make Vie a success. Still, I was full of confidence (perhaps a little arrogant!) after my time with McKinsey.

Management controlled the agenda. We were spiralling out of control

---

McKinsey, widely regarded as the world's leading management consulting company, has great experience and knowledge in understanding successful management techniques. One of the projects that I had worked on during my time with McKinsey was the development of a sophisticated dashboard of key management metrics that were designed to ensure that the management team of a multinational corporate were able to overcome the very issues that I was facing at Vie. Surely it would be simple to translate these skills to early-stage ventures like the far smaller and ostensibly simpler Virgin Vie? The answer, as I found out, was it's not.

At Vie I had always found it impossible to get clear and concise answers to my questions. I could see the bank balance going down but no one could provide me with a proper explanation of what it was precisely being spent on or, more importantly, why! Large capital expenditures and marketing spend were interlinked and mixed together with explanations buried in large reports, I always felt the management were controlling the agenda. When I was physically present they would go out of their way to be charming and polite, but I was sure that as I soon as I left the room an order would go out to return to precisely what they were doing previously. I never received information in a way I could digest so I struggled to provide input into decisions (probably just as the management wanted!).

Things continued to spiral out of control until I finally lost it at that board meeting and found myself standing in the corridor fuming. The real reason I felt so angry was that instinctively I knew that something was wrong but I didn't feel like I had the right information to make the necessary decisions, which left me feeling frustrated and out of control.

If the business fails, you fail. In a start-up, there's no one to bail you out

Vie did survive, but only just. It took significant surgery, including large new investments from the shareholders. What struck me then – and has stayed with me since – is that, regardless of management's good intentions, if the business falters and fails, you fail.

Now consider this in the context of a startup. The position is magnified because there is no one to bail you out. The buck stops with you.

As unpleasant as the Vie experience was for me, I wasn't going let it all have been in vain. I realised that if I wanted to be a successful business-builder I needed to develop two skills:

- First, a methodical, no-nonsense way to make every decision. I craved the unruffled, clear way that Richard Branson approached each decision without distraction and perceived interdependencies.
- Second, an ability at all times to quickly and easily assess the financial health of a business. This would mean less time wading through thick reports and instead concentrating on problem areas before they get out of control.

So, what did I do after coming to these realisations? I licked my wounds and set about acquiring these skills. This chapter describes them, and is divided into three parts: achieving clarity in decision-making; keeping ahead of the game by having the information for a quick financial health-check; and making the best use of accounts as a tool of management and analysis.

1. Getting the big decisions right

So, how do entrepreneurs like Branson (and now myself) achieve the necessary clarity and simplicity in their decision-making? Well, they ask simple questions every time they consider a business decision (usually when they are spending their precious cash!). The questions are: 'If I spend this, what will I get back?' and 'How quickly will I get it?' It's the payback principle.

The sarcastic, over-educated sneer is a sure sign of the triumph of theory over practice

Sometimes impressively trained people – some of whom may even be in your own management team – will sneer and look at you in a way that lets you know you obviously don't understand … you clearly don't know that all decisions are interrelated and there's a hugely complex matrix of consequences that you couldn't begin to comprehend. Rubbish! Look at each issue on its own merits. That was the secret to Richard's absolute clarity and ability to constantly progress his projects step by step and lead from the front.

You should do the same. Consider each decision by itself. Let it stand its own two feet. Forget the alleged interdependencies. Your goal is profit.

The payback principle sounds simple, doesn't it? Well, if it was, this chapter would be over! But unfortunately it isn't all that easy. It's the implementation that's critical, and having the discipline to use the principle always.

The best way for me to help you to get the hang of this is to bring it to life through the use of some examples, after which I'll summarise the steps that you will need to apply to every decision.

So, there I was, sitting at my desk, under a barrage of PowerPoint presentations and high emotion. One of the marketing agencies we used at my property company was trying to convince me to spend my hard-earned money on what they described as a 'truly unique marketing opportunity'.

They wanted to hold a promotion at Heathrow Airport whereby individuals could sign up to attend a sales presentation in return for a chance to win a four-bedroom house in Florida. They waved a thick folder full of 'detailed analysis' in the air and threw a stack of mock-ups of colourful flyers onto my desk. There was excitement in the air. This 'highly original idea' would provide 'fantastic marketing exposure' and the whole promotion would be 'entirely self-funding'. They appeared to expect me to either simply accept them at their word and hand over the cash they needed, or to spend the next two weeks of my life working my way through the reams of paper they kept waving in the air like madmen.

If adrenalin and emotions are high, that's precisely when bad decisions are made

I'd been through this before at Vie. So, before that sinking feeling in my stomach could take hold, I sprang into action. I was ready this time. I knew that I needed to understand my payback. I also knew the questions I needed to ask.

First, I needed to understand what it would cost. It should be no great surprise that this is usually significantly understated! I also needed to break those costs into fixed and variable. My fixed costs were those that I would still have to pay even if I didn't get a single sale. Variable costs are only paid if I secure sales. Because of this, I always start with the fixed costs and am extremely nervous about any idea that has a high fixed-cost component.

Now listen up, I am about to explain an important point: the only costs and revenues that I am interested in are those that specifically relate to this project. Accountants call these 'incremental' costs and revenues. If I was going to incur the costs or revenue anyway (i.e. regardless of this project) then they should not be included.

Let's now pick up from that point in the conversation:

Emotion and hype: Show me the value!

Marketing agency (MA): Fixed costs? They will be around £100,000. You have the cost of renting the space, the cost of producing the stand, the …

Me: Hold on a minute, I want to be thorough here. Let me get out my pen and write each of these down. I want to make a list. OK, start again …

MA: Well, we have … the cost of renting the space … the cost of producing the stand … and the marketing materials.

Me: That's it? What about the cost of airport security? You do realise that you have to pay to have each staff member pass security clearance? [The marketing agency obviously didn't, as they were looking blankly at me] What about the property that you are giving away? I would have thought that was a fairly significant fixed cost. [My list began to grow]

I was told the costs were about £100,000. In fact, they were £363,000 – and rising!

MA: Well, the clever thing is we are only going to pay for the deposit on the property, which will be £60,000. The purchaser will pay for the rest through a mortgage.

Me: Pay for the deposit of a property but force the person to get a mortgage? Surely you can't do that legally! Have you checked that with a lawyer? Besides, who wants to win a deposit on a property and then have to incur hundreds of thousands of pounds of debt? Hardly the most alluring prize in the world is it!

MA: I agree that it's not as strong an incentive to enter as giving away a full house but we thought it would keep costs down … and no I have not run this past our legal team.

Me: Right. So, if we add in the cost of security and assume that we are going to have to give away a full house. What will the total fixed costs be?

MA: Well, if we have to offer the full house as a prize, then the fixed costs are likely to come to about £350,000.

Me: OK. So, when you came in here today, you told me that I would need to spend only about £100,000 in fixed costs. We're now up to 'about' £350,000. You can probably excuse me for wanting to be as precise as possible here, in case there is a further missing £250,000! Let's pause for a moment while I add up all the costs on my list. I make it £363,000. All agreed?

MA: OK. It will be £363,000. But don't worry: it will all still be self-funding.

Ninety-nine times out of a hundred, the halo effect is a con

Don't worry!? They were asking me to spend £363,000 of my own money before I had even sold a single ticket and were telling me not to worry! Not the answer I was looking for. I want the cold hard facts that McKinsey's 'fact-based analysis' required. I certainly wasn't going to throw out this discipline. I wanted to know exactly what my exposure was. Judgements could come later.

Now that I understood the total fixed costs, my next step was to understand my 'incremental' profit margin – that is, the amount of revenue that each sale would generate less the variable costs associated with the sale of that product. We were looking to sign people up for a free introductory workshop, so I knew that this would not generate any revenue. But some of the individuals attending the sales event would then progress further to ultimately purchase a property. I knew that each individual who progressed would generate approximately £12,500 in profit for the business. (I had already netted off all associated costs like pay-aways to staff in the forms of commissions, etc.) However, I found that the marketing agency had a rather more generous view of how to calculate the profit margin. I wasn't going to let our marketing friends get away with their own style of voodoo accounting!

MA: Don't forget that there will be a whole host of 'halo' effects from the promotion. We believe that it will help strengthen the brand and lead to a large number of subsequent attendances at future sales events from people who have been exposed to the brand at the airport but who take a little more time to register for the events.

I couldn't believe what I was hearing as they mumbled on about these nebulous benefits. The team at Vie had used these same arguments. There, proposals were always a muddle of various anticipated benefits and miscellaneous expenses. Let me be very clear: you must isolate your decision-making. You must be absolutely disciplined here. You're only interested in measurable results. How on earth was I supposed to allocate a value to the perceived improvement in the brand? I wasn't even sure that this was true. What I did know was that I would generate approximately £12,500 profit per paying client. That was measurable.

Just tell me how many sales I need to get my money back

Now it was time for the main act. I needed to understand exactly how many places at sales events I was going to have to fill to get my money back. Accountants call this break-even analysis. So I picked up my pen and paper once again. To cover the £363,000 in fixed outlay that this project would cost I would have to ultimately sell thirty properties with each generating an expected £12,500 profit. I knew that to achieve thirty sales I would need to fill 600 places at the sales event with a net conversion rate of 5%.

What about the time to get my payback? Well, it would take up to three or four months for the first revenues to flow into the business' bank account and then up to twelve months for the late purchases. So I might have to fund the cost of the promotion for up to a year before I got my cash back.

The marketing agency was telling me that it was a 'home-run' to hit break even. I wasn't so sure. I had already caught them out low-balling the costs of the whole promotion, so their credibility was somewhat tainted. I pushed on with our decision-making. I now wanted to understand whether we had any reference point to compare our target with. A comparison would help my judgement call. Had we run a similar promotion before? How successful had it been? I put this question to the marketing agency.

MA: Well, we ran a promotion at the airport previously, offering people the opportunity to sign up for a free sales event, but we didn't really push it very hard. We had about thirty people sign up over the course of three weeks.

Right, so I have to outlay some £363,000 on a promotion that is untested and for which my only reference point suggested I might sign up about thirty people for the free event, which was likely to result in only one conversion! I had to let the facts guide me. I wasn't interested in the excitement and ego massage of running a high-exposure campaign in a national airport and neither was I interested in vague associated benefits such as a potential increase in brand equity!

Five minutes later the agency guys were packing up their fancy Macs and heading for the door

---

I shut out the 'no guts, no glory … we will all be winners here' mentality that had plagued me at Vie. Despite what the agency was telling me, the facts before me suggested I was going to lose

£300,000! Time for a judgement call. My gut instinct was that this promotion would be an abject (and costly) failure. That was it. I wasn't going to do the deal. Five minutes later the marketing agency team were packing up their fancy Apple Mac laptops and heading for the door. I, on the other hand, was already on to the next project to see if it would help grow the business.

Implementing this decision-making philosophy requires you to be ruthless, objective and like a dog with a bone until you get the answers you need to understand your payback. It's very straightforward, but it requires some real focus and attention. At the same time, one of the key advantages is that it should take no more than thirty minutes. Don't let them fob you off with reams of paper and long-winded explanations; don't get caught up in the moment or sucked into a turf war. You are a professional and you're not going to be a hostage to fortune. Once you have the facts it's time for an informed judgement – and then time to move on.

The payback principle can be summarised in a series of well-drilled steps.

Decision-making philosophy: The payback principle

1. **Do everything on a cash basis:** Only cash – no promises. This means you estimate the timing of your cash payments and receipts only when they reach your bank. A sale is not a sale until the cash appears in your account.

2. **Only consider incremental costs and revenues:** You are only interested in those costs and revenues that you incur solely as a result of this specific project. No complex made-up allocations, please!

3. **List all fixed costs:** Be thorough. Get out your pen and paper and make an exhaustive list. Learn to loathe fixed costs.

The higher the fixed costs the project entails, the higher the costs you incur regardless of whether you sell anything or not.

4. **Calculate your profit margin:** Estimate the incremental revenue from the sale of a single product and then subtract the variable costs associated with the sale of that product. Only include revenues that are directly measurable – no incidentals or knock-on benefits.

5. **Find out exactly how many items you need to sell to recoup all your costs:** This is your break-even. It's calculated by dividing your fixed costs by the profit margin per sale.

6. **Compare your break-even with other points of reference:** To assess how realistic the break-even is, look for data points or other evidence that is comparable (e.g. perhaps the idea has been trialled previously or a competitor might have launched a similar promotion).

7. **Make a judgement call:** Make a call based on your analysis and gut instinct. Is the return worth the risk?

8. **Don't look back: move on!** You've made your decision, now show leadership.

Once you take away the hype and emotion, you'll be able to find clarity in your decision-making. Whether you're being intentionally misled or not, now you're in control of every single decision – you can demonstrate leadership. The hidden beauty of this method is that it helps you ensure that every initiative works. It's not a question of look at propositions and saying 'Reject, reject, reject'; it's about looking for ways to make a good idea work for you. That's your job – to make things work, to make money.

Leadership entails fearlessness and absolute clarity

The payback principle forces you to consider the cost and revenue elements in turn, thereby enabling you to review each, and look for ways to improve them. Improvements can be made by asking questions such as: How can I reduce my fixed costs? How can I increase the percentage of variable costs in my cost base? How can I generate additional revenue so that I can reduce my break-even level?

Running a business is not all weddings and no funerals. You will inevitably make mistakes. But I have now given you a step-by-step methodology that will enable you to approach decision-making with confidence. Ultimately, though, you are still going to have to use your judgement and trust your instincts. You will have to take a risk but this is now a calculated decision and not a pure gamble.

Let's consider a few cases where you might not think the payback principle applies, but in fact it does:

> **Recruiting a sales person:** At my property company, I interviewed a highly experienced sales woman for a position with our in-house property sales team. When I asked her what she was looking to earn, she said she was after a retainer of £4000 per month for a minimum of twelve months and then sales commission on top of that, with an OTE of £100,000. She also wanted a laptop and a company car.

Enter, stage right, the payback principle.

The first step was to list the fixed costs. As she had been talking, pretty much all I heard was 'fixed cost, fixed cost, and then I would like some more fixed costs'. I had been busy scribbling these down on my notepad. The base salary would be £48,000 over the year. The laptop and IT probably another £3000. The company car another £7000. More than £58,000 in fixed costs before she had made a single sale!

The second step was to calculate the profit margin. When I met her I had immediately thought that she might be the right individual to finally crack the high net worth segment that we had been unsuccessfully targeting for some time. I knew that this segment could be highly lucrative. It would enable us to sell higher priced property and earn larger commissions.

High fixed costs? Don't want the exposure? Manage it down! I made a quick calculation: if she could average two sales per month, on stock that we were being offered commissions of £12,500 per unit, she could earn me £240,000 in her first year. It looked like a pot worth going for.

The third step was to conduct my break-even analysis. She would only need to sell five units over the course of the whole year for me to break even – that is, to recoup the £58,000. That seemed eminently achievable if she was even one tenth as good as she claimed to be.

But was I happy? Hell, no! I still wanted to reduce my potential exposure. I didn't like the pile of fixed costs that she'd asked for, and I didn't know how good she was. Sure, she had good experience, but she hadn't yet proved to me that she could sell the property I had, to the target segment I had in mind. I wanted to be fair to her, but I simply wasn't prepared to commit to £4000 per month. If things did not work out, I would likely lose six months of pay, some £24,000, and have nothing to show for it. I wanted to keep my costs as variable as possible. I only wanted to pay her if she was successful.

I wanted to keep my costs variable and only pay her if she was successful

So I offered her a retainer of £1000 per month for the first three months (which was to be offset against future commissions earned) but also offered her a much higher commission rate than she had expected. The car could wait; I sat her down and ran through my expectations of her selling two properties per week and showed her that she could expect to earn well into six figures. She was delighted. Now my exposure in the first three months was only £7000. She would only have to sell one property to generate a profit over the three-month period. That was a chance worth taking!

Buying a new accounting system: In every business that I have worked with, there comes a time when I have been accosted by the finance director demanding a new accounting system as the old one is 'creaking at the seams' and we are 'just moments away from doomsday'. I am always sceptical, probably the result of lingering trauma from the massive over-investment in IT systems at Rocket.

Again, the payback principle applies. By now you'll know the first step: list the fixed costs. When I ask the cost of the new system, I will normally be told a figure that has more zeros than the English cricket team scoreboard! As you can imagine, I don't respond to these requests particularly well. I always grab my trusty pen and begin writing out an exhaustive list of all costs. Usually, I will find costs that have been 'overlooked', such as the cost of installing the system and the cost of training people to use it!

If you can't see a pay-off, don't invest

The second step is then to seek to calculate the profit margin. Now, for something like an accounting system, this may not be immediately as obvious as if you are simply selling a product to a customer. I always begin by asking: 'What will this new system do that the existing system cannot?' Inevitably, what follows is a long list of relatively minor new features (e.g. slightly easier report production) and the claim that the new system is scalable so that we will still be able to use it when we have 250,000 clients (which seemed some way off when we had about 2500 clients at the time!).

I am not going to invest in a new system simply to make the life of the finance team a little easier and have reports generated in an hour rather than two. So, my next question is: 'How will this actually generate additional revenue for me, save me costs, or improve the experience of my customers?' If I can't see a pay-off in additional sales, savings through reducing required staff, or a major improvement in productivity or because it will alleviate some concern of my customers, then I won't invest – at least not till the very last minute before doomsday.

The third step is to conduct a break-even analysis. If I can't
see a clear payback in a relatively short period of time, I won't
invest. I'm not going to wait the twenty years until our business
achieves its 250,000th customer! My tell-tale sign to invest in
a new system is when my finance director begins to talk about
having to hire additional staff. At that point, the
implementation of a new system will often help
to offset the additional staff costs. Until then,
I would wait.

**Twelve months to
payback? That's too
damned long!**

Hosting a summer party for customers:

At my property business I was presented with a proposal to host a
summer party for clients. I liked the idea. It seemed like a great way
to meet many of the members face-to-face and hopefully to build
some loyalty. It was something that Virgin had done with many of its
businesses to great success. But, before I signed off on the plan, I
wanted to know exactly what I was committing myself to.

As always, my first step was to list the fixed costs. I summoned
the event coordinator to my office to take me through the costs
of the event. She arrived smiling, clutching a detailed budget and
description of the agenda for the day. It looked like an extravagant
children's birthday party! Bouncy castles, inflatable pools, flying-
foxes, magicians … I half expected her to then tell me that I was
going to have to climb into a gift wrapped box and jump out
halfway through the day! I wanted the day to be enjoyable for our
members but all I could see was a mountain of costs. This might
have been acceptable for the deep pockets of Virgin but it wasn't
going to work for us.

The second step was then to seek to calculate the profit margin.
Now, at first blush, you might think that the purpose of a
summer party is pure enjoyment. But I was sure that there would
be some way for us to use the day to actually deliver tangible
benefits (and ultimately sales) for the business. I began to pare
back some of the more ridiculous activities (e.g. did we really
need to offer people the opportunity to roll down a hill in a giant
inflatable ball?). I also vetoed the extensive alcohol budget. There

did not seem much point in holding the day if people would be too drunk to talk sensibly with staff about their investments. Then, on the revenue side, I began to think about how we could use the day to drive sales. We had recently taken on a fantastic new development scheme in the US. The picnic seemed like the perfect place to launch the development and to offer some 'Christmas' incentives to purchase.

A great party and a profit – win-win

The third step was to conduct my break-even analysis. With the picnic estimated to cost £40,000, I knew that I would only need to sell four properties to more than cover my costs for the day. Four sales to more than 250 attendees seemed eminently achievable.

The day turned out to be a great success. Clients had a great time, it was a valuable opportunity for our staff and clients to spend some face-to-face time, and we ended up making a profit.

So, now you don't need to procrastinate or agonise over decisions. You can make informed and rational decisions and then simply move on. But you must have a firm grasp of the financial health of your business so that you know where to focus your energies. And if this means some decisions, don't forget to apply the payback principle.

Let's keep going.

2. Keeping ahead of the game

To stay ahead of the game, you need the right information. I'm going to provide the basic tools to match your information needs as the business grows. Simple, straightforward and easily understood, they guide you to areas where you should spend time. Perhaps there's an opportunity to exploit, or a hole to fill. They also ensure you have an accurate picture of your operation.

Where does everything begin and end in a business? Cash in the bank.

The ultimate judge: Cash in the bank

Remember this, and don't ever forget it. Your first point of call is always your business's bank balance. It will not lie. So, when it comes to understanding the financial health of your business, the one true test could not be simpler: 'How much cash is there in the company bank account?' If I look at the bank account and see that I do not have enough money to pay my staff, then I know that I am in trouble, and that I had better get on the phone to my bank manager. If I look at the account and notice that the balance is higher than I expected, then I wonder whether some of the expenses that should have been paid have been overlooked.

Cash in the bank. Ultimately, that's all that matters

The company bank balance is still (and always will be) the fundamental test for any business I'm involved with. I still check the bank balance of my businesses every day and know instantly when something looks amiss. It takes just thirty seconds at the end of the day to do this and will give you a better understanding of how your business is trading than spending an entire week with your management team! Over time, you will come to know instinctively when something isn't right and whether the account is too high or too low. That's a sign to start digging.

Sales – but where's the cash?

The sales director of one business I was involved in once told me proudly that sales were rising solidly, but when I looked at the bank balance I could not see any change. This prompted me to dig a little further. A few probing questions later and I unearthed the reason for the miraculous rise in property sales. The sales director was using gross sales figures and not net figures. It was true that gross sales were rising but cancellations were rising at an even faster rate. So, the net effect on our cash position was negative rather than the positive, back-slapping outcome he had been claiming.

But while the cash in your bank account is critical, it is a somewhat blunt tool and might notify you of a serious issue too late. It will also highlight that something is wrong but will not give you an insight into what's actually amiss.

So, what other tools do you have at your disposal that are going to keep you focused on the right issues and highlight potential problems before they irreparably damage your business?

A 'to do' list with bite: The budget

Let's move to tool number two: the budget. This will be your most valuable tool during the early stages of your business. If used correctly, it will help to keep your business on track and keep you focused on the most important activities. It will also help you identify opportunities to reduce costs and increase revenue.

A budget that's more than two pages? Shred it!

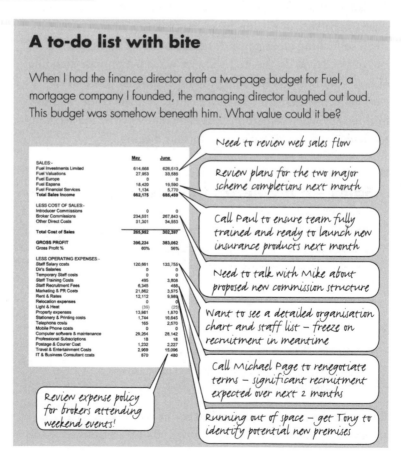

A to-do list with bite

When I had the finance director draft a two-page budget for Fuel, a mortgage company I founded, the managing director laughed out loud. This budget was somehow beneath him. What value could it be?

Need to review web sales flow

Review plans for the two major scheme completions next month

Call Paul to ensure team fully trained and ready to launch new insurance products next month

Need to talk with Mike about proposed new commission structure

Want to see a detailed organisation chart and staff list – freeze on recruitment in meantime

Call Michael Page to renegotiate terms – significant recruitment expected over next 2 months

Review expense policy for brokers attending weekend events!

Running out of space – get Tony to identify potential new premises

	May	June
SALES:-		
Fuel Investments Limited	614,668	626,513
Fuel Valuations	27,953	33,585
Fuel Europe	0	0
Fuel Espana	18,420	19,590
Fuel Financial Services	1,134	5,770
Total Sales Income	**662,175**	**685,459**
LESS COST OF SALES:-		
Introducer Commissions	0	0
Broker Commissions	234,681	267,843
Other Direct Costs	31,301	34,553
Total Cost of Sales	**265,982**	**302,397**
GROSS PROFIT	**396,234**	**383,062**
Gross Profit %	60%	56%
LESS OPERATING EXPENSES:-		
Staff Salary costs	120,661	133,755
Dir's Salaries	0	0
Temporary Staff costs	0	0
Staff Training Costs	495	3,808
Staff Recruitment Fees	6,345	488
Marketing & PR Costs	21,862	3,575
Rent & Rates	12,112	9,989
Relocation expenses	0	0
Light & Heat	(39)	(25)
Property expenses	13,981	1,870
Stationery & Printing costs	1,744	16,645
Telephone costs	165	2,570
Mobile Phone costs	0	0
Computer software & maintenance	29,264	28,142
Professional Subscriptions	18	18
Postage & Courier Cost	1,232	2,227
Travel & Entertainment Costs	2,969	15,096
IT & Business Consultant costs	870	480

I thought of it as a 'to-do list with bite'. It reminded me what had been promised, agreed to be spent and not, and who was doing what. The laughing soon stopped when I made the team sign the budget, and they noticed I repeatedly and stubbornly went back to the core, money-generating issues time and time again. We also used the two-page budget to solve problems on the spot, brainstorming what we could do differently.

Watch them squirm when they sign the budget

I knew I'd won the war and took great pride when the managing director revealed to me when it was his time to launch a business that he's used my to-do list with bite.

As your budget will only have value if it is prepared carefully and implemented effectively, you must observe the following principles:

- **Build it on a cash basis:** As a start-up, your only concern is with actual cash collection (i.e. when are you actually going to get the cash from a sale into your bank account?). A sale is not a sale until you have the cash. If you believe it will take sixty days to get the cash from a sale, then show the sale sixty days later.

- **Don't hype the numbers!** A budget will only work if it reflects the reality of your business. You can prepare a budget that looks brilliant by assuming you'll have 10,000 new leads a month of which 100% will be converted to high-value sales. Don't! Be realistic in your assumptions. You have to deliver the numbers so don't stick your head in the sand and hope for the best. You need to ask tough questions and provide frank answers. You're the one who needs to get the job done.

- **Always apply your decision-making philosophy:** You haven't forgotten the payback principle already, have you? So, apply it to any cost before you put it into your budget. Only activities with a payback should be included. Also, be careful not to overlook costs – a common error. To be effective your budget must reflect all your costs. You don't want any nasty surprises, so be thorough and list all your costs.

- **Make your management physically sign the budget:** You are committed to the budget's delivery. Your management team must also be, so make them physically sign their name on it. They'll hate it, but, believe me, it will focus their minds and will avoid any disputes arising at a later date about exactly what they had committed to deliver.

- **Don't spend on items not in the budget:** I don't care what the argument is, if it's not in the budget, then I'm not going to spend it. This is critical. You wouldn't believe the number of times I have seen business-builders spend months preparing detailed budgets, only to then leave them in their desk drawer and later find that the people around them have been spending money like they were possessed. Preparing a budget is a discipline that forces you to think through your expenses and then hold you to that carefully laid out plan. Don't waste it.

If it's not there in black and white, you can't spend it!

- **Drive profit, challenge costs and enhance revenue:** Use your budget to drive increased profit – that is, boost cash-flow – by identifying costs that can be reduced and finding ways to grow revenue. Don't think of the budget as lifeless. Each line on it represents an activity. Focus on shaping activities to directly improve the bottom line. For example, at Cashback Kings, a cash-back site that's part of a loyalty group, I would always use the budget to constantly challenge myself and the team to find ways to drive new registrations. I'd put myself in the customer's position, and try to make registration as simple and hassle-free as possible. I would also use the budget to identify potential cost savings such as outsourcing particular activities and the potential automation of other processes.

- **Revise your budget regularly:** You should update a budget every week. You absolutely must use it to understand your cash position.

There comes a time when you outgrow your budget as a management tool. As your business grows, the budget will become too long and cumbersome. It will be relegated to an annual objective-setting exercise. It's a dangerous time. You want to scale fast, but effectively. Complexity is high; staff numbers are growing; politics are rife; and time-management is critical. Fortunately, there's a tool, often misunderstood, that can and will enable you to keep ahead of the game – the *key performance indicator* (KPI).

Heat-seeking missiles: Key performance indicators

I don't want you to be confused or overwhelmed by the jargon of 'KPIs'. Think of them as heat-seeking missiles, programmed to detect your trouble spots and opportunities. KPIs are nothing more than numbers that reflect performance in each area of the business and which give you an indication of whether the business is performing well or poorly. If they indicate the business is performing poorly, then you have the opportunity to dive deeper, identify the root cause of the problem, and remedy it before it gets really serious. KPIs will also help you identify strongly performing areas, which probably warrant higher investment.

> **KPIs are heat-seeking missiles. They'll find your trouble spots**

My objective here is not to turn you into the head of the World Bank. I simply want you to understand what constitutes an effective KPI and how KPIs can be used to manage your business. It will be your management, led by your finance head, who will propose a list of KPIs to analyse the performance of the business and key personnel – including your management team! Your team may have its own agenda or propose a long list of KPIs that – intentionally or unintentionally – bury the truth, so watch out. To manage effectively, you need to be able to judge the worth of the KPIs.

Eight, good; thirty-four, bad!

I had sat down to go through the list of KPIs with the managing director of a division of one of my companies. We had had a brief chat, set the objectives, and here he was to show me the fruit of his labours – thirty-four KPIs! Clearly, this was too much information.

Just as he was explaining one KPI that dealt with a sub-menu of a sub-menu on the retail website, I interjected. 'Praise, praise – never criticise!' That's Richard Branson's mantra, but enough was enough. I asked him to get a clean piece of paper, and we attacked the problem together. The solution had to be simple. In effect, the business had two parts: new customers and what they spend; existing customers and what they spend.

KPIs' ruthless detective ability means they work while you sleep

For new customers, I wanted to monitor total new hits, conversion to membership, spend and average margin. For existing customers, I wanted to monitor their number, the percentage purchasing, what they spent and average margin.

He looked at our list of eight KPIs. He was a little hurt and bewildered. He'd wasted his long night agonising and finessing his huge list of KPIs. I explained he'd missed the objective – the KPI should give a high-level warning, at which point you dig.

His bewildered look remained, which worried me, as did the fact I was late for a tricky and potentially lengthy management meeting, which might wreck my diary for the day. However, I decided to invest a bit more precious time with him. He had to buy in to our new, shorter list. That way I could be confident he'd focus on the right issues.

I took one of the new more generalised KPIs, which showed the percentage of existing customers buying. I explained we only needed to drill into finer detail, such as email and newsletter response, copy on the latest promotion, etc. when there was a problem. Then we had to find it, fix it and move on. It was all about focusing to make a difference. I saw his mood change. It was reassuring to know the penny had dropped for him and I knew I'd sleep a bit easier that night because we'd developed a tool that was going to keep me ahead of the game.

These are the key principles of effective KPIs:

- **They should relate directly to net profit:** You are only interested in those metrics that significantly drive profit. That is, they lead directly to higher revenue or lower costs. For example, a KPI such as the conversion rate from sales leads to paid sales always has a direct impact on sales revenue.

- **They should be cash-based:** KPIs will only give you a true reflection of performance if they relate directly to cash. It is, after all, cash that pays your dividends. There's no conflict between this criterion and the one above – think of net profit in cash terms. For example, I'm interested in paid sales, not invoiced sales.

- **They should be ratio-based:** Clearly defined ratios will enable you to review trends in performance quickly, accurately and objectively. You will become accustomed to ratios. They'd better reflect success or failure. You'll be able to translate that ratio (for example, the ratio of sales conversions per consultant) into money.

- **They need to be high level:** You only need a small set of KPIs. It's a judgement call, but, typically, four to six for each major area will do the job.

Lastly, understand you're in a strong position. You know what keeps you up at night. Give the KPIs a once-over. Do they cover the key issues? Get to the essence of the business. Effective KPIs will blow the whistle and do the work for you, allowing you to get a good night's rest.

I could have stopped this chapter right here. I haven't because that would be doing you a disservice. The biggest mistake budding entrepreneurs make is misunderstanding accounting statements.

3. Making the best use of accounts as a tool of management and analysis

Accounting statements *can* (and should) be used to demonstrate financial strength, and to help with the following:

- Obtaining a bank loan.
- Securing equity funding.
- Building credibility.
- Negotiating a deal.
- Seeking external validation.
- Selling your business.

Accounting statements must *not* – ever – be used for:

- Managing your business on a day-to-day basis.
- Making investment decisions.
- Assessing the true financial health of your business.

Surprised? Accounting statements are reported widely in newspapers and on television as a reliable indicator of the financial health of businesses. So, why are they totally inappropriate for actually running a business? Well, despite what the various accounting professional bodies might have you believe, accounting is an art not a science. The various accounting regulations set out rules that are open to interpretation. The same set of financial facts can be presented in many different ways. This is why accounting statements are a significant cause of disastrous decision-making. But don't worry, I won't let this happen to you.

Let me give you an example that had a huge impact on my life:

The (dark) art of accounting

My first job after finishing my MBA in the United States was with
Bond Corporation as executive assistant to the managing director.
After six months in the job, I was handed a critical assignment: write
a defence to the Lonrho Report. The Lonrho Report was a document
that had been sent to every bank, partner, supplier and individual that
had a key financial or trading relationship with Bond Corporation. The
report's central message was simple but devastating: Bond Corporation
was technically insolvent. The mastermind behind the report was Tiny
Rowland (the infamous British businessman and chairman of the Lonrho
conglomerate from 1962 to 1994) who had prepared the report
together with the management consulting company LEK and one of the
big four accounting firms. Ultimately this report was the catalyst that
caused the entire Bond Corporation to collapse. But all this was ahead
for me. My first job was to prepare a defence to this claim.

Accounting statements – don't confuse them with reality!

Tiny Rowland was no fool and was absolutely ruthless. The UK Prime
Minister, Edward Heath, criticised the company and described it in
the House of Commons as 'an unpleasant and unacceptable face of
capitalism'. Indeed the phrase 'the unacceptable face of capitalism'
came to be associated with Tiny Rowland personally. This was the
man I had to go head to head with.

Still, how hard could it be? Surely I couldn't lose this one. I had
seen the accounts of the Bond Corporation and the P&L statement
showed very clearly that the Group was making a profit. It was there
in black and white. And when I looked at the balance sheet, I could
see that the group had billions of dollars' worth of blue chip assets.
The Lonrho Report was obviously wrong – just a cynical attempt by
a business rival to damage the reputation of the Group. But as I
began to dig a bit further and saw the looks on the faces of senior
management when I asked certain questions, I began to have a
rather uncomfortable feeling that all was not as it appeared. A year
later, Bond Corporation drowned in a sea of controversy. The Lonrho
Report had been right. I was barely out of nappies at the time, but it

left a lasting impression on me of just how dramatically accounting statements could be manipulated to present a view of a business that was little, if anything, to do with reality.

With this warning ringing in your ears, I want to take you through the salient points you need to understand to get at the reality behind accounting statements. Let's begin with the *profit and loss statement* (P&L). A profit and loss statement is exactly that – it is a document that is meant to show you how much money you are making. It takes your revenues and subtracts your costs. Ostensibly, lots of profit means all is well … or does it?

Accounting magic means you can report massive profits, yet have no cash in the bank!

There are two important concepts that you need to understand when looking at a P&L:

- **'Accrual accounting':** This means that a business is able to recognise revenue at the point of sale rather than at the point it actually receives the cash into its bank account. So, translated, this means a P&L might lead you to believe you have received more cash than you really have.
- **'Matching':** This means that expenses can be 'matched' with the revenues they relate to, even if the timing of the two is different in practice. So, for example, if an expense was paid up front for a full year but related to six separate events held over the course of the year, a company might recognise the expense in its accounts at six different times throughout the course of the year. In some cases, the matching may take place over a period of many years. So, translated, this means a P&L might lead you to believe you have paid out less cash than you really have.

These concepts mean that a P&L could be misleading. I can ensure this will not happen to you. Simply ask yourself the questions in the box below.

Interrogating the profit and loss statement

Revenues:
- How much of the revenue has been received in cash?
- How much am I still owed? Will I actually receive it?
- Will revenue owing be paid in cash?

Expenses:
- Have the expenses been paid?
- How much is outstanding?
- Are there any expenses paid but not recorded?
- Are there any expenses owed but not recorded?

Once you have found the answers to these questions – which could involve some relentless interrogation of the Finance Director – you will be closer to understanding the true profit (or loss) position of the business. It is yours after all.

Time to turn to the balance sheet. A balance sheet is meant to show the net worth of a business. It does this by taking the business's total assets and subtracting total liabilities, leaving something called shareholders' equity, which is meant to show how much the business is worth. If it is high, then you should have no problems … at least in theory.

Recorded value $1.3 billion. Market value? Zero!

An asset is anything owned by your company – computers, furniture, cars, cash in the bank, any stock held as inventory, any machinery owned by the company and any customer payments outstanding. A liability is anything your company owes outsiders, whether bank loans, unpaid invoices or income taxes due.

Once again, the commonly applied accounting rules are open to interpretation about how assets and liabilities are presented on balance sheets.

There are two vital rules. Firstly, you have to understand what historical accounting really is. This means that assets on a balance sheet will often be recorded at their historical value, that is purchase cost. Translated, this means that a balance sheet might lead you to believe you are able to access significant value through the sale of your assets when in fact they may be worth very little. The second rule is the principle of matching. Let's avoid the detail here. You just need to understand that you may list assets that are grossly overvalued, or possibly non-existent. Your business may also have liabilities that may not be recorded.

So, let's consider the potential practical implications of this. You might one day find yourself in a position where you need to realise the value in some of your assets to provide urgent cash-flow, but when you come to sell the assets you receive a nasty shock. Those assets that you had listed in your balance sheet as being worth hundreds of thousands of pounds are actually worth far less or even zero. Furthermore, an asset only has value if there is a willing purchaser. If you are forced into a fire-sale of your assets, you may find either that you have to reduce the price dramatically or you may even simply not be able to find a buyer.

To understand the true financial position of your company, ask yourself the questions in the box below.

Interrogating the balance sheet

- How much is the asset worth in the market today?
- Could I actually sell it if I wanted to?
- How long would it take me to actually receive the cash from the asset sale?

Liabilities:
- Do I have to pay that liability?
- When do I have to pay it?
- Are there any other debts not recorded?
- When are the debts due to be paid?

Once you have found the answers to these questions you will have a much clear understanding of the asset and liability position of the business.

As for Bond Corporation's collapse, it's the perfect example of the dangers of relying on accounting statements.

Loss not profit

In June 1988, Bond Corporation released results showing a 70% rise in after-tax earnings (to A$224 million) and operating revenues of A$1.4 billion, up 100% from the year before. So a cursory glance at its P&L would have suggested that the business was in fantastic health. But, in reality, the revenues were overstated and the expenses understated. This meant that the business couldn't actually meet its debt-servicing obligations. Finding itself in this quandary, the business looked to quickly sell some of the assets that were listed at impressive values on its balance sheet.

Unfortunately, many of the assets had been recorded at historical values, which vastly inflated the price that could realistically be achieved in the current market. Furthermore, once potential purchasers caught wind of the urgency of the asset sales, the negotiating balance of power shifted dramatically to their side and they were able to push for even lower prices. In November 1989 Bond reported losses of A$928 million – the worst in Australian corporate history. Bond Corporation was caught in a downward spiral, and unable to pay its debt commitments. In mid-1991 Bond Holdings was declared bankrupt.

Now that you understand what accounting statements do and don't tell you, feel free to use them as a tool. This generally means using your P&L and balance sheet to present your business in the strongest light possible. Everyone does it. However, don't be fooled by your own PR. You know the information that you should be relying on to make decisions and to stay on track.

The last word

You've reached a milestone. It's now time to scale your business, which means increased complexity, more staff, different agendas and massive time pressures. Many start-ups fail this test and lose their way. Not you – you now know how to make decisions under pressure and find and use the right information to keep ahead of the game. This ensures you'll be able to identify problem areas fast, before they spiral out of control, and capitalise on opportunities with speed and precision. As a result the realisation of your vision is close, but to get there, you'll need the right help at the right time at the right price. Let's go do that.

Dos and don'ts

1. **DO** make every decision in isolation. This makes for clarity.

2. **DO** base every decision on payback. If incremental profit exceeds set-up cost, do it.

3. **DON'T** take your eye of the cash balance in your business. It's the ultimate barometer of your financial health and the outcome of your efforts.

4. **DON'T** prepare budgets on anything other than a cash basis. A budget should be a 'to-do' list with financials.

5. **DO** use the budget to focus your efforts, control spending and highlight ways to improve your financial position.

6. **DO** use KPI when scaling your business to provide a guide to where you must investigate activities that may have significantly adverse or positive effects.

7. **DO** make sure your KPIs are cash-based ratios directly related to activities having a significant effect on profit covering each area of the business.

8. **DON'T** use accounting statements as a financial health check for your business, or for decision-making purposes.

9. **DO** use accounting statements to obtain credibility when securing outside investment, negotiating a deal or selling a business.

CHAPTER SEVEN **STEPPING STONES: GETTING THE RIGHT HELP**

It's plain and simple: we must get this part right. It doesn't matter how well you've started, it's game over if you screw up this stage. After all your hard work to reach this point, you simply mustn't crash and burn now. This chapter is going to ensure you can answer a critical question during the development of your business: 'How do I get the right help, at the right time, and at the right price?' Get the right help and your business will grow exponentially. Fail to find the right help and you can kiss all those plans of yours goodbye. As we're about to discover, it's a cruel, do-or-die business.

Time to change

As I looked out of my office I could see our marketing director making his way across the floor. He looked exhausted. He'd just returned from the final meeting with our direct mail supplier, a company that had been with us since the launch of our business, one that had been integral to our survival and growth over the previous three years.

Heartless? Maybe. Ruthless? Probably. Good business? Certainly!

The meeting had been the culmination of several months of heated discussions. He had finally told them that we would no longer be working with them. We'd achieved our objective but our marketing director had received a torrent of abuse in return.

The previous few months had seen the supplier try to play on our heart strings ('We helped you to grow your business'), play on our sympathies ('You just used us as stepping stones'), play on our fears ('No-one else knows your business like we do – everything will fall apart') and even try to bluff ('We are the best in the industry').

We hadn't reached this point lightly. We'd genuinely looked for ways during the previous months to continue to work together, through price restructuring, changing roles, etc. But there was simply no way that this supplier could service our changing needs and offer us a price that was competitive on the enormous volumes of mail we were now sending every week. As soon as I realised this, the die was cast and they had to go. It was time to change.

Was the supplier a 'stepping stone'? Damn right. Heartless? Ruthless? Maybe from one perspective. Should we have felt guilty about doing this? Absolutely not.

Listen up, because we've touched on a fundamental principle that you need to learn and apply at all stages of business development when dealing with those that are helping you. Your job is to survive and grow the business, service your customers as best you can, and protect your employees.

You must and will have the right help, at the right time, at the right cost

You're going to need to be brutal and ruthless in the pursuit of this objective. There is absolutely no scope for sentimentality in this game. You need to be constantly reviewing anyone or anything assisting you. Who is best-suited to help? Who can best get you through the next stage? You need to be ruthless not because I want to turn you into some Machiavellian megalomaniac but because the survival of your business depends on it.

Help can come in three forms: employees, suppliers and business partners. It's critical that in each category we understand what the ideal characteristics are, where to locate them and how to attract and motivate them – and if and when you need to upgrade them and move on.

Ensuring you have the A-Team: Employees

Who are the best and where are they?

The rough and tumble of start-ups suits few. You need a certain set of skills and personal qualities – quite different from the conventional, pretty CV-type qualities that suit other walks of business life. I found out as much when I joined Virgin ...

Goodbye to box-ticking

Shortly after I joined Virgin as group corporate development director, I remember talking to Richard about the reasons why he had hired me. I expected to Richard to say that his eye had been caught by my academic credentials – the degree, the MBA – and also by my experience with McKinsey in the London office, during which time I worked on some of the largest corporates in the world.

Branson wasn't sure what a CV was!

Wrong. Richard hadn't heard of the university I graduated from, didn't know anything about the business school I went to and had no idea who or what McKinsey was. But what had caught his eye was the fact that I had worked successfully with another leading entrepreneur and that I'd shown I could simply get on with things and persevere until I made them a success. Richard was looking for an attitude and ability to deliver rather than ticking off qualifications on a CV. And, I could easily be replaced if it didn't work out!

So, the message is clear. For a start-up, you need strong, often unconventional, people with some or all of the following characteristics:

- 'Doers' rather than 'thinkers' – you need results rather than detailed reports and comprehensive analysis. You need individuals who'll run through walls, leap over tall buildings and put their lives on the line.

- A real 'can do' attitude – people who will not rest until they have found a way to push through and achieve their goal.

- Entrepreneurial drive and a willingness to take a risk.

- Great persuasive skills – people who can sell a product to people who don't even realise they need it.

- Comfortable working in a fast-paced, dynamic, results-focused environment.

- 'Street-smart' and creative.

As you can see you are looking for individuals who are not entirely from the mainstream, so you need to look beyond traditional blue-chip CVs. People with the skills you require will not always have been to Oxford or Cambridge; nor will they have spent the previous four years as a management consultant.

Get the right start-up employee

Traditional employee	Start-up employee
University-educated	Practical experience and attitude
Risk-averse	Entrepreneurial
Highly analytical	Highly persuasive
Perfectionist	Close enough is good enough
'Thinker'	'Doer'
Comfortable work environment	Comfortable working in a mad house
Process- and procedure-driven	Focused entirely on result – the sale

---

That's who you're looking for – but where will you find them? Good question, and difficult to answer because the people you need are not easy to find. Typically, recruitment agencies aren't going to help you. Besides, you simply can't afford the exorbitant fees they charge. Furthermore, you don't have the time it takes to find the perfect candidate.

But all is not lost. They do exist. You'll simply have to use your nose and be opportunistic. You must rely on social and professional networks and keep your eyes open. Being entrepreneurial, my contacts book has been built up over the years by pursuing the following leads:

- **Competitors:** Define your competitors broadly.
- **New/fast-growing industries:** Look for new industries or industries that have grown dramatically but now face slower future growth.
- **Word of mouth through friends, family and former colleagues:** Let friends, family and former colleagues know the type of people that you are looking for and follow up recommendations.
- **Trade shows:** Look particularly for presenters and quality sales staff.
- **Professional associations:** Network at association events. Review lists of members.
- **Chance:** Look everywhere and be alert every day – you may find your future best sales person working at your local corner shop. Talking to other entrepreneurs can help.

Over the years, the three most fruitful areas have been competitors, fast-growing industries and chance.

Your competitors will always be an excellent potential source of employees. The tip here is to think of 'competitors' as widely as you can. They might be direct competitors in your own industry but they might equally be companies in other industries that have practices you want to replicate. When we were building the property group and looking for employees, we naturally looked at competitors in the property investment industry, but we also looked at time-share companies, stock trading companies and independent financial advisers who were running sales events. You should take every opportunity to attend your

> **Top sales people persevere, find creative ways to sell and make a small fortune**

competitors' events as a 'customer' and lurk around or visit their places of work and surreptitiously meet as many of their employees as possible. You will quickly come to know who the star performers are.

So, keep your eyes open and remember, employees come in many shapes, sizes and colours ...

Our risk, our reward

He walked into the office in his purple suit. I chuckled to myself. What a find this guy had been. I reflected on his past: he'd worked in double-glazing and as a furniture salesman. Each time the story had been the same. He'd overcome adversity and silenced the critics of his unconventional approach.

Double-glazing? Purple suit? Perfect!

He was an honest doer with the common touch. As a sales guy, he attacked difficult new industries with gusto. No matter how many doors got slammed in his face, he always found a way through. When we discovered him, he was restless but in need of shelter (other corporates had spurned him). We took him on, gave him some top-quality, intensive training and he became our top salesman. Our risk was our reward.

New, fast-growth industries that have run out of a bit of steam can be a great source of talented staff, particularly sales staff. Take the time-share or double-glazing industries, for example. When these industries first emerged, imagine what it was like for the sales staff. They were asking people to pay substantial sums of money for products that the individual had never heard of and had lived perfectly happily without previously.

Sales staff would often have had to trudge door-to-door attempting to find creative ways to sell their product. Can you imagine the number of doors they must have had slammed in their face? Or the number of bored people they must have endured long and fruitless conversations with? Yet, the top sales people in these industries persevered, found creative ways to sell their products and made a small fortune.

Every new product has a limited initial growth phase. If you can identify an industry that's beginning to wane, there's a good chance you'll be able to pick up some excellent sales staff if you can convince them that what you're offering them is the next new thing in the market.

Finally, what about chance encounters? Think of yourself as being constantly on a recruitment drive. Take an interest in people you meet and always look for skills or talents you might be able to use in your business either today or in the future. One of the most successful sales people I ever hired was working as a bank teller when my partner encountered her. He could tell that she was chirpy, cheeky, had a bit of a spark and was clearly bored senseless as a teller. We offered her a job on the spot and she began work with us the very next week. She went on to become one of that business's greatest assets. So, I'll say it again: keep your eyes open!

You want to take on the VAT man? Good luck!

From the outset, I have maintained that you must have an absolute focus on the front end of your business – and you still must. However, while you are out hitting the pavement, doing deals and securing large orders, someone must be holding the fort, even if it's just to check employees are coming to work. You're going to need a safe, cost-effective pair of hands who can do all of the operational work, from VAT returns and supply contracts to agony aunt. It's a false economy and a waste of your time for you to do it.

So, here's one of my most powerful tips and something that I am certain will work brilliantly for you. What you need to find is a single individual, an office manager, whom I call the 'office doctor'. I mean someone beyond an administrator, someone who is capable of performing most of the legal, financial, human resources and administration functions on their own. This individual will play an absolutely vital role in your business during the start-up phase. The ideal individual will have an accounting or perhaps legal background and will often have worked for one of the large accounting firms up to a middle level. He or she will be hard-working and able to deal with everything from preparing the books to resolving employment issues – including the hire of an assistant or an external supplier when your growth means the burden of work becomes too great. It's no exaggeration to say that during the start-up phase, your office manager or right-hand person will be the glue that will keep your business from falling apart. I cannot launch a business without one.

OK, you've found someone, but your work isn't done yet. You still have to convince that person to join you.

Sealing the deal

It sounds simple. What could be better than joining you and the excitement of a start-up? Well, you could be asking an individual to choose a role with you over a role with a well-established company that provides a good salary, health care, a company pension and the security of knowing that the company will still be there in a year from now. What do you think the individual's partner might say when asked for advice on which job to take?

Corporates offer good salary, health care, pension, security. You can do better than that!

Recruiting staff into a start-up is not easy. They need to be made to feel special and confident they're making the right decision. In other words, you need a convincing sales pitch. What better teacher of the art of persuasion than Richard Branson?

Branson's A-Team invites!

Before I joined Virgin, I'd always believed that money talks and that getting employees to join any business was simply a matter of getting the price right. (Maybe I was simply projecting my own motivations!) But I was wrong. One of the most important things I learned from Richard was his ability to recruit talented staff on the fact that they would be joining the Richard Branson/Virgin 'Train'. People believed that they were joining an exclusive 'A-Team' of incredibly talented staff whose days were full of madcap fun, stunts and satisfying work. Staff genuinely felt like they were a part of something that was changing the world. Of course, they weren't about to become volunteer workers – they still wanted to be paid a salary, but this wasn't their only motivation in joining. And, of course, as obvious as it sounds, isn't this exactly what a start-up is? Your chance to change the world?

Richard Branson taught me that a successful pitch to recruit any individual has two inseparable elements: the intangible and the financial. I have used this distinction to great effect ever since.

Your mavericks want to feel empowered, and have ownership and control over their own destiny. They are special and you must leave them in no doubt as to the uniqueness of the opportunity:

■ **A compelling vision of what the business will become and their role within that success:** You need to convince them that they are going to be a part of something that is different and that is going to radically change the world. They must believe that your business is going to be incredibly successful and that they will be rewarded many times over for their initial sacrifice.

> **Call them anything you like – just not 'an employee'**

■ **Conviction:** Leave them in no doubt that the journey they are about to embark on will involve hard work but that it will be fun and that they will be joining an elite group with fantastic team spirit (e.g. socialising and drinks after work will be a regular occurrence).

■ **A sense of personal value and development:** Make them feel important and excite them with the prospect of the role they will be performing. Within a start-up there will usually be an opportunity for staff to assume greater responsibility than they might be trusted with in a more established business, as well as opportunities to perform new roles as the business grows. Your staff should feel that joining you will enable them to leap-frog the bureaucracy of traditional companies and that they will be able to achieve their goals in a much shorter time.

- **Comradeship:** Never call them 'employees'. You want each individual you are attempting to recruit to feel like they are an integral part of something special – they are a fellow world-changer. So, call them 'partners' or give them titles that suggest ownership of their project ... anything that will make them feel special ... because they are special and important!

The salary, house and car will be bigger and better – but it's all going to be self-funded

So, now they're buzzing with excitement – but they still want to be paid, which leads us to the financial element of sealing the deal.

The financial side is just as important. After all, they can't help you rule the world without a big house and a nice car. They're just going to have to wait a little while until they've earned it.

The financial promise that you make to your employees in a start-up is simple: 'You'll earn more here than any other place you could work, but it will take time. You're going to have to back yourself.' Let me take you through an interview conversation I've had many times. It will bring out the key elements of the financial deal. My part in the conversation goes like this:

What are you looking to earn over the next few years?

- 'This is a very entrepreneurial place. People come here to have fun, become masters of their own destinies and make a lot of money. Our philosophy is that we reward success handsomely but don't believe in paying basic salaries. The same applies to me. I am paid barely enough to cover my Tesco bills. If the business has a good month then I get paid well. If we have a bad month then I have to put my hand in my pocket.'

- 'If you're successful – as I believe you will be – then you'll be earning two to three times today's salary within a couple of years. That's way more than you'd get elsewhere. Of course, there is no cap on the upside. The more successful you are, the more successful our business is, so it's a win–win.'
- 'See that guy over there? When he joined us I paid him just enough to barely live – but still more than I paid myself! Now he's earning more than £100,000 a year and set to do even better next year. Not bad for someone in his twenties. Actually, why don't we get him over here and he can tell you a little about his own experience.'
- Because I believe that you can make this a great success, and in order to make you rich, I am going to develop a bonus structure for you that will be tied to performance.'
- 'Naturally, we will have to review the particular mechanics of the bonus structure as the business grows but you have to admit that earning two to three times what you are earning now is quite attractive.'

Having read my pitch above, I hope that I've got you thinking of dusting off your CV and looking to join one of my new ventures! Now, what are the salient points that you should take out of the conversation and apply in your own recruitment discussions? First, understand this is a very personal deal. Once you have them on side, make the following points very clearly:

- There is an opportunity to earn significantly more than they are at present.
- They'll earn more than anywhere else.
- The upside is unlimited.
- Remuneration will be directly tied to success.
- They can meet other 'real life' staff who have joined on a similar understanding and have enjoyed enormous success already.
- The upside will be delivered over the 'next few years' – it is not an immediate pay-off.
- Little or no basic will be paid.

Employees: Honest toilers – keep them motivated

You probably now have a disparate group of mavericks in your employ: entrepreneurial sales types, 'doers' and individuals with non-traditional CVs.

Be the fearless leader. Inspire! No weakness allowed

Sales guys are typically energetic but have a tendency to be lazy when not supervised; they are often emotional and tend to lose interest quickly in things like administration. These are the individuals who are most likely to thrive in a start-up, but they aren't the easiest to manage. You're going to have your work cut out getting the best from them. They need to be given a lot of direction and shown how to do things. Then you'll need to watch them like a hawk.

The emphasis at the very early stages must be on motivation. Use our two pillars (the intangible and the financial) to motivate your employees, with an obvious emphasis on the intangible, as the big bucks are a little way off yet.

Here's a real challenge to you as an entrepreneur, a business person, a leader and a motivator. This is what you've got to do – and it's quite a list!

- **Be the fearless leader:** Your role is to be the 'inspirer' and to constantly motivate your staff. Remind your staff regularly of the grand vision for the business, of the successful progress towards that vision and their role in that success. Your staff should be able to feed off the energy, excitement and enthusiasm that you display. You must lead by example, leaving your staff confident that success is inevitable with you at the helm.

- **Downplay business set-backs:** Your staff have made a big decision – it's been a sacrifice to join you and they are conscious that their future success is intimately tied to yours and that of the business. So don't give them anything that will make them question that big decision – or indeed leave! You must provide a confident exterior regardless of what might be thrown at you.

- **Celebrate success:** You should always look for examples of success within the business. Perhaps the business has won a major contract, or just passed its 100th customer, or perhaps one of the sales team has just smashed the previous sales record. Celebrate these with your staff to reinforce their confidence that things are moving in the right direction. Keep your eyes open for opportunities to celebrate both the business's success and also the success of individual employees.

- **Take a personal interest in lower level staff:** As I learned, you'll sometimes need the understanding and help of senior staff to do this ...

The invisible man

As I sat in my office, Richard Branson stumbled in. He'd been out a bit later than me. He turned out his pockets, stuffed with crumpled bits of paper – the hopes and dreams of the people he'd met the night before. At one point the preceding evening, Richard had looked through me as though I wasn't there. The bits of paper solved the mystery; that party was the chance to ensure everyone got a chance to make a difference, and to be heard. He knew all about my views: I was around him in the office all day. He expected me to be quicker on the uptake.

- **Always look for ways to connect with your staff:** Remember the negotiation chapter and the importance of taking a few minutes to break the ice and build rapport? Are they married? Do they have kids? Most importantly, remember their names. This is so simple but is so incredibly powerful. At Virgin, Richard Branson was terrible at remembering names but he knew how powerful this was in building rapport and so would always furtively ask his closest staff for reminders of people's names. Every time Richard would mention someone's name (apparently unprompted) you could see the individual visibly swell with pride.

- **Provide fun activities outside of the office:** This is one of the most important motivating factors for most of your staff. I once thought 'heart for the family; head for business'. Maybe that works in a faceless corporate, but not in a start-up. So, don't ever underestimate the importance of organising events such as a drinks night, office party, or an event to recognise exceptional performance. Put some money behind the bar and reward your staff for all their hard work. You will also learn a lot once the alcohol begins to flow. Virgin is the best I have ever seen at this. In fact, I am not sure I've totally recovered from some of their parties more than a decade ago!

These intangibles will help to ensure that your employees don't skive off, get bored or become disgruntled. But you can see that the intangibles are also reinforcing the fact that the business is growing and will be successful, and thus is feeding their financial appetites too.

Stick to the deal – even if you go hungry!

To deliver on the financial promise, just stick to the deal and pay them, even if it means you go without pay to pay them. That kind of sacrifice will be noticed and the payback will be massive.

Lastly, lest you think I am going soft, you are going to have to watch your employees closely. It's human nature to take the path of least resistance and your employees will do the same if they feel they can get away with it. You need to keep them on their toes by making them aware that they are being closely monitored, so walk past their desks, talk to them, make surprise visits. Keep them sharp.

This can work to your advantage. A great method I learned was to give employees tasks and ask them to report back, sometimes within hours. They'd feel empowered. This stretches your influence and ability to control quality. With technology such as SMS and email, this process can be as simple as a daily text of the sales results. By applying this approach to a number of staff and different projects, you can maximise your influence on a wide range of projects with the limited time that you have available.

You now have the A-Team, but priorities change. How can you ensure your team is still the A-Team?

Keep the production line running: Stepping stones

In reality, you're likely to have ended up with a rather motley group of employees, particularly in the early days. This is simply the reality of having to get the best help that you can as you start and grow. You will have some staff who struggle; others will be star performers.

> **Move on non-performing staff. Fail, and it can cost you your business**

You're unlikely to have difficulty identifying the strugglers. The difficulty is actually taking action and moving them on from your business. This is a key point. You must have the courage to act and be absolutely decisive. It doesn't benefit you or struggling staff to keep them on. Be careful here about the temptation to simply move a non-performer to another part of the business. Shuffling weak staff around is simply moving the problem to another part of your business. It's no exaggeration to say that the failure to be ruthless and move on non-performing staff can literally cost you your business and, ultimately, the jobs of many more employees. The discipline of reviewing your staff regularly and removing non-performers is one that you must maintain for the rest of your business life. You will need to follow your instincts and then act decisively.

One of the critical tasks in the weeding-out process is to find and eliminate 'shop stewards'. The 'shop stewards' are those who spend their life agitating and 'representing' staff rather than actually delivering anything. It is how they seek to mask their poor performance or bargain with you over it. They slow progress, demotivate staff and undermine you. Show them no mercy and get rid of them yesterday. They are poisonous. And, typically, they are poor performers – the ones with the worst sales figures, etc.

Although they are likely to be far fewer in number, your star performers will have managed to grow and adapt as the business has grown and are now excelling in their roles. You must make these individuals feel special to ensure that you retain them.

You will want them to focus on what they have excelled at but they will probably be looking for new challenges.

You'll have to allow the stars a degree of freedom. Give them some additional responsibility, stroke their egos by giving them a new title, let them swan around the office a little, provide some public recognition of their success and turn a blind eye if they turn up late to the office occasionally. Don't get bogged down in these minor details. If they are star performers, they're making you a lot of money and you wouldn't want to jeopardise that, would you?

Protect the mavericks. Broker peace between them and the professionals

At some point your new senior team (see chapter 9 for detail on them), which admittedly is critical to your growth, is going to come into conflict with your mavericks. But your mavericks are valuable. They're in touch with your customers. They keep you grounded. Do NOT let senior staff bully or belittle the mavericks.

The professionals and the mavericks rarely understand each other. The professionals have a knack of letting the less formally educated know where they stand. You need to be there to keep the peace.

Employees provide half the help in the early stages, but what about suppliers?

Suppliers

Who are the best and where are they?

All companies work with suppliers. However, choosing which suppliers to work with is fraught with danger. A key supplier who fails to perform can literally send a start-up bust within months. But the perfect one . . .

The perfect supplier?

When my property group was still in the survival stage and struggling to make money, we realised we needed to look for a supplier to assist us with our IT. The last thing I wanted to do was to spend a fortune on building an in-house IT department, but we needed a skilled team who could provide us the basics immediately and then help us as we grew. I turned to my Rolodex and found a business card I had collected from a chance encounter with a former colleague of my wife. The guy was a very smart IT manager who had worked in large financial institutions but who had since left to form his own IT consultancy. He was perfect. He was very bright and hugely ambitious.

Size does matter. But in this case, big is not better

His business was very young and he could see the potential of our business. He believed that he would be able to grow his business on the back of ours. Our business would also account for almost all of his young business's revenue, so if we failed he would fail also – quite an incentive.

As a result he was prepared to come into our offices at short notice, work weekends, and was incredibly responsive to our demands. Whenever we phoned, the call was always taken by the owner, not a junior account manager. Within eighteen months, he and his team were no longer simply providing us with basic IT services, but were developing a £250,000 bespoke online customer management system that was the most cutting-edge system in the UK residential property market at that time. It was an incredibly successful partnership, but took a huge amount of hard work, attentiveness and close cooperation. He now has a large, successful business – partly because of his own ability, but also, I think, because of his growing experience with us.

Perfect suppliers do exist, but they are not necessarily what you'd expect them to be. Use the following questions as a guide:

- **How big are they?** Like so many things in life, size does matter. However, in the case of your start-up, big is not better. The IT consultancy I used at my property company was just one bright guy and some part-time help from university students. Your first intuition may be to find the largest, best-known supplier that you can. But a start-up business has different needs to those of a well-established company. There will inevitably be twists and turns during your first years of operation, so you need suppliers who are extremely flexible. Whenever your demands change, you want a supplier who is able to immediately respond. Ideally, you want your supplier to act just like an employee and be available at your beck and call.

- **Do I trust them and can they perform?** You can check their references, but in reality this is a very subjective test. You are going to be working closely with the supplier and so it's critical that you can envision having a good relationship with the owner and members of the senior team. So spend some time getting to know them. Are they likely to inform you of a major problem or will they try to cover it up until it's all too late? This doesn't mean that you'll then leave the supplier unsupervised. You're still going to have to watch them like a hawk at all times.

> Driving per-unit costs down by a few pence can make the difference between profit and loss

- **How important am I?** At this stage of your business development you need to know you're important to the supplier. Ideally, if your business fails, the supplier's will suffer enormously and possibly fail. If something goes wrong or you want to make rapid changes, then you need to know that the supplier is going to respond quickly. If they don't, your business may not survive. Ask the supplier how many clients they have. Find out exactly who will be managing your account. An easy test of your relative importance to the supplier is whether the owner of the business will spend significant time with you.

OK, you understand the type of suppliers you need during survival stage, but where can you find them?

Again, as with finding employees, there are no hard and fast rules or magic solutions. You'll simply have to follow your nose. You could use a phone book, but there are better ways. I've found my suppliers through all of the following channels:

- **Competitors' suppliers:** Review your competitors for work that has impressed you, and then find out which supplier was responsible.
- **Industry trade fairs:** Visit trade fairs either for your own industry or those of the specific supplier you're looking for.
- **Industry journals and magazines:** Check out the journals of your own industry or those of your target suppliers.
- **Industry league tables/awards:** These offer good independent assessments of supplier quality.

Finding top-quality suppliers is not simple. You need to use your wits, think creatively and be opportunistic. One of my favourite approaches is to simply keep your eyes open for work that impresses you and then find out which supplier was responsible. Ultimately, you'll simply have to make a decision and take a risk. However, the deal you strike is key.

Sealing the deal

Many of the methods of dealing with suppliers echo the ways to deal with employees. However, there are subtle differences. One of the more marked contrasts is how you structure the deal. Achieving the right deal structure is really important.

The key reason for using suppliers is to avoid the considerable set-up costs of performing the service in-house – costs that you simply can't afford during the survival stage. However, most businesses get charged these costs indirectly and don't even know it. I'm going to show you how to ensure you don't pay out unwittingly. The survival of your business depends on it, after all.

A gammon steak

It was a bitterly cold and rainy evening as I waited for the AA with my finance director by the side of the motorway. Still, I had a smile on my face.

The deal had been signed. The supplier was pleased with his upside. I was delighted with the low costs during our start-up phase. Driving the per-unit costs down by a few pence had given us a fighting chance to make a profit at low volume. It had been a two-month process – and it had it all started over a gammon steak.

I didn't like the steak, but what I did like was the start of the negotiation. I began to build empathy with the supplier by explaining the vision and the backers using each and every credibility tool. The supplier was sceptical at first, but gradually began to believe we were going to be big – which was absolutely critical if he was going to go for our proposal.

It was then that our detective work began. We spent days poring through lists of accounts, asking questions along the way, haggling over late-night beers and pizzas, being walked around factory meat-cutting areas in blue plastic shoes and hair nets to see exactly where the extra space was needed. We did price checks on all ingredients and took nothing at face value. Eventually, the supplier simply gave us access to any information we asked for. He truly opened up his books.

Pare down supplier profit as close to zero as possible

In the end, we got there. The contract prices were as close to his pure incremental costs as possible. If volume grew, the unit price would grow, fully compensating him for his earlier lack of margin.

It was still raining as the AA man arrived, but I felt warm and happy. As an epilogue, the supplier got his profits and eventually we both moved on. He found a client we introduced him to. We went to a larger supplier, with better economies. We're still friends today.

As with your employees, the pitch to your suppliers is going to be that they should accept less now because they will be rewarded with a large upside later. The problem with suppliers, of course, is that because by definition they are external, you don't have access to their cost information. Still, your objective is clear – get them to accept very little profit now in return for a large profit later.

To become an insider and structure a deal purely based on upside, follow this four-step process.

1. List your supplier's costs

Ask your supplier to provide you with a detailed cost breakdown, dividing costs into fixed (those that don't change because of your project) and variable (those that do).

2. Strike out your supplier's fixed costs

Fixed costs will include overheads such as rent, rates, management salaries and so on. Your supplier's going to incur these whether or not they work with you. By charging these they are indirectly making a profit. You don't want to pay for this in the early stages of your deal.

3. Challenge your supplier's variable costs

Variable costs will include any specific input required in the production of your product, including delivery costs and additional workers. Your objective here is to ensure your supplier's not inflating these costs.

4. Agree a profit margin

You've taken out the profit from the supplier's costs. Now you need to consider how and when your suppler will make a profit. This should be based on volume and how well your supplier performs. In the early stages of your contract, insist the cost is equal to the variable cost. When volumes grow, add a profit margin.

Suppliers will only agree to this if they believe that your business is going to be enormously successful, and that, as your business grows, their business will grow too. You want the suppliers to become so enthusiastic about how profitable the relationship will be in the future that they're prepared to make the short-term sacrifice.

It's back to credibility. (Review the funding chapter and the credibility tools we used there.) Why? Asking a supplier to take no or reduced profit for a higher return later is exactly like asking for funding. The same credibility test applies.

Your supplier is on the edge. That's now your management challenge

In reality, it is almost impossible to truly achieve a 'zero-profit' deal. Even in the case of Rocket outlined above, I am sure that we did pay a little above cost in some areas. However, your goal is always to get as close to zero as possible. How close you will come to achieving such a deal with your own suppliers will depend on how good your pitch is and how unique the skills are that your supplier possesses. If they have skills that are truly unique, it will be harder, but not impossible. Either way, you are going to have to work hard and really dive down into the detail to achieve your goal.

Driving a hard bargain comes at a cost. You'll need to work hard to ensure they perform.

Suppliers: honest toilers – keep them motivated

Now that you've negotiated the lowest price possible, your supplier will be on the edge, and will be looking for reassurance that they have done the right thing. The motivation, or intangibles, will be critical in reassuring your suppliers that they have made the right decision in working with you and will help to minimise potential fall-out during rocky periods – for example, if you're late paying an invoice.

Again, this is a management challenge. Even though you don't technically manage your suppliers, so many of the techniques are the same as the ones you need to get the best out of your employees. The objective is to ensure your supplier has empathy with you, to view your arrangement as a partnership. The suppliers need to feel important and part of the inner sanctum.

Nothing in a start-up progresses perfectly. There will be times when you need your suppliers' understanding. Make sure you get it by communicating key views and developments they will be particularly interested in.

- **Share success stories to demonstrate growth potential:** Your initial pitch to the suppliers was that they should work with you and offer you the keenest price possible. Why? Because you are going to become so wildly successful that they could grow their own business on the back of yours. So, take the time to keep your supplier abreast of your business's growth and share your success stories.

- **Help them grow:** If you can identify ways you can help the supplier to grow, you can use that as leverage to foster goodwill and maybe negotiate a better deal. Growth might be in the form of the lure of future work within your business as it grows or through commercially useful introductions.

What about the financial element? Well, the intangibles should reassure the suppliers that the business is growing and they will ultimately make a fortune. Your contract will have set out the deal, the service quality aspect and the potential penalties. A clearly drafted contract should help to minimise any potential disagreements about these key elements of the relationship.

However, you must closely monitor your suppliers' performance (just like you would with an employee) to ensure you both succeed. You must have your supplier report against an agreed set of metrics on a weekly or even daily basis. Once you have agreed these metrics, you should constantly be looking for ways to work with your suppliers to improve on them. You must scrutinise these reports to ensure that they tally with your own records.

Your attitude? Suppliers are ... lazy! They overcharge and under-deliver

Any deviation from the agreed targets must be immediately explained, remedial action taken and, if repeated, have financial penalties imposed. You must be persistent. Remember: if they fail, you fail.

So, in the early days it's all about keeping the motivation. But remember, your supplier is in business to make a profit. Once you have romanced your suppliers and got the deal, your attitude should shift to one that they are fundamentally lazy, that they will overcharge and under-deliver, and that their constant objective to is screw more money out of you. You need to manage them closely and adopt the view that there is always someone better out there.

But how can you really keep them honest?

Keep the production line running: Stepping stones

The only way to keep suppliers honest is to put their business out to tender every twelve months (you might even consider six-month contract periods), although it may jeopardise the effort you have made at creating a harmonious relationship. Yes, it sounds harsh. It is. But there's just one thing: you did a deal. They will earn a great return on the back of your growing business – a reward for being both competitive and best in class. By now they've made their return for giving you a cost break in the early days.

Reckless loyalty to suppliers will not go unpunished

If the suppliers are able to offer the best price in the industry, then fantastic, you can continue the relationship. If, however, they are uncompetitive, then you need to change. Furthermore, as the needs of your business change, you must ensure that your suppliers are still best practice. This is no time for a misplaced sense of loyalty. Scaling a business is fraught with danger and you must manage the risk. Remember our story at the beginning of the chapter. Changing our direct mail supplier ultimately saved over £1 million per year, and brought new ideas.

This war of attrition must be continued right throughout the life of your business. Not only will it ensure that you're always paying the lowest possible price, it will also ensure that there is a fresh flow of ideas and expertise into the business. It's common to find that the original supplier may be struggling to provide the increasingly sophisticated skills that you need as your business grows.

We've dealt with two forms of help – employees and suppliers. Now we move on to the third, more permanent, form of help: business partners.

Business partners

Partners are different. You don't have to have one – and if you fall out with them, it'll make divorce look cheap and painless. Before we go through our usual drill, there's an anterior question to be asked: 'Do you need a partner?' Other things being equal – yes!

Branson always partners with people who know an industry better than he does

The benefits of having a partner strongly outweigh the disadvantages of having to give away a slice of your profits and a degree of control. I've had both good and bad experiences with partners. I've been ripped off by some, but benefited greatly from others. They've always required a tremendous amount of hard work, time, effort and trust. But almost every business that I've been involved in has had entrepreneurs who've had partners at the helm.

At Virgin, although it's Richard Branson's name that's usually the most high profile in his ventures, Richard will usually partner with someone who knows the industry better than he does.

It's not a decision to be taken lightly. Let me take you through the thought process. You need to ask yourself whether the partner is going to bring something into the business that you don't have, something you believe is so crucial you wouldn't be able to capture it simply by recruiting an employee or hiring a supplier.

I have found that there are typically two scenarios where business-builders rely on partners for key input. The first is where the entrepreneur is a successful trailblazer but is poor at focusing on what he or she considers to be matters of detail. If this is the case, a partner might perform a 'sweeper' role to ensure that ideas are followed through to completion. The partner must be someone who has gravitas, someone who can take an idea or concept and make it happen – not simply someone who will blindly do your bidding. The partner must be able to sift the good ideas from the bad and execute those that have a high likelihood of success. This type of partner will often be called the 'right-hand man' (or woman, of course).

A partner will possess a ruthless ability to succeed – to get the job done

The second scenario is where there's a fundamental shift in the business and the skills required are different to those that you needed to launch the start-up. A good example is the change in business requirements once the business has got over the survival stage and the foundations are starting to be laid for a potential sale.

This process requires a very different skill set to the trailblazing start-up days. Suddenly you need someone who can bridge the gap between the 'suits' and the entrepreneur, someone who is skilled at selecting an experienced senior management team, someone who knows what aspects of the business must be invested in to make the business sustainable. Many entrepreneurs are poor at managing this transition. A partner can often bring the skills that are missing to ensure this transition progresses smoothly, freeing the entrepreneur to focus on areas they thrive in, such as new business development.

A critical question is whether you can really work with a partner. If not, your business could fail …

The self-chilling partner

The memories arrived in a landslide. It was the unhappiest moment in my business career. The divorce was through. We were no longer partners.

I should have seen it from the start. I'd been completely blanked and left out to dry. I had been shielded from information, not allowed to meet employees or suppliers, and constantly undermined. It was horrid. My sense of loyalty meant I stayed longer than I should have. His personality was based on paranoia. He trusted no-one, and felt vulnerable all the time. Perhaps that was why he always seemed to be on the attack.

If you constantly undermine or double-check your partner, the business will fail

A brief look at his history gave some clues as to why. Previously, he'd almost lost his business. That had made a lasting impression on him. So he spent ages devising strategies that made him a key player in any deal.

Blinded by the wondrous upside in the project, I'd not done my homework. There was no precise set of rules in the shareholders' agreement. This was a hard introduction to the real world. I'd fallen for the 'we're all friends here' line. This experience didn't put me off partners, but made me re-think how to select them and what rules to play by.

So, there's a massive caveat. Bringing a partner on board will only be successful if you are the type of individual who can work effectively with a partner. Are you really going to accept your partner and bring them into the fold? Not feel threatened? Not be competitive? Not undermine your partner at every opportunity? Are you going to be able to leave the partner to make decisions and get on with things? Will you accept their inevitable mistakes? I have seen many businesses where a partner was brought in only to have the original partner ride roughshod over the new guy, with disastrous – and sometimes fatal – results for the business.

Still convinced you should have a partner? If you are, now you pretty much know the type of person you're looking for. The next question is, where will you find one?

Who are the best and, especially, where are they?

A phone directory won't help here, so you're going to need to do some research, begin networking, keep alert to opportunities and use your nose to sniff out likely individuals. At some stage, you'll have to take an instinctive leap. You might find a partner using these ideas:

- Ask your lawyers and accountants for introductions.
- Seek out people who have established their own businesses and either sold them or been unsuccessful (although not too often!).
- Look out for people who have fallen out with their previous partner (although, again, not too often!).
- Check out networking events.
- Sound out competitors (who might offer the opportunity to put the two businesses together).
- Run an advertisement in the financial press seeking a business partner.
- Your friends might have suggestions so ask them.

Once you think you've found the right person, check the potential partner's previous dealings – at Dun & Bradstreet, Hoovers, Companies House, other credit-checking agencies. Ultimately, you're going to have to make your choice and take a calculated risk. Now, if you're like me, you're probably still nervous about bringing in the wrong partner and giving away control and profits to someone who turns out to be a lying, cheating, buffoon. Don't worry. Just read on.

Sealing the deal

You're excited – you've found a potential partner. But, how can
you be sure they'll be any good in the heat of battle? A subtle
test is to ask who's selling to whom? The new partner must sell
himself to you. You've already sold him the company vision.

It's important not to rush into anything, especially if you're at a
low ebb – a particularly dangerous time. Hold your nerve. Back
yourself. Still, it's an almost impossible decision to make, right?
Relax. It's actually not as tough as you think. There's one device that
will ensure that you get the right partner: the use of a trial period.

Before I became a partner in my property company, I agreed to
work in the business for six months. I was prepared to do this
as I knew that I would be able to prove my worth and it also
protected me in that I could ensure that I would be able to work
with my partner. The key here is ensuring that both sides have
a very clear understanding of what the deal
will be if both sides are keen to progress at the
conclusion of the trial period. The deal is agreed
but not crystallised.

**Trial inconclusive?
The partner walks.
It'll cost you, but it's
worth every penny**

You'll obviously need to convince your new
potential partner that you're not simply trying
to use them for a period of six months. Once your partner has
completed the trial period and come on board, then you must
embrace them fully and give them space and freedom. If at the
end of the trial period you have concerns about your partner, then
do not bring them into the business. You may have to pay them a
substantial fee but it's worth every penny.

Sealing the deal with a partner could not be more different to
sealing the deal with an employee or supplier. Sealing the deal
with a partner is actually a test for both of you – it's all about
ensuring that both sides are satisfied with the deal structure and
understand the 'rules of the game', which must include protection
for both sides.

You will need to thrash out a shareholders' agreement with your new partner. This will set out the rights and responsibilities of both of you and is critical to avoid misunderstandings or arguments at a later stage. This is also a good test of your partner. If the two of you can't agree on the elements of the shareholder agreement then you've no hope of working together.

If you can't finalise the shareholder agreement, you've no hope of working together

Your lawyer will be able to discuss this in detail with you, but you must make sure that you have workable solutions to the following questions:

- **Who gets what?** If you give away too much equity now, you will likely regret the decision later and begin to resent your partner. But if you give your partner too little, they may come to resent you and feel that they are being poorly rewarded for their contribution to the growth of the business.

  You will only be able to maximise the effectiveness of the partnership if both sides feel they are being sufficiently compensated to justify giving every ounce of energy they have to making the business a success. This needs careful thought. The only rule I would give is that you should not give away control (i.e. own less than 50% of the shares).

- **How much will you both be paid in salaries?** Agree a reasonable sum and then stick to this. You both should be getting rich through dividends and the ultimate sale of the business, not your salaries.

- **What is the expense policy?** Only business expenses should be payable. Be very clear about what constitutes a business expense. Always provide for the finance person to administer this.

- **What is the dividend policy?** When will dividends be paid? While maintaining sufficient funds in the business to ensure that it can meet its obligations and grow, partners will often

agree to pay out the maximum possible in dividends, subject
to the point below.

■ **What types of business will be invested in?** Agree whether
you will reinvest profits into the existing business, invest in
new businesses, take profits as dividends or a combination of
each. Be very specific about which types of business can be
invested in. Typically you want to keep them closely related to
what you are doing.

■ **What other deals can partners work on
independently?** You must have a clear
understanding about what deals outside of
the core business each of you can be involved
in. It can be very damaging to the business if
a partner spends a lot of time on other deals.
A good practice is to require each deal to be
first presented to the other partner.

**Who can work
on which deals
independently? It's
contentious – but
vital – to agree this**

■ **What protections do you both have?** It is critical that
you ensure that you have sufficient protection should the
relationship sour. The legal agreement that you negotiate will
be vital in protecting your interests to a large degree. You also
need to be aware of the broader protections automatically
provided by the law for both sides. These protections imply
restrictions for both parties. If you hold less than 50% of the
shares, then you are a minority shareholder and you're going to
need to make sure that your interests are carefully protected.
Having less than 50% of the shares will mean that you won't
have day-to-day control. If it is the intention that day-to-day
control is to be shared, then make sure that your lawyer puts
appropriate provisions in the agreement

■ **Under what circumstances can I buy my partner out?** It is
impossible to see the future and so you must make sure that
you are adequately protected in those circumstances of death,
disability or relocation of your partner. You don't want them

to suddenly sell their share of the business to a third party you don't want to work with. A buy-out clause – at market rates and after a minimum period – will ensure you have the first right of refusal to buy your partner out.

If things go wrong, you might have all sorts of rights to remove or penalise your partner. But, in doing so, you might destroy the business. Make sure the clause is fair, and then move on. Better still, if you have concerns about the integrity of your partner, it is far better simply not to do the deal. Go with your gut instincts.

After six months, you're in it together – common problems, common solutions. Now how do you keep your partner motivated?

Partners: Honest toilers – leave them alone

You don't 'manage' partners, like employees, and you shouldn't try. You brought the partner in for their skills. Now you must give them the opportunity to deploy those skills. Don't second-guess and don't undermine. Give them the freedom they need to make a real contribution. You must make them feel comfortable at all times, including during the trial period when they are likely to feel the least settled.

> **You don't manage partners – you work with them**

Bearing this overarching philosophy in mind, there are two other important points to make about 'managing' a partner.

A business partnership is not the same as a friendship. Of course, every relationship is easier if you have a good rapport and it's important that you and your partner have a good working relationship. But you don't need to be best friends and socialise together. Some of the most successful partnerships I have seen involve two people with very different personalities who rarely socialise outside the office. Yet they have complementary skills and each has a great respect for the abilities of the other.

In every partnership there will be times when one partner makes a poor decision or error of judgement. You must be able to let these slide. There is nothing to be gained from ranting and raving. Both of you should review the reasons for the failure, learn from it and move on. You must never resent your partner. Accept that some mistakes are inevitable – even the ones made by you, dare I say it!

But what if those mistakes keep piling up, or your partner loses it?

The production line halts: Stepping stones

I began our discussion about business partners with the warning that bringing a partner into a business is like an engagement and then, after your six-month trial period, a marriage. It should be viewed as something you intend to respect for the rest of your life. If the relationship unravels, it can be extremely messy and expensive.

Pause and take a deep breath. Good partners are hard to find

Nevertheless, relationships can run their natural course. You may find that your partner is no longer as committed to the business as in the early days for a whole host of personal and professional reasons. Alternatively, you and your partner may have quite different views on where the next phase of growth for the business will come from. In the worst case, the relationship may have soured so much that you simply do not want to work with your partner any longer.

My advice is that you first pause and take a deep breath. You need to consider such a situation free of emotion. If the relationship is under pressure because the other side feels that they are not being adequately rewarded for their efforts, then look to buy them out. Look at the buyout clause in the contract, but remember: be generous because, believe me, it is best to avoid a long drawn-out legal battle.

The last word

Scaling a business is difficult. It can't be done without substantial assistance. Four in five businesses fail this test. You won't because you now know how to find the most appropriate employees and suppliers, how to keep them loyal, highly motivated and productive. Critically, you know when they need to be changed. You also know if and when a partner becomes critical to your success. Furthermore, you understand the rules of engagement with a partner, guaranteeing you work seamlessly together. In short, you know how to get the right help at the right time at the right price, to ensure you power forward. As you scale your peaks, you need to be able to use your brand as a weapon. Let's learn how to do that. The battle is ours for the taking

Dos and don'ts

1. **DO** look beyond traditional CVs when hiring. You're looking for entrepreneurial drive and street smarts.
2. **DON'T** rely on traditional labour sources and be constantly on a recruitment drive. Introductions, trade shows, competitors and plain chance come into play.
3. **DO** offer incentive-based financial packages that can beat the competition. You've got to motivate employees through opportunity and excitement at joining you.
4. **DO** manage employees by demonstrating leadership – downplay setbacks, celebrate success, take a personal interest in staff, be vigilant in review and weed out the disruptive/poorly performing.
5. **DO** use these criteria for identifying the right supplier: small, trustworthy, needy, close to you.

6. **DON'T** pay suppliers a penny more than you need to. Cut a deal where they make their money as your business grows – not right from the start.

7. **DO** constantly review suppliers' performance. Put contracts out to tender every twelve months – or maybe even six.

8. **DO** find a partner with ability that can't be found among suppliers or employees. Ensure they're trustworthy, resilient and able to make things happen.

9. **DON'T** court partners. The new partner should sell to you after you've explained your vision, not vice versa.

10. **DO** insist on a six-month trial period for partners. Thrash out the key terms of your agreement – drawings, salary, expenses, working on independent projects.

11. **DON'T** try to manage a partner. Trust them to deliver.

12. **DON'T** undermine or run roughshod over your partner. If you can't work with a partner, don't have one.

PART THREE
FLOG IT

CHAPTER EIGHT **BUILDING A VALUABLE BRAND: SURVIVAL, DEVELOPMENT, 'DIVORCE'**

Brands are an important influence on our lives. They are central to free markets and democratic societies. They represent free choice … they reflect the values of our societies. Mega-brands … can even embody the spirit of many nations, if not the spirit of an age ..

— From www.interbrand.com

Your brand and survival

The pressure on today's companies to have a brand is overwhelming. The brand gurus at agencies like Interbrand argue that only strong brands survive.

You'll build and use the brand as a weapon in the sale process – but not at the expense of survival

The media preach the virtues of branding – often without actually having a true understanding of what it involves. A strong brand is viewed as synonymous with unbridled success. It is a panacea for all a company's woes. Only companies with weak brands are destined for the scrap heap.

But is that really the case? This chapter will help you understand and build a brand, and use that brand as a tool in the sales process – but not at the expense of building your business.

Let's start with the kind of cautionary tale that's meat and drink to the branding experts (who shouldn't get too much – if any – of your money, by the way).

A case of premature branding

Rocket, as you may recall, was a business that I became involved with after leaving Virgin. Rocket offered time-poor professionals ready meals that were made from high-quality fresh ingredients. The idea was that it would be possible to get the meal from packet to plate in six minutes.

Rocket chose to focus on its brand development from day one. My goodness, the level of detail was overwhelming – branding agencies, a fancy brand document, point-of-sales materials, elaborate print campaigns, development of colour schemes, logos, uniforms … you name it, they spent money on it. Hundreds of thousands of pounds were spent on materials and design before a single sale was made.

Rocket was crippled by its brand obsession

The only thing the company wasn't spending sufficient money on was survival. The management team didn't understand how to generate sales. So while Rocket won praise for the look and layout of their stores and the well-dressed staff, sales remained shockingly low. The business was going under at a rate of knots.

Realising that there was no time to be lost, I began developing plans to ensure the business could survive. But when I raced in with the blueprints, a huge debate with the management ensued about whether these ideas were consistent with the brand strategy. The business was haemorrhaging cash and going nowhere, yet the management's main concern was that we didn't contradict any of the brand attributes that they had spent so much money on.

Inaction is the death knell for any start-up business, and Rocket was crippled by its brand obsession. The obvious truth was that the brand was defined too early, before the team knew what the key elements were that would drive revenue. The fact was that they had not spent enough time on working out how to convince customers to buy their product. Rocket's management team did eventually come to its senses, but not before it had wasted a huge amount of time, effort and money. If its parent, Unilever, had not had such deep pockets, Rocket would have crashed and burned.

During the dot-com boom I was approached by a venture capital investor to see if I would be interested in taking a senior position (a very lucrative one, I might add) at Boo.com.

Boo.com – a classic case of style over substance. It crashed and burned

The chief executive of the business was proudly proclaiming that 'with a marketing and PR spend of only $22.4 million, we have managed to create a worldwide brand'. My instincts were to immediately say no to the job offer – the business seemed like a classic case of style over substance. As it turned out, my instincts were right – the veneer of the brand covered a fundamentally flawed business model. By the time Boo.com went under, more than $130 million of investors' money had been spent and the Boo.com name and images were sold for just £250,000.

There are countless other examples like Rocket and Boo.com where businesses have put brand (or at least their understanding of brand) before commercial business. Too many start-up companies are led to believe that 'brand' is a panacea for all the issues that the business will face. I'm dismayed and outraged by the so-called brand experts who hire stalls at start-up exhibitions and insist that it's vital for would-be business-builders to spend thousands of pounds on a brand they just don't need. I can't tell you how many times I have been frustrated by aspiring entrepreneurs telling me that they could launch their business if they could just raise, let's say, £250,000 to establish and build the brand.

Sales – not branding – are the imperative in business-building. Successful entrepreneurs know that a brand is no good without sales. The new business's initial efforts must be focused on driving sales and meeting customers' expectations. As sales increase, the

brand becomes established. If customers buy the product and
are satisfied with it, they will encourage others to buy too.
At the end of the day, a brand is nothing more than a promise
that is consistently delivered. Just like the culture within
a business, you will always have a brand. It is an inherent
philosophy. It's either rubbish or it's good. Either way, it's led
by your customers' experience of your business, and will take
time to develop, change and evolve.

But before you jump in your car to go and protest outside the
office of your local branding agency, let's look back on some of
the experiences I've outlined in the foregoing chapters.

I remember sitting in a Mayfair bar sipping vintage champagne
and celebrating the successful securing of a 50% investment
in Virgin Direct by joint venture partner AMP, the Australian
financial services group, for £900 million. And why did AMP
invest £900 million? They wanted permission to use Virgin's
brand. So, in practice, all Virgin brought to the Virgin Direct
venture was its name.

The deal wasn't easy. It took seven months and an armoury of
negotiation skills and tactics to pull it off (see chapter 4). The truth is
that it would have been impossible to achieve without the attraction
of the Virgin brand. The first meeting involved me
clutching a signed copy of Richard Branson's book
extolling the virtues of the Virgin brand.

**AMP invested £900
million essentially
for a brand!**

But wait a second, I can almost hear your cry.
Just a brand? Did I not just state in black and
white that a start-up must avoid the pitfalls of
investing in brands like the plague, yet here is an example of a
brand generating hundreds of millions of pounds' worth of value?
Haven't I just contradicted myself? Actually I haven't. Brands
do have value – there, I've said it! Listen, I was the new business
director for Virgin and lived and breathed one of the world's
strongest brands, spending years selling that brand for as much as
I could at every opportunity.

My concern is that you will be sucked in by the slick marketers who will encourage you to waste a huge amount of money, time and effort trying to build a global brand from day one. That's the surest route to a failed business. There's a time for brand investment and the building blocks that don't require significant investment should be put in place from the start. Smart entrepreneurs know a strong brand can add significant value to a business on sale – provided the business is making money, of course. I want you to have your cake and eat it. So, the trick is to create a brand with minimal investment.

To ensure you survive, prosper and ultimately end up with a strong brand, I am going to share direct insights from one of the most successful brands of the past thirty years – Virgin.

Understanding the role of your brand

This will dispel some of the most popular myths about branding. I am going to take you right inside Virgin to get behind the hype and mythology to show you how it really was. I want you to have a concrete understanding of the role of brands in start-ups, all distilled into practical lessons based on the way it actually is in the real world.

Virgin's history dispels the myths behind start-ups and brands

Inside the Virgin brand

In 1995, I was plucked from relative obscurity as a management consultant at McKinsey to become the group corporate development director for Virgin. My brief was to work closely with Richard Branson to shape one of the UK's strongest brands. Indeed, so closely would I be working with Richard that I was to be based in a room at his own house.

Richard's brief to me was clear: find new business start-up opportunities and secure the best possible deal for the Virgin Group.

I had the use of the Virgin brand and the rest was up to me. It was an exciting time, as Richard was looking to expand the group into as many new businesses as made commercial sense. The more successful deals I could conclude, the better. This was an ideal opportunity for me as my ambition was to start and run my own business one day. What better way to continue my training (and understand the role of brands in start-ups) than to learn at Virgin? Here I was on the inside, working with one of the most respected entrepreneurs in the world, and with responsibility for taking one of the strongest brands in the UK into new areas of business.

Theory told me that all companies with strong brands would have detailed brand materials that explained and set out the rigid rules that would protect the company's crown jewels. Indeed, that's how they got to have a strong brand in the first place. At any rate, I needed evidence of the strength of the Virgin brand to negotiate the best possible deals for Richard.

Virgin, one of the world's most successful brands, didn't even have a briefing note!

I approached all the business units within Virgin to gather up any documentation that they might have about the brand. (As you'll recall, the ready-made meals business, Rocket, drew up an incredibly detailed (and expensive) brand book before it had even sold a shepherd's pie.) Richard and the heads of Virgin's business units were bemused by my request. Virgin, arguably one of the most successful brands of the past four decades, didn't have a brand book. Not even a one-sheet briefing note! They had more notes on the staff roster than they had on the company's single most valuable asset.

I thought this was rather curious. My real-world introduction to brands and how they are applied to start-ups had begun in earnest. It was time to roll up my sleeves.

I was wondering how I was going to communicate the value of Virgin's brand to the potential business partners from whom I was trying to prise large piles of cash for the use of the Virgin name without any documentation. I decided that I would find out about the brand's evolution and prepare a summary. A presentation that could be tossed onto the boardroom table during negotiations would be useful. I found Richard's explanations of the history of the evolution of his businesses and the role of the Virgin brand compellingly insightful and could see that it was the perfect example of the role that a brand should play in a start-up.

So let me take you through my journey.

Virgins in business

As most people know, Richard began his entrepreneurial life with the launch of a student magazine. During this period, he was also a prominent figure in anti-war demonstrations. Richard's attendance at these events was certainly driven by his convictions but they also served perfectly to raise his profile and provided excellent PR for the magazine – something that was not lost on Richard.

Richard's next venture involved importing records from Belgium. This was his first foray into music and fitted nicely with the customers he understood so well from his student magazine. Music was also cool, fun and potentially irreverent – much like the student magazine.

Richard's instinctive genius told him he needed a single name for his business ventures

---

The Virgin name was not born until 1970, when Richard set up a mail order record retailer. Not long afterwards, he opened a record shop in Oxford Street, London.

Richard is the first to admit that Virgin was not a brand that was carefully planned and documented. Indeed, even Richard can't quite remember exactly when or how the name came to be used, although more than one person has claimed credit for it. The story goes that the name came from a discussion where they referred to themselves as 'virgins in business'. Even though Richard did not set out immediately to create a brand or even understand exactly what brand attributes were, his instincts told him that it would be a good idea to have a single name for his business ventures. He had a vision. But he didn't know what the brand would look like or even what to call it. And he certainly didn't think that the name might be applied to an airline, trains and hot air balloons. He simply wanted all his hard work and goodwill to begin to accumulate around a single name. After that he could try to ensure that his business ventures actually worked.

So here's a simple lesson on brand-building. When you start the process, pick a name and business logo that suits you and your company. The name and logo should be distinctive, be able to grow with the business, accumulate goodwill and build brand identity. This can be done for almost no money. But that's it. Remember that this is not the same as investing heavily and building a detailed book on brand attributes that will suffocate growth.

But let's get back to Richard Branson, who's still in the foothills of building on of the world's greatest brands.

Getting to number one: A hit and miss business

Richard soon realised that record stores didn't make spectacular amounts of money. Finances were still a little rocky and he was eyeing, with some jealousy, the money he perceived that the record labels made. So, in 1972 Richard built a recording studio and launched his own record label. Richard was pursuing first and foremost a business opportunity but he was also deepening the perception of the Virgin brand as being fun and cool.

The established record labels may have been making a lot of money, but that didn't mean it was easy for a newcomer to break into the industry. It was harder than Richard thought. He struggled to sign up his first acts. Eventually he stumbled upon Mike Oldfield, who had approached (and been rejected by) many other established record labels before arriving at Virgin Records. Richard was desperate to sign up his first act and Oldfield was desperate to release an album.

Tubular Bells *was rejected by every other major record label – it sold 15 million copies!*

There are those who might like to believe that Richard was a visionary who had observed a mood swing in England at the beginning of the 1970s that saw an increasingly disaffected youth keen to assert their opposition to the 'establishment' through music, but I can assure you that the decision to sign Oldfield was driven purely by business survival.

Oldfield's *Tubular Bells* became Virgin's first record release. At the time, the album was quite unusual. Oldfield played most of the instruments on the album, recording them individually and then layering them to compose the pieces. Despite the unusual nature of the album and the combined wisdom of the A&R managers at the major labels who believed the album would flop, *Tubular Bells* became a phenomenon. The album stayed in the British charts for more than five years. It sold more than 2 million copies in the UK alone and an estimated 15 million copies worldwide. Part of this success was no doubt due to the use of the opening theme from the album in the movie *The Exorcist*, which itself was also highly controversial. Let's face it, all start-ups need a lucky break.

Tubular Bells was a spectacular success but no record label can survive on one hit alone. It was not long before money became tight again and Richard was forced to set about cutting costs at the record label. Once again, Richard was desperate to find a new act that would ensure the survival of the record label, so it was with some relief that Richard signed the Sex Pistols in 1977, a band previously dropped as too anarchic by well-known labels EMI and A&M.

Richard lamented the tortuous negotiations with Malcolm McLaren, but he had to roll the dice . . . there were bills to be paid, a label to be made. The band immediately released the single 'God Save the Queen'. The record reached number two and was banned by the BBC.

McLaren was a nightmare, but the Sex Pistols saved the day

What a coup! Richard's reputation as an anti-establishment 'rebel entrepreneur' had been growing but this now sealed it. Some wondered whether this was all part of a carefully orchestrated plan. Absolutely not. Richard didn't set out to be a rebel entrepreneur. He just wanted to be a successful entrepreneur!

He was, simply, desperate to survive. There was no great plan of image or brand design. He had signed Mike Oldfield and the Sex Pistols because he was struggling to fill his stable of bands, saw an opportunity and believed he could make some money – that simple.

The second moral in our brand story is this: start-ups must concern themselves with survival above all else. Brand should never dictate the product or opportunity. Find an opportunity and build an advantage. In the early days, let the brand take care of itself.

Let's fast forward to the end of the 1970s, when Virgin had been trading for more than a decade.

An emerging identity

Over this time, whether Richard and Virgin liked it or not, three lynchpins of the Virgin brand had begun to emerge: 'anti-establishment', 'fun' and 'irreverence'. Richard had never made a conscious decision that the brand would encapsulate these values; he had simply capitalised on business opportunities and had delivered a customer experience that reflected these qualities.

At this time, Richard and the Virgin brand were almost indistinguishable. His lifestyle, actions and the regular 'stunts' he performed exemplified the brand in every way. Richard's unique gift in understanding that PR was the best way to promote his companies was legendary, even in those days. He never let an opportunity pass him by. Some critics suggested that it was a case of style over substance, but they couldn't have been more wrong. No business survives and prospers if it doesn't meet customers' expectations over the long term.

When the BBC banned 'God Save The Queen', Richard seized a golden PR opportunity

A great example of Richard's unique understanding of the importance of PR was the launch of Virgin Bride. I remember sitting in the back of a cab with Richard's wife and several members of the senior management team about a month before the launch. Richard's wife was pleading with me to talk some sense into Richard and convince him that dressing himself up as a bride on launch day was a ridiculous idea that would be personally embarrassing and potentially undermine the credibility of the new business.

But there was no dissuading Richard. On the day of the launch, Richard was standing on a podium in central London dressed up in a top-of-the-line Virgin wedding dress surrounded by the world's press. The stunt was reported as a leading news item around the globe and Virgin Bride received millions of pounds of free publicity. Virgin Bride was ultimately one of Virgin's less successful businesses, but Richard's stunt at the launch of the business was a perfect example of how to promote a brand.

There are countless other examples of Richard's bravado and daredevil stunts earning Virgin millions of pounds of free publicity. Richard tried anything from throwing Ivana Trump into a swimming pool to using Melinda Messenger (a former Page 3 model and winner of the prestigious 'Rear of the Year Award') to launch Virgin Trains.

One stunt I particularly liked was Richard's recruitment of a good female friend of mine, Freya Swane, to infiltrate British Airways' press conferences.

Richard stood on a podium in a wedding dress – and got millions in free publicity around the globe

---

My friend would arrive looking very demure in a fashionable overcoat, only to disrobe during the press conference to reveal red and white clothing plastered with the Virgin logo. She would then be promptly escorted out, but not before stealing some of the thunder of the event and always ensuring a reference to Virgin in the press coverage.

So, here's another lesson from the Virgin story: as your business begins to establish its brand values, you must use them to your advantage to grow the business. Nothing will build brand awareness and credibility faster and more cost-effectively than PR (see chapter 3).

After the Sex Pistols, Richard was on a roll. The Virgin brand became a magnet for anti-establishment bands such as Human League, Culture Club and Simple Minds. The record shop chain was also expanding rapidly. And then, in 1984, to the amazement of outsiders and the horror of his fellow directors, Richard announced he was launching an airline . . .

Onwards and upwards!

Virgin had developed a strong brand in the music industry but it was a rather large stretch to suddenly enter the aviation industry. However, Richard had identified a clear business opportunity. Surely he could leverage the existing attributes of the Virgin brand – and, boy, what great PR, to own an airline!

Richard's business brain had observed both that air travel for business was booming and that it was forecast to continue to grow, and also that the routes from the UK to the USA and Hong Kong were particularly popular and growing rapidly.

Richard played a David versus Goliath PR game – and Virgin Atlantic succeeded because it delivered

He believed that many business travellers desperately wanted to travel first class but were only permitted to travel business class by their employers. His ingenious solution was to offer 'first-class service at a business-class price'.

As Richard rolled out this customer proposition for the new airline, he played on the brand lynchpins that his music ventures had established. He presented his fight with British Airways as a David and Goliath battle with the brash newcomer taking on the stuffy establishment that was ripping off travellers. The fact that British Airways was found guilty of a 'dirty tricks campaign' – something that nearly ruined Virgin Atlantic – only served to reinforce this perception. It turned into a PR godsend, gaining Virgin the sympathy of the masses. It made the brand legendary.

In addition, Richard made sure that Virgin Atlantic was perceived as a fun way to fly by ensuring that the Virgin cabin crews were young, outgoing and friendly, and by the introduction of little touches like handing out ice-creams during the flight.

Behind every successful brand, there's a great, well-executed business idea

So Virgin Atlantic was 'anti-establishment', 'fun' and 'cheeky', but the core of the proposition – and the reason it was able to take on British Airways so effectively – was the fact that Upper Class represented such excellent value for money. Richard had to be true to his existing brand values but he was able to provide a price element that was attractive to customers. Richard did not deliberately set out to craft a fourth cornerstone to the Virgin brand when he launched the airline – he simply saw a very clever way to steal a march on the established airlines and to carve out a successful business. Nevertheless, Virgin was now viewed as a consumer champion, a business that would shake up the cosy world of the established corporate and deliver 'superior service at a lower cost'.

There are two morals to draw from this tale. The first is that behind every successful brand, there's a great, well-executed business idea. The second is that once a brand has been established, you must be true to its cornerstone values and only make changes that are consistent with them.

Virgin was starting to mushroom. It had many businesses and thousands of employees. Richard had to make sense of all of this.

Living the dream

When Richard began to realise the value of the Virgin brand, the need to meet customer expectations became a fixation. He knew that if Virgin disappointed its customers in any one of its business ventures, then it would affect the value of the brand. Richard did not believe in brand books (I doubt he knew the term), but he did believe passionately that, in order to protect the brand, the whole company had to live and breathe it at all times. This became increasingly difficult as Virgin grew in the UK and around the world.

To protect your brand, the company has to live and breathe it

Richard developed his own approach to achieve this. He always sought to foster a culture that was dynamic and entrepreneurial, giving all of the Virgin businesses a feeling that they were exciting start-ups even when they were well established. He also ensured that all the businesses were extremely careful about who they hired. He wanted every staff member to personify the brand. He took what appeared to others – but not to Richard – to be a risk in hiring unconventional employees. He was interested in the employees' attitude. Did it fit the brand? Attitude plus basic competence were all Richard required.

He also sought to foster a strong camaraderie among staff by regularly hosting parties and fun events. He developed the mantra: 'Praise, praise – never criticise'. The parties that were hosted by Virgin Atlantic at Oxford Place were legendary ... my headaches after these events were testament to that!

And the moral in this tale? Simple: you must find ways to ensure that your company lives and breathes the brand – through yourself and your employees.

I now understood the Virgin brand and what it stood for. Richard and I agreed that the Virgin brand had four key attributes:

1. Fun/irreverence (what's the point if no-one's having fun?).
2. Anti-establishment (become the consumer champion).
3. Excellent products and services (exceptional customer experience).
4. Value for money (first-class service at business-class prices).

I put together a new presentation (my version of a brand book) describing the Virgin brand. The title might have been 'Virgin is the best brand in the world ... by far'. Now that I had this selling document, it was time to get out into the market and begin using it to secure all those new deals I had been recruited to find. But I soon realised that there were more key lessons to learn. My apprenticeship was not over yet.

Rags without riches

One of the new businesses that Richard and I were keen on was Virgin Clothes. Unfortunately, this was an idea which struggled from the outset and which ultimately failed. It always seemed like we were trying to force an industry on a brand. We struggled on nevertheless.

Virgin Clothes demonstrates that even a strong brand is no guarantee of success

But why did it fail? Perhaps with hindsight it was obvious. Let's begin by taking a look at the clothing industry and consider how Virgin Clothes fitted in. Fashion generally falls into one or a combination of four categories:

1. **Hip and funky:** Think of Diesel clothing. The Virgin brand was too well known and mainstream to have any street credibility.

2. **Catwalk:** Richard may have held a share in Storm Modelling Agency but the Virgin brand was hardly synonymous with glamour.

3. **Designer-led:** Unfortunately, Virgin didn't have a visionary designer at its helm. Designer clothing would also hardly fit with Virgin's reputation for providing excellent value for money.

4. **Low cost:** Virgin offered its customers value for money, but was never going to be a 'pile 'em high and sell 'em cheap' retailer. We couldn't and didn't want to compete with Tesco's pair of jeans for £3.

So, without a clear fashion segment to target, we tried to market Virgin Clothes with, amongst other things, images of Richard in fluffy jumpers.

The business flopped, because the market was hugely competitive and there was no clear market gap for the Virgin brand to exploit. We had tried to rely on the awareness of the brand alone.

Every time we brought a clothing industry expert in to advise us on what was going wrong, we found that we could not action their recommendations because we came up against the restraints of the brand.

> *Failure is branding catastrophe. Late trains?*
> *Not the Virgin experience!*
>
> As Virgin Clothes demonstrated, a brand (even a strong one) is not
> a cast iron guarantee of success. Indeed, the Virgin brand effectively
> restricted the opportunities for Virgin Clothes to change its customer
> proposition.

Virgin Clothes was not the only Virgin business that had suffered
because of attempts to force products to fit the Virgin brand.
Virgin Vodka was another good example of a business that failed.
It failed because there was very little scope for Virgin to deliver
something new and different. Virgin could not deliver the 'anti-
establishment', 'fun', 'value for money' product with excellent
service that people associated with the brand. It was simply
another bottle of vodka sitting on the shelf at the
off-licence. For the very same reason I was never
a fan of Virgin Cola.

**The opportunity
must fit the brand**

The moral of this narrative? See whether an
opportunity fits your brand. Don't see whether
the brand can be manipulated or massaged to fit the opportunity.
It will be like a straitjacket, constricting the flexibility so essential
to your start-up. If the opportunity doesn't fit, do not – repeat,
do *not* – pursue it. This is a re-working of an earlier moral.
Start-ups must be free to choose their own course.

Next stop: Virgin Trains. When Richard bought his train set,
the funders demanded that the trains be immediately re-branded
'Virgin' …

Late pulling out of the station

Failure has a catastrophic effect on brands. I remember walking into Richard's office one day and seeing mountains of paper, which turned out to be complaints from customers of Virgin Trains. Virgin Trains was no worse than its competitors at the time, but customers had such high expectations of the Virgin brand that they were disappointed when we failed to deliver something better. Virgin Trains had launched amid a fanfare of talk about high-speed tilting trains, luxury seating, a return to the classic days of rail travel.

The problem was that these things would take time to implement – some four to five years in fact. But customers expected their very first ride on the train to deliver the trademark Virgin experience. When it didn't, they wrote to Richard and he rapidly became only too aware that if customers were disappointed, then there was a risk of undermining the Virgin brand. The improvements to Virgin Trains had to be made as fast as possible in order to avoid this. In the meantime, there was a frenzied rush to implement some short-term improvements. But there was no denying the message from dissatisfied customers. It was clear that Virgin had lost them, possibly for ever.

The moral here? Once you have a developed brand, customers will have very specific expectations of your products and services. Disappoint them, and the consequences will be lost customers – and plenty of them.

Virgin Active fitted the brand perfectly – sales were turbocharged!

Undeterred by these setbacks, we continued to look for new ways to exploit the Virgin brand. Virgin Active was a great example of a success.

Reinforcing the cornerstones

Virgin Active offered a new take on the traditional gym. It offered a friendly, more fun environment than the traditional cold and often intimidating gyms. It was a social environment rather than just a place to work out. It also offered excellent customer service at a price that was highly attractive when compared with the larger chains, which often left members feeling like just another body crammed into an aerobics class.

Everything Virgin Active offered its members reinforced the cornerstones of the Virgin brand, from the giant toothbrush waterfall for children to the library and chill-out area. Our expectations were high; pre-sales good. And on opening, all our hopes were realised. The place had a real buzz and demand high; Virgin Active was turbocharged. In fact, not only did Virgin Active 'fit' with the Virgin brand, it was able to actually add credibility to it. Today, it ranks amongst the world's largest gym chains.

The lesson was fairly obvious: when a business opportunity and a brand are perfectly matched, when there is freedom to innovate, and when customers' expectations are met, you will be successful much faster, with less risk – and the brand image will be enhanced. Secondly, a strong brand provides great leverage when negotiating financial deals, particularly the price achievable when selling a business.

£50 million for a business plan – oh, and the brand!

A big part of my role was to negotiate major deals for Virgin. Richard and I both knew that the stature of the Virgin brand provided leverage in negotiating deals and sourcing funds. Just how much leverage it could provide was my job to find out and I intended to push the boundaries as far as possible. Indeed, I was the first person at Virgin to suggest that our goal on every negotiation should be to take 50% of the business in return for use of the Virgin name alone. The theory was sound – but I didn't know if it would work in practice. Then came the AMP deal ...

Deal heaven

The deal with AMP, where they provided the vast majority of funds in return for a 50% stake in the Virgin Direct joint venture, is a perfect example of how to exploit a brand. It demonstrated just how powerful a strong brand can be in securing the best possible price – £900 million to be exact. Virgin Direct was not the only the example of the Virgin brand proving invaluable at the negotiating table. I also managed to raise funding of more than £50 million on the back of little more than a business plan for both Virgin Clothes and Virgin Vie.

Would it be the same when we came to sell off businesses? Once again the theory suggested that it would. A strong brand should lead to customer loyalty, which in turn should mean consistent sales and expanding profits. Once again the theory was borne out in practice with Virgin One and Virgin Atlantic.

The Virgin One deal allowed Royal Bank of Scotland to use the Virgin name for just one year. This meant that the pricing of the deal was quite mechanical and based purely on the number of customers that we had at the time. There was no premium paid for the goodwill associated with the brand. In 1999, Virgin sold a 49% stake in Virgin Atlantic to Singapore Airlines for £550 million. This was an exceptional price given that the business only recorded profits of about £50 million (adjusted for sale costs) in the year to March 2000. Clearly Singapore Airlines was prepared to pay a significant premium due to the strength of the Virgin brand.

The resulting moral: a strong brand provides great leverage in any price negotiation.

The strength of Richard's personal brand was a real Achilles heel

There was, however, one key issue that was always raised whether I was raising funds or selling a business, and that was the strength of Richard's personal brand. Everyone wanted to know what Richard's involvement with the business would be going forward. The same questions were asked: Can I meet Richard? Will Richard do the PR for the business personally? Can Richard be the chairman of the business?

It was a real Achilles heel. We had to accept that Richard could only be in one place at a time. This led Richard to begin a concerted campaign to try to reduce his personal profile and to focus on the Virgin brand. Richard tried to do this by recruiting high-profile spokespeople like Will Whitehorn and encouraging them to assume higher profiles with the press. The senior management of the various businesses also found themselves more in the limelight. However, he would be the first to admit that he has only enjoyed limited success in actually achieving this objective – today, Richard Branson remains synonymous with the Virgin brand. The reality has been that without ongoing involvement from Richard, businesses have been sold for lower prices. But let's not feel too sorry for Richard – he is, after all, a billionaire!

To me, the above demonstrates the lesson that a strong brand will always create value on the sale of a business. But to achieve the maximum possible sale price, the brand must be distinct from the personality of its creator.

You now have an insight into branding from my own experience inside one of the world's strongest brands. Next I needed to know whether the Virgin experience was truly applicable to all start-ups as I began to set out on my own ventures.

Some brand lessons are pretty much universally applicable

As mentioned earlier in this chapter, on leaving Virgin, I worked with Rocket. As part of the elaborate (and hugely expensive) branding exercise they went through prior to launch, I was introduced to one of the UK's leading branding agencies – 'Dave'. The guys at Dave impressed me immediately. They had a very entrepreneurial and practical view of branding. I wasn't surprised when I learned that they had been the team behind the Orange brand. I have since become good friends with them and seek their advice on every new business that I am involved with. Given their expertise and experience with Orange, I wanted to test what I had learnt at Virgin. Orange provided the perfect test as not only was it one of the most successful brand launches in recent years, but it was also a single product (and therefore more like start-ups) rather than the broad range of products that the Virgin brand had embraced. Everything the Dave team told me reinforced perfectly my own experiences at Virgin.

I think, as the next story demonstrates, the Virgin lessons are pretty much universally applicable.

Orange or Microtel? You choose ...

When Orange first sought help with their brand, they had recently secured the fourth mobile licence and were lagging well behind the other three carriers. The intention was to call the business Microtel. Hmm, doesn't exactly roll off the tongue, does it?

Our brand experts wasted no time in telling the management of Orange that it would be difficult to build an exciting brand identity around the name Microtel, and that, with so many companies already using either 'micro' or 'tel' in their name, there was a risk it would be lost in the corporate jungle with no clear identity.

After some careful thought, the branding team returned with a shortlist of potential names including Pecan, Gemini, Miro and Orange. The guys recommended Orange, believing it was catchy and wide enough to act as a veneer while the brand took shape.

Orange started with a catchy business name and a logo – nothing more

This was a bold leap of faith as consumer research had been overwhelmingly negative about the Orange name. It just demonstrates, once again, why it does not pay to leave the fortunes of your business to small focus groups of students and bored housewives sitting in a market research office in Slough.

So, Orange now had a catchy business name and a distinctive logo – but not much more than that. Orange was still little more than a concept. It had few subscribers, was losing money and was in a frantic race with the other players in the industry to sign up as many customers as it could. It was in survival mode and lacked any real point of differentiation. It desperately needed a unique selling point to lure customers away from its three bigger rivals. It was floundering as it struggled to define exactly what this unique selling point was. If it couldn't find something, then there was every chance that the business would eventually fail. There was clearly no point in detailed brand books. The veneer of a brand would suffice for now.

And then a eureka moment occurred.

Its researchers came up with a technical innovation that allowed Orange customers to get 'per-second billing'. You could almost hear the collective sigh of relief from the management. They hoped that customers would respond to this innovation but weren't absolutely sure. Today it is almost impossible to appreciate how radical Orange's innovation was.

The fear was palpable: would per-second billing save the day?

But the mobile phone market in 1994 was characterised by three-year contracts, high monthly rental fees, expensive call tariffs and little flexibility over the services on offer. The market was littered with high-tech jargon and complicated pricing. And Orange's competitors charged by the minute.

The fear was still there, how would customers react? The customer response to 'per-second billing' was phenomenal. By the end of 1995, Orange's customer base had more than doubled to 785,000 from 379,000 a year earlier. Orange had offered its customers a real benefit, and as the first mobile phone company to make such an offer, Orange grabbed an edge over its competitors while they all raced to copy the proposition.

But Orange did not rest on its laurels. It began to believe that it could really take the whole mobile phone market by storm. The management were also acutely aware that once its rivals launched similar products, they would lose their key advantage. So they went back to the drawing board and challenged themselves to come up with a new market-changing innovation. Once again their marketing department did not let them down – they came up with the idea of offering customers free handsets. Once again, this was truly revolutionary and again the market response was phenomenal, forcing its competitors onto the back foot.

Orange was by now beginning to stand for something – it was viewed as a consumer champion, innovative, challenging convention. Just like Virgin's most successful ventures, it was the business that was leading the brand. Just as important – it was substance over style. Orange was not simply making empty promises; it was delivering real value to its customers.

Orange could not (and did not) ignore its developing brand attributes. Quite the opposite. The team defined what the brand stood for and took advantage of these qualities, aggressively using them to grab market share. Orange embarked on a high-profile national advertising campaign with the memorable tag line: 'The future's bright ... the future's Orange'.

Orange brand loyalty was valuable – to the tune of £27 billion!

Orange was also a big believer in using PR and set about grabbing any opportunity it could in the media. All sound familiar? By taking advantage of its brand once it was established, Orange was doing exactly what Virgin had done.

Orange hoped that having a strong brand would have a positive impact on costs and top-line revenue growth. Orange customers were more loyal than its rivals' – of course, that is why brands are so valuable. And Orange customers spent more, as measured by the industry's all-important average revenue per unit (ARPU).

The real value of Orange's brand was demonstrated in May 2000 when France Telecom paid just under £27 billion for the mobile phone company. As a result of Orange's strong brand and high degree of customer loyalty, France Telecom paid twice as much per customer as Deutsche Telekom paid when it acquired the One-to-One network a month later. The price that Orange was able to secure was due to the strength of Orange brand, but in addition (unlike Virgin) it also had no affinity with owners or management, enabling it to achieve the highest premium possible.

The experiences of Virgin and Orange clearly reinforce each other. The key Insights into the development of a brand, in rough summary, are:

- At the beginning, you only need the veneer of a brand. Don't spend too much money on it.
- Get on with what you need to do – whatever it takes – to survive.
- At some stage you will identify that your business has come to stand for specific values: understand them and exploit them, using effective PR.
- Actions always speak louder than words, so always find a way to meet your customers' expectations. Disappoint your customers and brand loyalty will disappear and sales will fall.
- As you grow, make your company live and breathe the brand. It's an important way of keeping your customer promises.
- Use your brand to drive price increases and negotiations.
- Separate your own identity from that of the brand. This will help you to achieve the maximum possible price on sale and minimise your post-sale involvement.

Congratulations: you are now a branding expert! You will not fall for those slick marketeers selling false and expensive dreams.

Let's use these brand morals as a practical guide to when, how and what to spend money on in developing your brand as your business grows. You're going to do this without wasting time, effort or money – and end up with a brand that's a powerful weapon.

Establish your brand on a shoestring

The imperative here is to establish your brand for £5000 – absolute maximum! You might be able to spend even less. Either way, the effect will be worth substantially more.

We know that during the survival stage, so far as your brand is concerned, all you are looking for is a 'veneer'. Your objective is to present a credible face to the world and allow goodwill to build as you provide a good service and amass a body of satisfied customers.

A clue on image: don't get confused with a condom!

All you really need are four simple things: business name and logo; business cards; website; PowerPoint presentation. Choosing the right name for your business is crucial. Everything you do will be associated with this name. You want to grab attention and generate empathy with customers. Here are some tips to help you through this process.

- Try to choose a name that is catchy and memorable and that is associated with what you are doing. Ensure that the name is not already in use.
- Think carefully about whether the name could be distorted or have a meaning that you didn't intend. Does it mean something quite different in another language? Alan Bond found this out the hard way when he named his boat XXXX

after the beer company he owned. When he tried to moor it in a marina in the US, he was denied access because XXXX was the name of a brand of condom and was regarded as an offensive name for a boat.

- If possible, register and trademark your chosen name to ensure it is protected. You might be able to do this at a later date but be warned that you might suffer the same fate as the branding agency Dave, which is currently engaged in a legal battle with another company that has been using their name and logo. If they had taken the right steps to protect their corporate identity, it might have saved them a great deal of time and money.

- Use a professional graphic designer to help create the logo for your business.

- Consider the practical side of your logo. How easy will it be to reproduce on letterhead, posters, clothing, badges, vehicles etc?

- Choose a name and logo that you have an affinity with and that you will be proud to see every day.

To see this in action, let's look at the successful launch of Fuel.

Fuel on fire

Financial services is a highly commoditised industry where trust is a major factor for consumers. A strong, clean brand can help customers navigate the confusing array of offers and begin building the trust in the brand that is so important. We needed to create a name that was short and easy to remember but that also conveyed a little bit about our brand and business. The name and identity needed to be clear and easy to understand.

We drew up a shortlist of ideas and then hit on Fuel. One of the main reasons we liked the name Fuel was that it enabled us to develop a clever campaign based on variations of 'fuelling' investment returns.

The name very effectively conveyed the business's ultimate client promise: to maximise investment returns by supercharging their property investments.

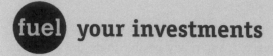

fuel your investments

Fuel also ticked all the main boxes identified above. It was catchy and memorable. It was hard to distort and meant exactly what it was intended to. The logo was memorable and easily replicated for use in the company's marketing materials. I really liked it. It seemed to capture the energy and raw power of what we were setting out to achieve with the business without narrowing down our future options as the business grew. This was all achieved at virtually no cost. Not bad for a business that went in a few short years from being a mere concept to writing £600 million of loans per annum. It was named 'Buy-to-let' broker of the year in the UK several times.

Let's now look in more detail at the other tools in brand-building – business cards, website and presentation.

A business card is often the first moment that a customer will see the name and identity of your business and brand. It is vital not to skimp on the quality of your business cards. Handing over a flimsy piece of paper that you had printed from a machine in a tube station is never going to impress a potential client or supplier. Name (a personal preference – I never use job titles), address, solid texture, and that's it.

Today, a business's website is quite often the first port of call for prospective customers or just about anyone you become involved with. Your business needs to be seen as solid and exciting.

At the same time, your business is still evolving and you can't afford to waste any cash. You are in survival mode and not exactly sure what you stand for. Remember, the last thing you want to do is to box yourself into a corner. So – like your brand – your website will evolve. Begin with a simple and effective website design.

The graphic below sets out the structure and content that I believe every site should have as an absolute minimum.

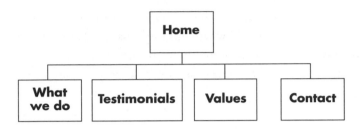

Let's look at each of these pages in a little more detail:

- **Home page:** This is the first page people will see. It should provide:
  1. A concise summary of what it is that your business does, focusing on the benefits it delivers rather than the technical aspects of the product or service.
  2. Some form of third-party endorsement to help build credibility.
  3. A clear call to action, for example an incentive to call a telephone number or a form that should be completed and emailed.

- **What we do:** It is essential to describe your product in terms of 'benefits' and not 'technical features'. You have a bit more room here than on your home page, so use it to develop your key messages and support them with some sales figures or other statistics.

- **Testimonials:** Testimonials from satisfied customers are really powerful. That's why you should put them up front. To portray them with maximum effectiveness and credibility, make sure you display the customers' names and photos with their quotes. Positive press comments must also be displayed with a quote from the article and the logo of the publication. If you can't find any customers or press coverage, then use an endorsement from suppliers, government bodies or any well-known individual.

Display the customer's name and photo with their testimonial – otherwise, people will think it's made up!

- **Values:** This is your opportunity to tell the world what your business stands for. It builds further credibility and trust by stating the principles that you hold dear. You may be an organic food producer, sell 'fair trade' products or simply believe in delivering the finest level of customer service possible. It is important to convey these messages to potential customers.

- **Contact us:** It is important for the business to look as large and reputable as possible so do not use PO Box addresses. Ensure you give people a range of options to contact you, including phone, fax, email and, of course, the option of a meeting.

Before you design your website, do some homework and then stick to the design rules outlined below.

- **Check out the competition:** Look at the websites of your competitors and see what works and what doesn't on their sites. See what ideas you can use and what you can improve on. If there are elements that are common among all the sites, then they are probably worth using. Here's a great tip: if there is a particularly successful competitor, watch carefully for the changes they make to their website. If they keep the changes after a trial period, then it is probably worth imitating the changes because they will probably have proven successful.

- **Keep site design simple and clean:** Research has shown that users will make a judgement about the site (and, by implication, the business too) within the first three seconds, so it is not a good idea to bombard them with images and text. You must always keep text on your website concise and compelling. Your customers don't want to have to spend time scrolling through reams of items. Remember, your website is there to inform and sell product.

- **Have a clear call to action:** You want any viewer of your website to actually do something. It might be to give you a call, place an order or register their details on the site. Whatever it is, you must have a clear way of driving people to actually take this step. Incentives always help here.

> **In Web World, you have three seconds to impress – otherwise, the customer leaves**

- **Avoid fancy animation:** You don't have to use animation. I don't want to go into too much detail here, but suffice it to say that a simple site without complicated bells and whistles is best – that is the message that you need to give to your web designer. The longer it takes each page to download, the higher the risk that people will lose interest and leave your site. An old partner of mine would ask his PA to print out suppliers' websites. If it was tricky (because of the fancy graphics) she ignored it. Hence the supplier lost out.

Now run your own experiment. Look at some sites. Compare them. Which are interesting enough to keep you there a while? Which ones make you want to buy? Which site do you want? You're in business. Your objective is sales. Fancy designs are just decoration. Follow our principles at R-Points: the designers got just £4000; the company got a straightforward, effective website. It's now the largest cash-back community in the UK.

> **Develop an 'elevator pitch' – by the time you reach the top, you must have a sale**

In the early stages of your business, building credibility through your brand is almost entirely dependent upon you. One tool that will be vital to help you is a simple but effective presentation document. I want you to take it everywhere you go. It should concisely state the benefits of your business and explain why people should work with you.

Virtually everyone I meet thinks that they can prepare and
deliver good quality presentations. But, at the risk of sounding
condescending, most of these presentations are poorly conceived,
overly complicated, and unpersuasive. McKinsey, where I
worked for a number of years, is much admired worldwide for its
approach to preparing presentations. I have taken
the key elements of the McKinsey approach and
adapted them specifically for start-up businesses.

**Your presentation
will only be as
powerful as the
quality of your
delivery**

So that each presentation you give has the
greatest chance of achieving the outcome you
desire, I want you to use the following rules
of thumb.

- **Identify three key messages:** People will only remember
  three things from a presentation, so think carefully about
  what your three key messages are and build your presentation
  around these points. Typically, the three points would be:
  (1) what is the unique selling proposition (USP) of your
  business/product; (2) show what you have achieved through
  case studies and examples; and (3) what action you want the
  audience to take as a result of the presentation.

- **Don't crowd slides:** Use only about three or four bullet
  points per slide. A slide covered in bullet points becomes
  impenetrable and the key messages will be lost.

- **Use action headers:** A presentation will be more powerful if
  the headers you use on each slide are insightful and analytical
  rather than mere a description of the content. So, don't simply
  have a headline stating: 'The Market from 1999 to 2008'.
  A more powerful headline is: 'The market has grown by
  7% p.a. over the past decade'.

- **Use graphics that reinforce the headline:** For example, if the
  headline states that the market is in decline, then the graph you
  use to support this point must clearly show a downward trend.

■ **Cite your references:** Always cite your references at the bottom of every page where you have drawn on other materials or data.

■ **Put additional information in an appendix:** If you have additional information that you want to provide, put it in an appendix and provide this separately. Don't try to cram your presentation with every piece of data that you have. The appendix also serves to show the amount of work you have put in and are prepared to do. It will help to establish credibility.

Even the best-written presentation will only be as successful as the quality of your delivery. To ensure your delivery oozes confidence and knowledge, and inspires your audience:

■ Do not read the slides. Your audience can do that for themselves. You'll lose them. Use the slides to provide you with structure, but talk around the bullet points.

■ Use graphic examples as often as you can to bring the key points to life.

■ Lead into the next slide before showing it. If you don't, they'll read it.

■ Pause from time to time. Recapitulate your arguments every now and then.

When establishing a business, I can always be seen clutching my presentation. I'm like a broken record – constantly evangelical. When I launched Fuel, the eight-page presentation contained the key messages for potential funders. Every presentation improved and finally I was able to allow others to do the presenting. I moved on.

Your presentation is a device you can use to get the price you deserve

Your extended brand development – and 'divorce'!

Your objective now is to maximise the business value on sale. This is the brand's moment. It will be the glue that holds your business together and a powerful weapon to increase its price.

Why does a strong brand mean higher exit value? We've already stated that a brand is nothing more than a promise that is consistently delivered. So, if you have a brand, then you've got satisfied customers who understand your product. A would-be purchaser of your business sees an entity with a clear purpose and loyal, satisfied customers. This is good. Your business is easily understood and hence easily sold. Purchasers will line up. The 'strong' in 'strong brand' means your business is satisfying many customers and there are many more waiting in the wings. There's your price premium on sale.

But we're not there yet. To be in that happy brand position, we're going to have to apply our brand 'morals' to answer the following questions – and then act on those answers.

- 'What does the brand stand for? How can I take advantage of this?'
- 'How can I get my people to live and breathe the brand?'
- 'How can I build my brand so it's widely known and independent of me?'

If you hear disappointment, confusion or disillusionment, fix it – and fix it fast!

The first question will involve some market research among your customer base. Don't be shy to call a number of your customers and ask them what they believe you and your business stand for. Compare the response you get from your customers with your own view of what the brand stands for.

It is important to understand why your business has been successful. Once you understand the key reasons why customers have purchased your product or service, write them down. You'll have started with certain objectives, but now you need the detail. (Remember, we did this at Virgin and came up with fun/ irreverent, anti-establishment, high-quality products and services offering excellent value for money.) What are yours? They become your guiding brand principles – they hold your business together.

During this process, you may receive some customer feedback you don't like. This will force you to take remedial action to improve your customer experience. So, go do it.

Once you've understood this, you can develop specific strategies to answer the remaining questions.

You must constantly look for ways to grow sales and profit. Keep the entrepreneurial drive. Simply do it within the confines of your brand principles. There'll be growth opportunities that just don't fit in with your brand guidelines. It will be a judgement call, but being all things to all people is an oft-travelled path to mediocrity and confusion. Remember, business-purchasers like it simple. So do customers.

Remember, too, the lessons learned from Virgin Trains and Virgin Clothes. If you break your customers' understanding of what the brands stand for, you hurt the brand. That means the customers become confused and disillusioned – and they will leave *in droves*.

Employ people who understand and will live the brand

Contrast that with Virgin Active, which fitted perfectly with the brand and was an enormous success. This is your moral for deciding whether or not to add a new product or service. Does the new thing fit – is it consistent with customers' expectations? If they expect low prices, give them low prices. Premium service? Give them that.

So, how do you get people to live and breathe your brand? For starters, you need to ensure that your staff understand the brand values and help to reinforce them. Virgin achieved this partly by being very careful about who they recruited.

The company understood that the staff it recruited must have a sense of humour and embody Virgin's values of fun and irreverence. Staff became brand advocates. Think for a moment about the difference between a typical British Airways cabin crew member and a Virgin Atlantic cabin crew member. Virgin also rewarded its staff with regular parties, drinks nights and other 'fun' social events. These events both helped to ensure that staff enjoyed working with Virgin and also provided opportunities to bring staff together to ensure that everyone within the company was moving in the same direction.

Other companies adopt a more formal approach and seek to formalise their **brand** values in a 'brand book'. This book will typically detail everything from the logo and its correct usage (colours, size, etc.), the typefaces to use (size, style, colour), right through to the way that clients should be addressed. This document is often used as part of the induction process for new staff and provides an ongoing reference tool for existing staff.

An ego can destroy your brand – and any hope of a price premium

You may decide to adopt one or other of these approaches or a combination of both. I don't much care, as long as the approach works for your business. Just ensure that you take a close interest and become the brand champion.

Now we move into brand awareness. Your objective is still to generate high sales cost-effectively. You can't afford to waste any money, but you are now clear about your brand values and your objective is to seek creative ways to get your brand broadcast to the widest audience possible, as quickly as possible.

It's brand-awareness with a twist. We're deliberately going to take you out of the spotlight and promote the company's brand. This is only possible if your ego allows it. For some, this is difficult

– which is quite understandable given that you led from the front throughout the hard times. But our goal is a high sales price, not ego gratification. So, let's review those tactics.

Word of mouth

Growth through word of mouth is one of the most natural and energetic ways to grow your brand. But you can be pro-active and help it along. You understand the value of testimonials, but also look for opportunities to encourage your customers to communicate word of your product to the wider community. Incorporate a referral scheme where clients are incentivised – the most powerful method of reward is by cash – to sign up new customers.

R-Points goes so far as to write a suggested email for customers to send to their friends. All they have to do is add the email address.

Use your customers to communicate their love of your product to the wider community

Advertising

Traditionally, marketers believed there were two primary types of advertisements: sales-focused and brand-focused. Sales-focused advertising incorporates a very specific call to action to purchase a product or service. Brand-focused advertising seeks primarily to generate awareness of a business and its core values.

Today, I think that distinction is irrelevant – at least for start-ups. I believe that all advertising should have a clear objective: building sales. Brand advertising, if that's what you want to call it, must work hard too. It may be focused on retaining customers, extracting additional value from existing customers or attracting new customers. But you should never forget the overarching objective of advertising: to ultimately make your business more profitable. There is no value in businesses investing vast sums of money in brand advertising if they cannot demonstrate a return. As your business matures, the tone of your advertising may soften somewhat, but it should always have a clear sales emphasis.

Consider Virgin, one of the strongest brands in the UK. It has never undertaken a pure brand advertising campaign. Rather, it always promotes an immediate purchase – but in a way that reinforces the brand values, often by being cheeky, irreverent and fun. Remember: be disciplined. Higher advertising costs that don't lead to new sales mean lower profits and a lower business-sale price.

PR

If you took my advice from the outset, you'll have been using PR assiduously to generate sales and build credibility. You'll have taken whatever you could get. The Virgin story clearly illustrates the moral that PR is a sensational tool to build brand awareness. So, if anything, your PR effort should now be redoubled as you approach sale. However, there are some subtle changes of emphasis.

One subtle change you may not like: You cease being the front man!

An important change to start with is to ensure your PR doesn't revolve around you. You must stop being the 'front', the spokesperson. The company and new management must stand on their own two feet, quite independently of you. Second, use your brand attributes to deliver stories. Finally, as you move to maturity, position the company as a vocal industry leader. Speak out on the latest events and trends. Do customer polls so that you can make insightful comments based on consumer habits. Business purchasers will enjoy (and pay for) the elevated status.

Showing authority

Aside from PR, we must find other creative ways to show authority. I have used a number of tactics: develop an industry magazine; publish strong corporate literature; establish an industry code; formulate an industry body.

An industry magazine should generate sales as well as promote your brand. It should at least break even. Corporate brochures and well-produced annual reports imply that your young company is growing up. Creating an industry code or set of best practices shows leadership, and will attract the positive attention of related government bodies and other industry associations. This can lead to creating an industry body. You can become the

founder and head of this – a particularly effective tactic in an
unregulated industry.

Brand association

The use of 'association' was brought up in chapter 3 as a great way
to build credibility. Any and all associations that promoted ability,
strength and size were fair game. The reality is that the closest
association is with the founder. The company has benefited from
the founder's PR by association. That's got to stop now.

It's time to be more circumspect. In the early days,
you may have found convenient associations that
generated sales. Now you'll be looking to refine
your associations so that the businesses, entities
or causes with which you are associated fit with
and further the development of your brand. You
need to be absolutely certain that your proposed
brand partner will be adding value through the
association and not weakening your brand.

> **The use of brand associations or 'the parasite approach' can significantly reduce customer acquisition costs**

But, again, be sales-focused, and be clever with your associations.
Central to successful association is a deep understanding of your
target market and their spending habits – what car they drive, the
shoes they wear or even where they go on holiday. In turn, this
can help you to drive the direction in which you develop your
brand and its associations with others. Vertu (the luxury mobile
phone maker) recently collaborated with Porsche by sponsoring
their GT Racing team after establishing that the typical Porsche
driver shared many of the same characteristics as the Vertu target
audience. The use of brand associations or 'the parasite approach'
can significantly reduce customer acquisition costs and bring
exposure to a wider audience.

The power of association goes beyond formal business
collaborations. Much of Richard Branson's early 'branding' was
a result of his active participation in various anti-establishment
movements and public protests. These high-profile activities
helped to reinforce the perception of the Virgin brand as being

anti-establishment. Had Richard spent the early years, or even the later years, of his business life sipping cocktails and smoking cigars in a Pall Mall gentleman's club, the Virgin group would have struggled to have any credibility as anti-establishment.

Sponsorship

Sponsorship can be a huge opportunity to build brand awareness. Consider Virgin's V Festival or Innocent's Fruitstock – both great strategies, both great brands.

Let's be both smart and disciplined here. You need to be cagey. Sponsorship is an investment, and you must be certain of a _____ payback. Otherwise, don't do it.

Don't be fooled: Only sponsor if there's payback

Virgin had existed for more than thirty years before launching the V Festival. Its sponsorship beginnings were much more humble, such as the Virgin Atlantic party, which was mainly for frequently flying Upper Class passengers. Eligibility was based on air miles, and Upper Class passengers tended to have most. As the party – hosted at Branson's home in Oxford – grew in popularity, people wanted to collect points, if only to gain admission to the gig. Consequently, the whole affair was self-funding because of the extra revenue it generated.

I still remember Richard lamenting that someone had talked him into sponsoring Crystal Palace FC in the 1990 FA Cup Final. The result? A draw. Therefore a replay – double exposure for Virgin. However, he still felt he didn't get his payback. And that's the point to remember: payback, payback, payback!

The last word

A strong brand maximises the price you'll get on the sale of your business. However, some people would have you believe that brand is a panacea for all of a company's woes. This is a myth. Anyone adhering to this myth will waste massive amount of time, effort and precious funds. In a worst-case scenario, it could cripple your start-up during launch. This won't happen to you – you understand the role of brands. Hence you know what to invest in a brand at each stage of your development and how to make use of it to smooth your path. In short, you know how to use your brand as a weapon at all times, culminating in the realisation of your dream – a sale. It's time to do exactly that – sell. Succeed in this and the battle is over ...

Dos and don'ts

1. **DON'T** invest serious funds in branding during launch. Concentrate on sales to survive. All you need is a brand 'veneer' for a credible face to show the world.

2. **DON'T** spend more than £5000 on your brand veneer. Focus on name, logo, website, business cards and a concise presentation.

3. **DO** build concision, clarity and comprehensibility into your brand. Purchasers will pay a premium for them.

4. **DON'T** disappoint you customers' expectations of your brand. If you do, they'll be disillusioned and confused, and leave in droves.

5. **DO** stay entrepreneurial and grow your business. Extra products and services must be consistent with and feed off your brand vales.

6. **DO** make your company live and breathe the brand. Become the brand champion and hire like-minded people and make sure they 'get it'.

7. **DO** broadcast your brand to the widest audience possible. Only use creative tactics that will pay you back.

8. **DO** separate your own identity from the company's brand. Step back, don't let your ego get in the way. It will maximise the price you get on sale.

CHAPTER NINE **SELL HIGH – AND SET YOURSELF FREE!**

Wow! What a roller coaster ride it's been. And now look at you … sitting in one of the swankiest bars in Mayfair, a glass of vintage bubbly in one hand and tapping away at the keys of your BlackBerry with another. You're relaxing in a Le Corbusier chair, thinking about all the hard work you've put in over the past few years to reach the point where your business is ready for sale. It's been a rocky road, but now it's time to reap the benefits.

New pad? 10,000 square feet! Gym? Private cinema? Of course!

And you just can't resist it – you're human, after all – you're updating your 'to do' list. Hmm, a bit of careful thought, but here goes …

- Pick adviser to sell business.
- Buy house in Chelsea. Not too ostentatious. Say, 10,000 square feet. Gym? Private cinema? Of course!
- Book holiday to the Maldives.
- Research private jet ownership.
- Trade wife/husband in for younger model.
- Call adviser, give details of new offshore account and ask for money to be transferred there.

You order another glass – oh, what the hell, a bottle! – and reflect on how exciting it is thinking up ways to spend the windfall.

Sorry to interrupt but I have a few questions. Nothing frivolous or complex, you understand, just a few basic queries about your business.

1. Who knows your business best?
2. Who can best communicate its strengths with the same conviction and passion?
3. Who knows the business-related issues that keep you awake at night?
4. Who would best make the required changes to address these?
5. Who is most critical to the business right now?
6. Who truly understands why you want to sell?
7. And, most importantly, who has the most to gain when the business is sold?

What's that? Did you just replied 'me' – seven times? Right! Now you should have realised that you'd better cancel the champagne order, get your butt out of that fancy chair and rush home to start preparations for the most important negotiation of your life.

You should be in absolutely no doubt that realising value from a business is hard work. And you – the person responsible for the establishment and sustainability of the business – will be the most important individual in the sale process.

In reality, few start-ups ever get sold, but there is a formula ...

Certainly you will need an adviser, and we'll get you the right one. But this is not the time to abdicate all responsibility to someone else. Their prime interest is to generate fees and commissions. You want the best possible price and you want to be free to do what you want to at the end of the process. Surprisingly, these two objectives might occasionally come into conflict!

The reality is that relatively few start-ups achieve a sale. Of those that do get sold, the conditions attached are often onerous and may mean a different – potentially arduous – role for you in what's now someone else's company. It can be done, and there is a formula, but it requires considerable effort. So let's be clear about our objectives. First and foremost, get the deal done. Second, do it at the best possible price. But third, you want to emerge from it all free to pursue a quiet life – or, more likely, other opportunities.

I trust I now have your attention. You should have a number of questions, including:

1. When is it time to sell?
2. What shape should my business be in?
3. What would be my role – or lack of a role – in the business?
4. What's my role in the sale?
5. Who's the ideal adviser?
6. What should I look for in my sales contract?

This chapter will provide the answers to those questions. It won't waste time delving into detail, but tackle the obstacles head on. We are interested in what you have to do. We're interested in results. There are two jobs of work still to do.

The first task is to position yourself and your business to get the best price and to retain your personal freedom. The second is, simply, getting the deal done.

Prepare your business for sale – and prepare yourself to go

When is it time to sell? Timing is everything, and the right time is when you're on the way up, still growing. Don't wait, or try to pick the peak. If you go into decline, it becomes virtually impossible to sell the business. You must sell on an upward trend.

Now for another big question: do you have what it takes to be an asset trader? Let me set the scene.

When quitting is winning

Alan Bond was riding high in 1985. He was Australia's national hero and regularly appeared on the front pages of the national press. Two years earlier Australia II, a yacht he had personally bankrolled, won the prestigious America's Cup.

Successful traders are like successful gamblers – they know when to quit and sell up

---

The trophy had been held by the US since 1852, and Australia II's success ended the longest winning streak in sporting history. And, on the professional side, Bond Corporation had just acquired Castlemaine Tooheys for A$1.2 billion in a transaction that was, at that time, the largest corporate takeover in Australian history.

The deal received the 'Australian Takeover of the Year' award from the prestigious Australian *Business Week* magazine. The following year, the Bond Corporation had assets of more than A$11 billion with free cash-flow of some A$200 million. It was huge and profitable, but in 1991 it collapsed in Australia's largest corporate bankruptcy.

While Alan Bond was breaking corporate records, on the other side of the world, Richard Branson's Virgin Group was diversifying away from his record-empire roots. In 1984 Virgin Atlantic took off and two years later Branson floated the Virgin Group on the London Stock Exchange. He even tried sailing, funding the Virgin Atlantic Challenger II, which in 1986 recaptured the Blue Riband for Britain, recording the fastest Atlantic crossing ever.

One year after the Bond Corporation's collapse, the Virgin Music Group was sold to Thorn EMI in a $1 billion deal. The deals have continued. A 49% share in Virgin Atlantic was sold to Singapore Airlines in 1999, valuing the fifteen-year-old business at a minimum £1.23 billion. That same year Virgin Mobile was launched. It was the fastest-growing mobile start-up ever in the UK, signing up one million customers in less than two years. It was sold to Japan's NTL for £962 million in 2006.

Richard Branson almost went bust in the late 1980s. The memory haunts him to this day

So, why did Sir Richard Branson and Virgin succeed while Alan Bond and his business empire collapsed? Both are hugely talented, charismatic individuals with an eye for a deal. But where they differ is that Branson recognises his limitations. He knows when to let go. He sells out.

An entrepreneur must be an 'asset trader'. The asset in question is the business or the business idea. Successful traders are like successful gamblers – they know when to quit and sell up. And there will always come a time when it's better to sell an asset than to hold on. Successful entrepreneurs recognise this and respond accordingly.

Others find it harder to accept. Entrepreneurs are self-assured, confident, possessive, persistent, adventurous, risk-taking and stubborn. They enjoy being in control. Some find it hard to relinquish this power. They are unable to delegate. They want to be involved in everything. But what they fail to realise is that the skills required to take a business from scratch to profitability are very different from those that drive the next stage of growth. The early days required the use of a sledgehammer. Later on, it's all about polishing. And the reality is that there are a lot of people who can polish but very few with the skills to build a successful business from scratch.

Don't let your own ego destroy what you've built

Richard Branson is constantly selling part or all of his businesses. I know that he didn't always want to, particularly when it came to Virgin Atlantic.

But he always recognised when he had to, perhaps for cash-flow purposes or to raise the funds for another venture. Why? Well, he almost went bust in the late 1980s and the memory haunts him to this day so he accepts that some sacrifices must be made for the greater good of the Virgin empire. But he is acutely conscious that the moment you stop adding value and start tinkering is the moment to move on. He is also a very hands-off manager. At the right time, he puts a management team in place to run a business and, apart from being very involved at launch, leaves them to get on with it.

This tale of two entrepreneurs reveals striking similarities and key differences. Entrepreneurs are typically supremely confident individuals. This is a huge strength. But there is a fine line between confidence and ego. And sometimes, as a business grows, this confidence is replaced by egotism. Entrepreneurs begin to believe their own PR and behave inappropriately. Decisions get made on the basis of ego rather than the best interests of the business.

If you talk to Alan Bond today – who, incidentally, is featuring once more in the rich lists – he'll tell you he should have sold his businesses when he had the offers. He held on too long for a variety of reasons – perhaps his ego came into play. Too many entrepreneurs fall into this trap. They start a business that eventually throws off lots of cash, they employ staff and begin to believe their own PR. They think they are invincible and that the business, which they established, can only benefit from their wisdom going forward. After all, haven't they just created an amazing business out of nothing? Well, if they continue with that attitude nothing is exactly what they will be left with.

Follow my road map to be one of the few who sell for a premium

If I've been able to persuade you it's time to sell, to move on, then I've removed one of the largest – if not *the* largest – obstacles. If your heart and soul want to achieve a sale, we're on track. Follow the road map I set out below, and you'll be one of the rare breed who sells their business for a premium.

We've established that you sell when you're growing. Yes, but when? After all, your business has been growing from day one, and you can't afford to miss the boat. So, when, precisely, is the right time to begin the process? Well, businesses that have reached this crossroads typically demonstrate certain common traits.

Your business will have a range of well-tested and proven sales pitches. It will be generating cash. In fact, your business will, by and large, have settled into a daily routine. The trailblazing of the early years has disappeared. But stresses are starting to emerge. The current systems are likely to be under pressure and beginning to feel out of control. There are many more employees and some senior management scattered around.

You must sell on the way up – don't miss the boat

The business is probably facing new strategic challenges, such as trying to work out how to harvest new value from existing customers. Customer service is becoming a critical issue, and the business is probably struggling to keep up with the demands of its rapidly growing client base. And, for better or worse, the business is starting to develop its own brand values.

There's plenty to do, and not much time – or space – to do it in. That thought came home very forcefully one time when I was locked in an underground mining lift …

Cutting the umbilical cord

I tried in vain to open the lift cage. I couldn't. I was the 'city slicker' surrounded by hardened coal miners having a joke. The cage door was air-locked. I couldn't have opened it if I'd been The Incredible Hulk!

But I didn't mind – I was on a mission. I needed one of the team leaders to step up to the role of general manager of Bond Coal. The guy I had in mind was in the cage with me, looking to see how I would react. We all laughed. The mood lightened. I'd passed the test. Several weeks later, he was the general manager.

Why was this important? I'd been given the task of selling Bond Coal – and fast. The Group was in trouble and needed the cash.

To be truthful, it wasn't perfect timing. Coal prices were down. The business should have been sold eighteen months earlier, when people were knocking on the door.

I had a job to do. If we were to get it away at a good price, it had to be perceived as able to stand on its own two feet. We had to cut the umbilical cord to the Group.

Over a period of six months, I set about doing just that. The beginning, middle and end revolved around ensuring the management team was perceived to be running the show. And, of course, they actually had to do it.

Alan Bond was replaced as chairman by the managing director. A relatively junior marketing and sales executive stepped up to become head of that division. My friend from the Newcastle coal fields became operations head. The colliery finance person became financial director. Despite the dramas and the politics, they ended up being a great team.

After intense coaching the team stood tall and proved their worth

Now we could market the business without Bond Corporation being involved. Potential buyers wanted to know who ran the business and all about operational costs. If the team couldn't answer the buyers' questions, a full sale was doomed. The team stood tall and – after intense coaching – proved their worth.

Not only did we have to demonstrate substantial value as a commercial enterprise – cutting coal, firming up reserves, sale contracts, etc. – we had to get what some people call the 'window dressing' right. That meant bringing all Group functions in-house, including treasury and all Group reporting. Intricate intercompany loans were repaid. HR, IT systems and the rest had to be supported from within the company. But, window dressing or not, that's what a purchaser wants.

It took many sleepless nights and lengthy negotiations, but in the end the business was believed to be completely independent of its founder and owner. The A$220 million banked proved that.

Now is the time to act. There can be no procrastinating if we are to sell on an upward trend. Purchasers are looking for what they call a sustainable business. So, what next?

Building a sustainable business is part art and part science. I am first going to define a sustainable business and highlight some wholesale operational changes – what I call the 'cornerstone changes' – that you will need to make to transform your business from its current position to a sustainable equilibrium. I will provide a framework and process for you to follow. If you do so, you'll be able to finally sell your business at the maximum price. You can use this framework as a checklist and with the right mindset you will be able to work through it.

Sustainability has a magnetic attraction for purchasers

So, what is a sustainable business? You need to know what you are aiming for. There is no one-size-fits-all definition, but all the businesses I have ever sold have had four common characteristics:

1. A sustainable business doesn't depend on any one thing for success. The business must not be reliant on a single individual, single customer or single supplier. It will have a team in place capable of running the day-to-day operations independently of your input.

2. A sustainable business will know how to make its core business work. The core business should be operating as an engine, with many people playing their part, trading successfully day after day and reliably generating cash. It faces new challenges, such as motivating staff to do tasks better rather than showing them how to do them. Any changes will be minor or marginal improvements.

3. A sustainable business no longer scrambles to find new customers. The business will already have a significant client base, achieving repeat sales, and have developed successful ways to 'farm' these for additional revenue opportunities. It will still be adding new customers, but this is no longer its sole focus.

4. A sustainable business can explore growth opportunities outside its core business. This needs careful definition. It doesn't mean that a restaurant proprietor should suddenly start designing and printing menus, but they may be looking at a second restaurant or, perhaps, a retail store selling its products. The growth opportunities will be a natural extension of the existing business.

Your job is to get your business into a position where it demonstrates all these traits. Your business is probably close to sustainability. Use the cornerstone changes set out on pages 260–261 as your specific 'to do' list. Some of it may look like window dressing, but what we're doing is tailoring the business to the purchaser's requirements.

Window dressing or not, It's what a purchaser wants

What Is your role in achieving the cornerstone changes? The answer is to hire a management team that will do it for you. Indeed, here is your opportunity to make yourself redundant, as Richard Branson was just about to find out ...

Up, up and away!

As Richard Branson and I sat around in Richard's office with other senior Virgin executives, my vote was for Steve Ridgeway to become managing director of Virgin Atlantic. A sale of some or all of the airline was in the offing.

Sir Richard Branson – make him redundant!

But there was a problem: people believed Richard ran the airline. For many years, Virgin Atlantic had been run by a gang of four, with no managing director. It had worked, but we realised no-one was going to buy a large, controlling stake and allow Richard to actively pursue other Virgin interests.

To facilitate a sale, Richard needed to be seen as largely an ambassador for the airline. Steve, as head of customer service – a lynchpin of the business – seemed to be the right guy.

So, after much trial and tribulation amongst the gang of four (they all wanted the job), Richard appointed Steve. Some executives left. There were some promotions from within, and the result was a much more conventional management team structure.

Richard observed that he didn't believe it would add great value, but he was always amazed what the corporate world needed to see – box ticking! He took a philosophical approach and ultimately admitted that things at the airline had moved on from the early pioneering days, and that maybe it was all for the best.

Singapore Airlines bought 49% for £550 million.

So, the moral is clear: if you want to sell the business, shoot the entrepreneur! The cornerstone changes are largely about polishing the business. A true entrepreneur prefers revolution to evolution. You simply won't have the skills to get the polishing and the window dressing done.

If you're intimately involved in everything, a purchaser will not allow you your freedom. They'll tie you into the business. Do you really want to have a boss? Constantly account for your time? Work in committee rooms?

Your management takes the glory – you take the cash

So, understand this: the person writing the cheque has the power. If you're seen as integral to the business, you're going nowhere. If you've resisted the urge to bring in a partner, perhaps now is the time to work with someone – unlike you – who can work through the cornerstone changes. It will take some time to implement these changes, perhaps as long as six months. A partner could be of critical importance – possibly the person to stay, post-sale, grow the business and buy you your freedom. It could also be the difference between sale and no sale.

The 'cornerstone changes' of building a sustainable business

Cornerstones	Objective	Start-up	Sustainable
Management	• Ensure business is not dependent on any single individual – especially you • Build a team that can both grow existing business and effectively farm existing clients • Conduct a general review of all management and ensure incentives are in line with the maturing business	• Weak or no senior management • Too many people reporting directly to founder • Inexperienced staff • No middle management	• Management take care of the day-to-day operations free of your involvement • Experienced senior management team in place, normally including a managing director and/or chief operations officer, finance director, sales and marketing director • Staff have appropriate experience for their roles • Clear lines of accountability and reporting • A partner with skills to take forward and sell the business • Timing
Finance	• Build systems to an appropriate level • Ensure robust financial controls are in place and accurate and timely information is available to help generate new clients and facilitate selling to established customers • Ensure no significant outstanding tax and VAT issues exist	• Accounting policies and procedures are weak • Limited financial information available • No tax planning at all • Outstanding VAT issues • No/small auditor	• Accounting policies and procedures are robust, well documented and stand up to external scrutiny • You know exactly where the cash is going • Detailed and accurate management reporting • No major taxation matters outstanding • Tax planning carefully considered • Respected auditor • FD maintains strong control over finance function and bank accounts

Cornerstones	Objective	Start-up	Sustainable
Information technology	Capture detailed customer information to better service and improve sales to existing customers, as well as generating new customers	• Information stored in multiple spreadsheets and databases • Limited management and financial reporting • Little known about existing customers • IT infrastructure and systems designed for a small business	• Customer information securely stored in centralised database • Sophisticated information about customers • Customer information is farmed to assist selling • IT infrastructure and systems reflective of size of business • Integrated financial reporting systems
Customer service	Ensure that you deliver high-quality customer service to encourage both repeat purchases from existing clients and sales to new customers	• No clear responsibility for customer services • Customer issues resolved on ad hoc basis • Customer complaints are common	• Evidence of the priority of your customers • Dedicated customer service team • Clear policies and procedures in place for resolution of customer issues • A brand that's independent of you
Human resources	Ensure that the business retains high-quality staff and that the business complies with all laws	• Much of HR is performed ad hoc by you (e.g. recruitment, dismissal, salary reviews)	• Often neglected but extremely important – they are looking after your most valuable resource: your people • Clear employee policies in place (e.g. dispute resolution, dismissal, terms of employment, confidentiality, etc.)
Legal	Protect the business from potential legal action and to provide certainty around key employee, customer and supplier relationships	• Customer/supplier/employee contracts are either non-existent or are poorly written • Intellectual property often poorly protected or not at all	• All key customer/supplier/employee contracts should have been reviewed to ensure they are watertight • Few or no outstanding legal matters that require resolution • Intellectual property appropriately protected – all patents, trademarks and domain names are properly registered

Partner or no partner, you'll need a management team and will work with them through the cornerstone changes. You need to educate them on the raw mechanics of the business and the path to growth. You must leave them with a complete, comprehensive blueprint. It takes time, but you must complete your 'to do' list.

If the business is sustainable and free of you, you've gained yourself a bargaining chip. You're now ready to get the deal done.

Doing the deal – the pay-off

Some believe that getting a deal is as simple as hiring an adviser. Not true. Who would entrust a third party with the most important negotiation of their lives? The objective here is to ensure that you lead the process, focus on the important issues and make the difference.

Let's break down getting the deal done into four parts: home truths, the sale options, choosing the right adviser and the sale negotiation.

1. Home truths to keep you honest

I know you're immensely proud of the business you have built – and rightly so – but you must have your feet on the ground. A successful seller has to have the right expectations. If those expectations are unrealistic, you'll drive the purchaser away and screw up the sales process.

Let's understand the position. The fact is your business is still relatively young. It doesn't have a long track record of profitability. The core business is now hopefully robust, but the growth initiatives are still in their infancy. You have probably only recently started to farm your old customers.

A buyer is attracted by a business that has grown rapidly, but, without a long track record, there will be concerns that it may tail off. Buyers will not pay for future growth but they need to believe it exists. That is the upside of the deal for them.

However, they will be aware that, as your business grows and matures, it is likely to go through some ups and downs. The management team, appointed as part of the process of making your business sustainable, is still relatively new and unproven. Thus, potential buyers will view you, and your wealth of knowledge, as critical to the ongoing success of the business. The more successful you've been in removing yourself from the business, the greater your freedom on its sale.

Buyers will wonder why you're seeking to sell. They may be suspicious that perhaps you know something about the business that may undermine its future value. Let's be honest. You have more information than they do and, therefore, they will never totally trust you. Don't take this personally. This may be your first time, but the buyers have been here before – and they may have been badly burned in the past. The buyers are likely to be cynical about all your claims, and will not believe everything you say. Come on, do you believe all the claims of a used car salesman?

Eventually, the buyer will have all the information. If they feel misled, the game's over

The buyer will expect some degree of sugar coating but, and this is critical to the whole process, never lie to them. When talks begin in earnest, the buyer will be given access to all the information about your company. They will soon find out if they've been misled and that will jeopardise any deal.

This knowledge is deal power. You must accept that the buyer's experience and beliefs have important implications for you:

- You are unlikely to be able to sell 100% of your business on day one; you will need to discuss your ongoing role with the purchaser.
- You are unlikely to receive all your money on day one.
- Your business may not be worth as much as you think it is – be realistic.

- Floating your company will typically prove to be fool's gold.
- Any sale will likely have significant conditions attached.

These truths go to the heart of structure and pricing

These home truths will go to the heart of the deal's structure and pricing. They will also help you select an adviser and avoid common pitfalls. They will also inject a healthy dose of realism into the process and that is absolutely critical. I have seen many instances where entrepreneurs, caught up in the hype of the sales process, have forgotten these truths and pushed for unrealistic terms or were just too greedy, or maybe they were just unable to let go and move on. In any event, they destroyed any hope of a successful deal.

Now that you understand the home truths, it's time to consider the main options that you have when selling your business.

2. Finding – and understanding – your buyer

We're going to look at three sales options in order of attractiveness. We'll help you list your potential buyers and explain their motivations – a key weapon in negotiating the sale.

Acquisition by a trade buyer is easily the most attractive option. A trade sale involves selling your business to another trading company, usually one that operates in the same or a related industry.

What motivates a trade buyer? They will purchase a start-up, like yourself, in the belief that by combining the companies, the overall profits will be greatly increased. Put two and two together and make five. You're looking for businesses that could combine well with yours. There are additional revenues or cost-savings to be had, which are often called synergies – a fancy and often over-used term.

To help you identify a potential trade buyer, I need to outline a comprehensive list of potential synergies. There are two main types: cost savings and revenue generation.

The cost savings include:

- Reduced need for senior management.
- Reduced need for administrative staff.
- Economies of scale.

The revenue generation includes:

- Sell their product to your customers.
- Sell your product to their customers.
- Combined stronger brand and presence.

Doing a trade sale gives the buyer the opportunity to put two and two together – and make five!

Often it's the cost savings that are easily identified, but the revenue adds real spice to the potentially increased profits. The trick is to be specific. This is an area where you, as the founder, can add value. It's simple: the greater the synergies, the greater the price.

In the sale of Virgin Atlantic, Branson was clever. He realised the synergies with Singapore Airlines were the highest on offer. There were a number of other sales options, including flotation, venture capitalists and other airlines. On looking at the market, Singapore Airlines was the natural choice. The feeder routes and IT systems were compatible. The combined companies now commanded a significant share of the Asian market, and an integrated and streamlined international route offering. Negotiations with suppliers, for example caterers, would lead to massive cost savings. The economies of scale were huge.

But there are a few important points to remember about trade buyers when negotiating with them. Trade-buyer management may lack deal experience. Corporate inertia, internal politics, funding and regulatory requirements are all factors that need to be considered.

Typically, however, they will be well-established businesses with sound reputations and professional management. If the company is quoted, shareholders and analysts will be scrutinising their every decision to ensure forecasts aren't missed.

To get the deal done, you'll need a 'sponsor' who will champion the transaction

Consequently, trade buyers can get nervous looking at very young businesses or those operating in industries that might be regarded as slightly contentious. They do not want to make mistakes, which would spark a negative reaction in the marketplace. They need to be able to justify their business decision.

So, the implications you need to understand and work around when dealing with a trade buyer include the following:

- A potentially higher price.
- A need to demonstrate good synergies.
- The deal will typically move at a slower pace.
- The trade buyer will need an adviser.
- You need a 'champion' within the buyer.

We like trade buyers. No doubt about it, they're our first port of call. The problem is, for the reasons outlined above, they may not buy a start-up. This leads us to the next-best option, private-equity buyers.

A private-equity company has shareholders who provide money to buy and sell businesses. It typically doesn't operate or manage those businesses – and it certainly isn't operating in your sector, as a trade buyer would.

So, what motivates a private-equity purchase? They have only
one concern: the ability to buy businesses at one price and sell
them on for more. The less they can pay you, the more they get
to keep for themselves. They're hard-nosed negotiators who aren't
interested in the long hours, sweat and toil you put in to building
your business.

To attract a private-equity player you need to address three
primary concerns. Is the business sustainable with credible growth
prospects? Will the entrepreneur put his money at risk? Are there
clear exit opportunities?

Private-equity companies will look at the key
performance metrics of your business, consider
the potential downside risks and then invest only
if they consider that the business performance
is sustainable. For them, knowing a business
generates a certain cash level limits their
downside. Then they'll invest some money in
you so you can grow faster, and appoint someone
to the board to supervise that process.

**Private-equity
companies are
hard-nosed and
heartless. It's tough
– but it could be
your only option**

They'll often demand that you re-invest a large chunk of the cash
they just gave you back into the business. They'll want you to put
your money where your mouth is. Suggesting that you want to
keep the cash is a total deal-breaker so don't even suggest it if you
want to keep the deal alive.

They need to believe there's a sale or exit plan. Ultimately, they'll
realise value from the deal by either flotation or selling your
business through a trade sale to the very companies you thought
would be a natural fit. If they don't believe there's an exit, they
won't do the deal.

So, you can see where this is going. They buy and sell. The less
they can pay you, the more they get to keep for themselves. They
don't have the luxury of potential synergies that trade buyers
do. They will be ruthless negotiators, perform a tortuous due

diligence process and refuse to pay any premium at all unless you have an exceptional business. And, throughout all this, they will act as if they are doing you a favour!

So where can you find a private-equity buyer? There's a national association and, despite their claims to be unique, stylish players in the market, they're basically all the same. Cast your net wide and you can narrow your options by looking at their typical deal size and the industries they prefer. Very occasionally, private-equity firms will develop a strategy of buying related businesses to group them. This puts them in the category of a trade sale so jump at any such chance.

Let's consider some more important characteristics of private-equity firms. They're owned by institutional shareholders and are FSA-regulated. If they can be shown to be negligent in their processes, they can be sued.

Flotations have a magic allure – but they could destroy all you've created

Private-equity companies have seen enough deals go wrong to be highly sceptical. They'll want to know why you're selling now. If your answer's not persuasive, they'll treat your deal like a bus – another one will be along in a minute.

So, when you snare a private-equity firm, you should keep the following points in mind during the negotiation:

- They'll offer a lower price than a trade buyer.
- The sale will involve less than 100% of the business.
- You'll be required to re-invest some of the sale proceeds.
- There'll be a tortuous due diligence process for the business – and you.
- There will be a clear role for you, post-sale.
- You must demonstrate commitment, at least for a few years.

Let's now consider what – for me, at any rate – is the least attractive option: stock-market flotation.

This is the biggest 'honey-trap' for start-ups. For reasons I've never been able to understand, flotations have a magical allure for many entrepreneurs. However, flotations should come with a huge health warning. You could destroy all your hard work in a moment of madness here – I should know, it almost happened to me …

Paper wealth, paper victory

While I worked at Virgin, I was involved in the flotation of Victory Corporation, the holding company for Virgin Vie and Virgin Clothing. Our initial preference had been to pursue a sale to a private-equity buyer. With £45 million committed after an exhausting series of road shows, an accounting scandal broke at one of the leading private-equity houses, which caused the market to dry up. It transpired that the fund managers interested in the private sale were also responsible for the management of IPO funds, and would readily change horse mid-race.

Victory Corporation failed to satisfy any of the investors' demands. It was punished in a textbook manner

Despite the very obvious enthusiasm of our advisers for the new plan, the Virgin team had serious reservations. We were aware that Victory Corporation was an immature business with no sales history and that, as a result, there was a very high risk of the company missing its forecasts during the early days. Notwithstanding these misgivings, we decided to be bold – or was that just a little bit foolish? – and a decision was made to float.

Victory Corporation listed at 58 pence per share. Shortly afterwards, Victory Corporation missed its first forecast. The shares were extremely thinly traded, so the loss of investor confidence in Victory Corporation had a disproportionate impact. Within a year the shares slumped to trade at less than 10 pence.

All Virgin parties had been subject to a three-year lock-in that prevented the sale of any stock. We watched helplessly as our paper profits slowly disappeared. Our hands were tied but, even if we had been able to sell our shares, it's unlikely we would have been able to find buyers in a downward spiral. It was an unmitigated disaster. Victory Corporation failed to satisfy any of the investors' demands and, as a result, was punished in a textbook manner.

From a management perspective, flotation was an executive straitjacket. We felt very limited in what we could do. The market was obsessed by the forecast figures and seemed ready to cane any turnaround plan. And we were subject to intense – and hostile – press scrutiny. It was the first Virgin experience of stock-market flotation in fifteen years. Everyone suffered from the pressure.

Despite marked improvements in its management and operations in recent years, Victory's share price continued to languish. The only way out of the City doghouse was to take the company private again. Branson took it back for a few pence per share.

OK, despite the shudders after hearing my cautionary tale, maybe you're still sitting in a plush stockbrokers' office. It's fraught with traps and difficulties, but perhaps a flotation route is the right thing for your start-up company – after all, the Alternative Investment Market (AIM) has attracted a lot of capital, so it's got to be right for somebody. So, read on, but with your eyes wide open …

What do you know about investors in listed companies? Well, for a start, they want businesses that deliver predictable, stable profits that will hit their financial projections every time. They want ironclad forecasts that are never missed.

Traders and analysts have extremely short-term investment outlooks. They want stocks that will generate strong returns over the next twelve months; they aren't particularly interested in stories about investing for future growth that might deliver returns three years from now. They want immediate results so that they can satisfy their own shareholders' demands.

Shares in start-up businesses are thinly traded, particularly those listed on secondary markets like the AIM. The shares are susceptible to large swings in value on small trading volumes. If your financial targets are missed by even a whisker, you could see large chunks of the value of your shares swiftly disappear – possibly permanently.

There will be restrictions placed on your ability to sell shares for a specified period after the flotation. These restrictions are designed to protect investors in an initial public offering (IPO) who put their money in only to see the management bail out on day one and the share price plummet. Consequently, you will have significant value locked up in the shares and will be trapped in the event of a stock market collapse. I have had some great friends who borrowed against the value of their stock, but then the share price plummeted during the lock-in period. They ended up in a very bad place. As forced sellers, they went bankrupt. You see why I think of flotations as 'fool's gold'. Please be very, very careful.

The City has a long memory. Companies failing to meet forecasts are long remembered

Yet, despite its short-term investment attitude, the City has a long memory. Companies that fail to meet forecasts or analysts' expectations are severely punished, and may face a long period of negative market sentiment even after the business gets back on track.

Floating a business is also very expensive. Not only do you have to pay the exorbitant fees of accountants, lawyers and investment bankers, you're also committed to significant reporting obligations every year. And, in the current regulatory environment, these are only going to become more onerous.

There are some more important points to consider. Floating a company brings with it disclosure of sensitive information. Again, that is only likely to intensify. If you are considering a flotation, you must be absolutely comfortable with the additional information you will need to disclose.

Meet your new best friend – he's going to make you rich

This information will include details not only of the company's trading and financial position but, more importantly, also your own financial situation and dealings. It's a good idea to consult with a lawyer to gain an understanding of just how intrusive this might be.

Secondly, if you are going to float, then you must be comfortable 'selling' the strengths of your company to a broad and demanding audience. Previously your only concern was selling your product to customers. Now your business is the product that you must sell to analysts and the City. And it's not a one-off process: you'll find yourself on the wining-and-dining treadmill. You have to keep on telling your company story, and selling yourself to the City – time after time after time. Slow up, or just get unlucky, and you'll discover your company's a 'sell'.

If you are convinced that the stock market is the right home for your business and you're determined to opt for an IPO, then make sure you understand:

- You'll be paid mostly in shares, with limited cash, and you won't be able to sell those shares for several years.
- Forecasts must be achieved on time. Every time. At least four times a year. And by that I mean four times in four – not three in four.
- Senior management departures or any other significant, unexpected events that happen during the lock-in period will damage the share price.
- You need strong shareholder demand for your company and analysts' coverage to ensure some degree of liquidity in the stock.

- You need to be able to sell the company and its wider vision – starting from IPO and all the way through to the end of your involvement.
- To maximise stock price, you must demonstrate a realistic prospect of moving up from the AIM to the main board.

I don't like flotations (in case you hadn't already gathered!). Time to choose our new best friend – for the next several months, at least – our sales adviser.

3. Selecting the right adviser for you

Selecting the right adviser for your sales process overcomes another obstacle. He or she will work intimately with you to secure a sale. The advisers who assisted me with the sale of Bond Coal and at Virgin became my right-hand men and women. They made the right introductions and orchestrated a well-planned negotiation.

Fins to the left, fins to the right ... transaction sharks!

You need to be super-cautious here. Why? Because for start-ups there are huge numbers of advisers who are better termed 'transaction sharks'. They're very good at getting your confidence. Their number-one sales tactic is to tell you what they think you want to hear. They charge high fees, with as much up front as possible, and will 'explain' how you'll get rich with minimum effort.

It's a sad reality that the smaller the business, the smaller the pool of available advisers. It's a rich feeding ground for transaction sharks. But you won't be their lunch. Why? Because I'm going to help you deploy the knowledge you now have to find the right man or woman for the job.

Cast your net wide. You want advisers with experience in your industry and deal size. Meet as many as you can and ask the following questions:

- Who might buy my business?

- What will be their motivation?
- Could I float my business?
- What are the implications?
- Would a venture capitalist buy 100% of my business?

These are all loaded questions. You know the answers. Are they suggesting that a VC will buy 100%, or that flotation is paradise? If they are, run a mile!

This will weed out the weak and the transaction sharks. But to ensure we get the right investor, you need to dig deeper. So, ask these questions:

- What specific trade buyers are likely to be interested?
- What specific private-equity companies are likely to be interested?
- How many of these do you know personally?

The last question goes to the heart of the decision of which adviser to choose. Once you've knocked out the pretenders, the key attribute advisers bring are their personal relationships with buyers. One thing you're paying for is their reputation. Do buyers respect them? Do they do deals with them? You should not expect them to know every last possible buyer, but they absolutely should know some.

No-one can sell something they don't believe in

Now let's consider how the adviser expects to be paid. If they insist that the fee isn't success-based you've got the wrong outfit. It isn't entirely reasonable that all of the fee be based on success, but the lion's share must be. It isn't unusual – it's the industry norm.

If your advisers are truly confident in their ability to get the deal done, they should be happy to put fixed fees at risk in return for an upside on a successful sale. Make the upside generous. It must be important to them. That way you ensure you get maximum attention from the best staff.

OK, you have found the right adviser, but you've one last job to do – you must prove yourself to them. No-one can sell something they don't believe in. An adviser who truly believes in the product always achieves the most effective sale. You must ensure you've sold your business and its unique features to your adviser. If they are to sell your business to sceptical purchasers, then they must be almost evangelical in his belief in your business.

4. Closing out the sale negotiation

Now it's time to get the deal done. But how? You create a bidding war – with at least two companies going head to head. This takes all you've learned, meticulous preparation and considerable creativity ...

Live the dream

To get a deal done at anything like a decent price for the coal business, I had to be creative. The bank's offer of A$180 million was derisory – and, coincidentally, the amount owed. What I needed desperately was some competitive tension. Competition amongst buyers would raise the price.

So who might buy? First, industry players – other coal companies, of course. But what about the Japanese trading companies? I decided to cast the net wide. Japanese trading companies bought the coal – why wouldn't they take charge of its source? That way, they could get an edge over their competitors. We knew C-Itoh wanted to push up the ranks and Sumitomo was always ready to push its weight around. I had to run very specific plans that showed real revenue and cost savings for them in increasing supply. The net was widening.

But the Japanese were often slow. I needed something else. But what?

A flotation was possible, but the company was relatively small – which in itself is unattractive for a flotation. At closing, we were going to be paid with little or no cash. Our pay-off, as is so often the case, was going to be in shares. There were also restrictions on the sale of the shares for at least two years. Venture capitalists never let all the money out in one go and we needed a 100% sale. So, a flotation and a VC sale were non-starters.

What, then? The managing director had me thinking. He would love to own the business ... Gotcha! A management buyout – the team could make a bid, and I would help them.

Deliver competition for your business – that will drive up the price

With enough players and detailed ideas of how the companies in the Group could operate with each owner, it was time to move to the process. We needed a well-orchestrated process that led the buyers to compete head-to-head at the right time. I had to manage the contact, nurse them, convince them – and get them to make bids at about the same time.

The key would be to ensure the team would live, breathe and eat coal. They had to be able to see every pothole and know how to fill it in. They had to know where advantages could be had. A key area of tangible growth was new open-cut mines. They were vastly more profitable than deep mines. I had to get them to express the dream at all times – in meetings, plans and presentations. They had to have a command of the detail and the numbers, yes, but also see the art of building the business.

The possible buyers could be left in no doubt as to the management team's vast knowledge and experience, which would let them live the dream.

So, countless presentation rehearsals and rewrites later, to war we went. It was a tortuous process because we had to constantly assess, re-evaluate and re-think how to work the deal. We had to work the buyers, draw them in, understand their concerns and address them. We had to make them part of Bond Coal – or, better still, they could christen the company with a new name: their own.

Competition pushed a 100% sale at the right price. The buyer believed in the project and the team and simply did not want to miss out. He didn't. He forked out over A$200 million.

What I learned is that you need to lead. You need to call the shots. The sales process described below is a cleverly orchestrated plan that subtly draws in dedicated buyers, resulting in an elegant and carefully managed shoot-out. The highest price wins.

Included in each stage of the process are tips on how you can add value and be proactive. Some contain technical detail that may make more sense as you progress in a real sale and you're sitting next to your adviser.

The sales process: making the difference

1. Select adviser	• As above
2. Select legal adviser	• You may already have a relationship with a legal firm, but you must determine whether they have the requisite commercial and transaction skills to advise you throughout this process
	• If the potential purchasers include large corporations and private-equity companies that hire leading City law firms, then you should consider using a similarly well-regarded legal firm. A more experienced firm will help build credibility throughout the sale process, and is also likely to have a better understanding of what is and is not acceptable during negotiations
	• I would always recommend using the best legal firm that you can afford
3. Prepare information memorandum (IM)	• The IM is your principal selling document, so it must be compelling and insightful. It goes to the very heart of your credibility – so you must get it right
	• You must be intimately involved in its preparation. No-one knows your business better than you do
4. Conduct vendor due diligence	• Vendor due diligence is a report produced by an external expert (such as a consulting or accounting firm) that provides a view on the business's financial and commercial status and prospects

	• It provides credibility if the business is young or in a new industry and can help to speed up the sale process
	• Read the report for inaccuracies, which could easily deter a purchaser if misunderstood
5. Brainstorm potential buyers	• Use the knowledge I gave you and work closely with your advisers
	• Think widely as the buyer may well come from outside your industry
	• This is where those close relationships of your advisers come in handy
6. Finalise list of potential purchasers; distribute IM	• The IM should ideally only go to a small group of serious potential purchasers who have all already indicated genuine interest in the business. It should not be a turkey shoot
7. Receive indicative offers	• You need to consider both the indicative price but also any terms and conditions that might be attached
8. Prepare shortlist of three to four top bidders	• Hopefully you are in a situation where you have sufficient bidders to create competitive tension
9. Conduct management presentations	• These provide the purchaser with their first real opportunity to gauge the calibre of your management team and assess their ability to run the day-to-day operations of the business without your watchful eye
	• So, the meeting is all about building the credibility of the management team. Make sure they are well rehearsed
10. Open data room	• The data room (either a physical room or online) contains large amounts of legal, financial and commercial information about the business
	• Prospective purchasers will require sufficient information to enable them to give a firm final offer
11. Receive final offers	• A judgment call – pick the one with the best price and the highest likelihood of success
12. Select preferred bidder	• Again, you must consider both the price offered and any conditions attached
13. Conduct confirmatory due diligence	• The preferred bidder will conduct their final due diligence checks
14. Negotiate sale and purchase agreement (SPA)	• Work with your advisers, remember your negotiation tactics, think it through, and don't let your greed ruin the deal

> - Purchasers will typically seek warranties from you about the current state of the business
> - Never give a warranty about future performance
> - You must negotiate hard, tell the truth and don't give them any excuse to come back at you
>
> 15. Sign final agreement • The most enjoyable signature you will ever give
> 16. Retire to the Caribbean or invest in the next big thing!

There you have it – all the answers in a box!

Let's reflect on the firepower at your disposal. You've built an exceptional business – sustainable and with tangible growth opportunities. You're well prepared, understanding the motivations of your buyers. You're involved in a process you understand and can be proactive in. And you have an adviser you can trust. So, can you perhaps relax a touch? Absolutely not! I'll tell you how to be perfectly certain that your sale happens: make a difference.

Your mission? Sell the dream – convert the buyers to your religion!

Your job is to ensure the purchasers buy the dream of your business, heart and soul. They must believe that you understand the business issues that would keep them up at night. They must believe you've got the answers – practical, detailed answers. You can drive the engine of growth and deliver that profit.

So, at every point of buyer contact – written or face to face – you're relentlessly striving to ensure you convey that message. Be honest. Speak from the heart. You know the business. You built it.

And so the moment of truth arrives. Can the management do it on their own – or do they need your help? How truly independent are you? If you don't believe the management can pull it off, you'll have to accept that a sale will necessarily include a future role for you. It may not be full-time, but there'll be something. I promise you: if you leave it to chance, you'll fail. Conveying the dream either kills or cures.

But I know you'll ensure the dream's delivered. It's your moment. You should get a sale. Should? Well, you definitely will if you can overcome that one last obstacle: greed. If you're too greedy for the highest price and unrealistic terms – or if you let your ego drive your actions – the deal will fall over.

So, remember the objective: a sale, a fair deal for all. Whether this is your first or fifth sale, be practical. Get the deal done. The competitive tension will reveal the fair price. Sale made, game over.

Well done!

The last word

Some think that selling a business simply involves hiring an adviser. This is a myth. First, we have armed you with the winning attitude. Second, you have learned how to position yourself and the company in the optimal position to attract the right buyers. Lastly, you can now lead the sales process and identify buyers and their motivations, so you can pull the right levers at the right time. You know how to make the difference, ensuring the highest price with the maximum post-deal freedom for you. In short, you got the deal done. Congratulations, the battle is won.

Dos and don'ts

1.   **DO** attack the sale process with the mentality of an asset trader. Park that ego – and throw away the key!

2.   **DO** ensure your business is a machine not relying on any one attribute for success. It's called sustainability – the greater the sustainability, the higher the price.

3.   **DO** manage yourself out of the business. Replace the central role you play to maximise the price – and your freedom.

4.   **DO** hire a trusted and diligent adviser who can introduce you to buyers they've done deals with before. Ensure their remuneration is largely success-based.

5.   **DO** create competitive tension. The only way to get a successful sale on the best possible terms is to have buyers going head to head.

6.   **DO** cast your net wide. Trawl the pool of potential buyers.

7.   **DO** consider trade buyers, who'll be enticed by the prospect of profitable synergies.

8.   **DO** consider venture capitalists. To excite their interest, you'll have to prove your absolute commitment, demonstrate your willingness to work with them and to re-invest sale proceeds with a view to a jointly profitable exit.

9.   **DON'T** consider a flotation unless your business is stable, predictable with year-on-year growth forecasts for at least three years from listing.

10. **DO** make sure potential buyers completely buy the dream, the vision of your business. You must demonstrate the management's intimate understanding of how to operate and grow the business.

11. **DON'T** – and I mean **DON'T**! – be greedy.

INDEX